OLIMPISMO

SPORT, CULTURE & SOCIETY

DAVID K. WIGGINS, SERIES EDITOR

OLIMPISMO

THE OLYMPIC MOVEMENT IN THE MAKING OF LATIN AMERICA AND THE CARIBBEAN

Edited by Antonio Sotomayor and Cesar R. Torres

The University of Arkansas Press
Fayetteville
2020

Manufactured in the United States of America

ISBN: 978-1-68226-110-1
eISBN: 978-1-61075-679-2
DOI: https://doi.org/10.34053/scs2019.o

24 23 22 21 20   5 4 3 2 1

♾ The paper used in this publication meets the minimum requirements of the American National Standard for Permanence of Paper for Printed Library Materials Z39.48–1984.

Library of Congress Cataloging-in-Publication Data

Names: Sotomayor, Antonio, author. | Torres, César R., author. |
  University of Arkansas Press.
Title: Olimpismo : the Olympic movement in the making of Latin America and
  the Caribbean / Antonio Sotomayor and Cesar R. Torres.
Description: Fayetteville : The University of Arkansas Press, 2020. |
  Series: Sports, culture, and society | Includes bibliographical references and index. |
  Summary: "This book explores the variegated ways in which Latin American and
  Caribbean societies have been made through their participation in the Olympic
  Movement since its beginning late in the nineteenth century. The study of the
  Olympic Movement, in its different manifestations, not just following its European
  origins, but also considering the agency, struggles, and contributions of Latin
  American and Caribbean societies to this phenomenon offers a more balanced
  perspective of the Olympic Movement's history and this region's role in it, while
  at the same time illuminating the role that the Olympic Movement played in the
  making of this region. Thus, the book provides potent vistas of the varied ways
  in which the Olympic Movement has played a significant role in broader social,
  political, and cultural processes in these societies, and occasionally beyond them.
  Similarly, it allows to observe and evaluate Latin American and Caribbean
  influences on the Olympic Movement, as well as the actors and actresses,
  rationales, and forces at play"— Provided by publisher.
Identifiers: LCCN 2019017229 (print) | LCCN 2019980355 (ebook) | ISBN
  9781682261101 (Paperback) | ISBN 9781610756792 (eBook)
Subjects: LCSH: Olympics—Participation, Latin American. | Olympics—Social
  aspects—Latin America. | Olympics—Social aspects—Caribbean Area. |
  Olympics—History. | Nationalism and sports—Latin America. |
  Nationalism and sports—Caribbean Area. | Sports—Latin America—
  History. | Sports—Caribbean Area—History.
Classification: LCC GV721.4.L28 S68 2020 (print) | LCC GV721.4.L28
  (ebook) | DDC 796.48—dc23
LC record available at https://lccn.loc.gov/2019017229
LC ebook record available at https://lccn.loc.gov/2019980355

To the people of Puerto Rico:
amid catastrophes and crises, your Olympic flame still shines.
—A. S.

In memory of my late father, Rodolfo,
and my late mother, Marta.
—C. R. T.

CONTENTS

SERIES EDITOR'S PREFACE

Sport is an extraordinarily important phenomenon that pervades the lives of many people and has enormous impact on society in an assortment of different ways. At its most fundamental level, sport has the power to bring people great joy and satisfy their competitive urges while at once allowing them to form bonds and a sense of community with others from diverse backgrounds and interests and various walks of life. Sport also makes clear, especially at the highest levels of competition, the lengths that people will go to achieve victory as well as how closely connected it is to business, education, politics, economics, religion, law, family, and other societal institutions. Sport is, moreover, partly about identity development and how individuals and groups, irrespective of race, gender, ethnicity or socioeconomic class, have sought to elevate their status and realize material success and social mobility.

Sport, Culture, and Society seeks to promote a greater understanding of the aforementioned issues and many others. Recognizing sport's powerful influence and ability to change people's lives in significant and important ways, the series focuses on topics ranging from urbanization and community development to biographies and intercollegiate athletics. It includes both monographs and anthologies that are characterized by excellent scholarship, accessible to a wide audience, and interesting and thoughtful in design and interpretations. Singular features of the series are authors and editors representing a variety of disciplinary areas and who adopt different methodological approaches. The series also includes works by individuals at various stages of their careers, both sport studies scholars of outstanding talent just beginning to make their mark on the field and more experienced scholars of sport with established reputations.

Olimpismo: The Olympic Movement in the Making of Latin America and the Caribbean examines in depth a topic that has largely escaped expanded scholarly inquiry. Editors Antonio Sotomayor and Cesar R. Torres help rectify this fact with a collection of nine essays by well-known academics that provide important insights into the development of the Olympic Movement in Latin America and the Caribbean and the cultural and economic impact it has had on those societies over the years. Noting that most scholarly studies on the Olympic Games have been limited to

Europe and North America, which has resulted in an unbalanced and limited view of the Olympic Movement, Sotomayor and Torres have assembled an anthology that furnishes details and cogent analysis of the origins and characteristics of the Olympic Movement in Latin America and the Caribbean as well as the challenges it has presented to the region's social, political, economic, religious, and cultural life. Indications of this reality are evident in essays on topics ranging from Olympic diplomacy in post-revolutionary Mexico and the Olympic Games and Nationalist Movement in Puerto Rico to the Olympic Movement and Argentine sport and the YMCA and Olympism in Uruguay. Importantly, these essays and others in the collection make clear in their assessment of the Olympic Movement in Latin America and the Caribbean that the societies that make up the region are similar and bound together in an assortment of different ways, but also possess unique national and regional characteristics that are sometimes not recognized and acknowledged.

David K. Wiggins

OLIMPISMO

INTRODUCTION

More than fifty years ago, Mexican president Adolfo López Mateos whole-heartedly embraced the bid to host the 1968 Olympics in Mexico City. He thought that hosting the event would bring attention and respect to his country on the global stage.[1] Not surprisingly, when Mexico City was selected as the host of the 1968 Olympics in October 1963, López Mateos declared that the achievement "is the world recognition to the effort of the Mexican People not only to maintain but also to elevate its international position in the sphere of sport, and to its conditions of economic and political stability."[2] Whether or not it is justified, sensible, or appropriate, this rationale has animated the efforts of regional elites who have successfully bid to bring the Olympic Games to Latin America.[3] Consider, for example, that the Candidature File to host the 2016 Olympics in Rio de Janeiro, delivered by Brazilian officials to the International Olympic Committee (IOC) in early 2009, argued that one of the "principal motivation[s]" to bid was that

> [the Olympic Games] will bring a new level of global recognition of Brazil. Super Games and stunning broadcast imagery will provide a long-term boost to tourism and Brazil's growing reputation as an exciting and rewarding place to live, do business and visit.[4]

Brazil underwent significant political, economic, and social turmoil before, during, and after the 2016 Olympics. Yet Michel Temer, the deeply unpopular Brazilian interim president who had replaced Dilma Rousseff in May 2016 when the Senate voted to impeach her, replicated the argument advanced seven years earlier in the Candidature File. Despite nationwide protests against what many believed to be an illegitimate government, including spectators at Olympic venues wearing anti-Temer shirts and displaying signs calling for his removal (Image Introduction 1), the interim president claimed a few days before the closing ceremonies that "there will be worldwide recognition on the Brazilian capacity for organization and the structure of government for an international event."[5] Temer's intrepid prediction, which could also be read as a desperate hope, came after a meeting with the officials of the organizing committee, cabinet members, the mayor of Rio de Janeiro, and the governor of the State of Rio de Janeiro—but, more important, after being jeered less

3

Image Introduction 1. A spectator protests against Michel Temer during
the 2016 Olympics in Rio de Janeiro. The sign means "Temer Out."
Courtesy of Camila Augusta Alves Pereira.

than two weeks before by the crowds during the Olympic Games' opening
ceremonies on August 5.

The conviction, and arguably hope, that the Olympic spectacle serves
as a global platform to bolster the image of the host city and nation was
also advanced by the organizers of the 2018 Youth Olympic Games
hosted in Buenos Aires in October of that year. Back in 2011, when
Buenos Aires announced that it would bid to host the event, Gerardo
Werthein, president of the Comité Olímpico Argentino (Argentine
Olympic Committee), proclaimed that even the announcement was significant, because such news has "an enormous audience and it will put
Buenos Aires and Argentina at the center of the world."[6] Six years later,
Horacio Rodríguez Larreta, Buenos Aires's mayor, reiterated the argument. In June 2017, he proclaimed that the 2018 Youth Olympic Games
were "a unique opportunity to be in the eyes of the world."[7] Shortly thereafter, at a ceremony in which the Olympic rings were set up at a famous
city landmark to mark the one-year countdown to the event, Rodríguez
Larreta insisted that in a short while "we will be the center of attention
of the world during those two weeks."[8] In line with past Latin American
organizers of the Olympic Games, he added that the 2018 Youth Olympic
Games "is also a unique opportunity to demonstrate what we are capable
of the Argentines."[9] Clearly, Latin American Olympic organizers, promoters, and hopefuls have been united in the notion that bringing the

Olympic spectacle to their countries would prove valuable, among other things, in terms of drawing global attention and recognition.

The Latin American persistence in bidding for and hosting the Olympic Games extended over the entire twentieth century. For instance, Mexican and Brazilian elites had previously bid for the event before eventually succeeding in hosting the 1968 and 2016 Olympics, respectively. Likewise, Argentine elites bid for the Olympic Games before Buenos Aires was granted the right to host the 2018 Youth Olympic Games.[10] The Olympic Games have also captured the imagination of the Caribbean. For example, Cuban elites unsuccessfully bid to host the event in Havana both before and after the revolution of 1959 led by Fidel Castro.[11] The Puerto Rican bid to host the 2004 Olympics met the same fate.[12] More precisely, Latin American and Caribbean elites have been seduced not only by the allure of and opportunities offered by the Olympic Games, but also by the event's underpinning philosophical vision, known as Olympism, and, more broadly, with the travails, aspirations, and various manifestations of the Olympic Movement.

The Olympic Games, Olympism, and the Olympic Movement are inextricably interrelated. Over the last hundred and twenty years, the Olympic Games have become, as John MacAloon aptly put it, "an international culture performance of global proportion," based on sport competition for elite athletes.[13] At the core of this culture is Olympism, a neologism coined by Pierre de Coubertin, the founder of the IOC at the end of the nineteenth century. In developing Olympism, Coubertin was inspired by different worldviews, including classic Hellenism, English Muscular Christianity, quintessential nineteenth-century liberalism, and French social reformism.[14] In essence, Olympism proposes to advance moral values through the practice of sport. While there is no consensus on its exact meaning, Olympism is typically articulated as a cosmopolitan, humanistic, secular, and egalitarian vision emphasizing "values such as holistic human development, excellence, peace, fairness, equality, mutual respect, justice, and non-discrimination."[15] Its moral foundation and amelioristic commitment provide Olympism with an unambiguous educational rationality. Emphasizing its educational role and potential, Coubertin argued that "Olympism is a destroyer of dividing walls."[16] Devoid of Olympism, the Olympic Games would just be, to use Coubertin's words, world championships.[17] By bringing together young athletes from the world over to compete under the values of Olympism, the Olympic Games represent, as the IOC's Olympic Charter clarifies, the pinnacle of the Olympic Movement.[18] The latter encompasses organizations, athletes, and everyone who embraces the tenets of Olympism. "The goal of the Olympic Movement," the IOC states, "is to contribute to building a peaceful and better world by educating youth through sport practised in accordance with Olympism and its values."[19]

The aspirations of the Olympic Movement are also promoted by and visible through the work of international regional sport organizations. In the western hemisphere these include the Pan-American Sports Organization and the Central American and Caribbean Sports Organization, among several others. Together, these international regional sport organizations form an important part of the Latin American and Caribbean expression of and involvement with and in the Olympic Movement. Countries in these regions have also actively sought to lead and participate in these international sport organizations as well as in the international sporting events they organize, which are patronized by the IOC and motivated by the same vision framing the Olympic Games, after which they are modeled.[20]

Latin American and Caribbean peoples have been envisioning themselves through sport and articulated in the global world of sport since the dawn of the Olympic Movement. Argentina's José Benjamín Zubiaur was among the thirteen founders of the IOC in 1894, and Latin Americans have participated in the Olympic Games since they first began in 1896, although athletes from this region only entered the festival en masse in the 1920s.[21] The oldest regional games patronized by the IOC are the Central American and Caribbean Games, which began in 1926. Previously, in 1910, Argentina hosted a festival known as the Centennial Olympic Games, and five years later the Dominican Republic held an event known as Olympic Games.[22] In 1922, Brazil hosted the Latin American Games; in 1935, Puerto Ricans organized their own Puerto Rican Olympic Games to determine the athletes that would compete in that year's Central American and Caribbean Games; and, in 1951, after a frustrated attempt a decade before, Argentina officially inaugurated the Pan-American Games.[23] The Pan-American Games have become one of the largest international sporting events, in terms of the number of countries represented and athletes participating, after the Olympic Games.[24]

Sport has increasingly been studied to understand the experiences of countries around the world.[25] In Latin America and the Caribbean, a generalized understanding of sport is typically confined to football and baseball, the two most popular sports in the region.[26] While football and baseball are crucial to comprehend Latin American and Caribbean societies, there are other sport organizations, events, and agents that have played complex and important roles in the "making" of such societies. The regional Olympic Movement, which spans three centuries, is certainly one of these entities. As the "concerted, organised, universal and permanent action, carried out under the supreme authority of the IOC," the Olympic Movement is particularly special because of its institutional reach and numerous manifestations.[27] As such, it is a platform that projects globally, impacting every aspect of the human experience. Recognizing the stature of the Olympic Movement, it is no wonder that so much is at stake for both supporters and critics.

In this regard, the study of the development of the Olympic Movement in Latin America and the Caribbean serves as an effective medium to explore the making of these societies. This is especially the case because, through the defense and celebration of the values of Olympism as a "destroyer of dividing walls," a project born in Europe that was meant to be exported and applied globally, the Olympic Movement progressively became a force that allowed Latin American and Caribbean peoples to not only envision themselves through their Olympic undertakings, but also to engage with the global Olympic world.[28] Yet Olympic studies have been usually confined to Europe and North America, which results not only in a limited view and understanding of the Olympic Movement, but also in an unbalanced perspective of how Latin America and the Caribbean envisioned and regarded their experience through their Olympic undertakings.[29] The study of the Olympic Movement in its different manifestations—not just following its European origins but also considering the agency, struggles, and contributions of Latin American and Caribbean societies to this phenomenon—offers a more balanced perspective of the Olympic Movement's history and this region's role in it, while at the same time illuminating the role that the Olympic Movement played in the making of this region.

In addition, the complexities related to the 1968 Mexico City Olympics, the 2016 Rio de Janeiro Olympics, and the 2018 Buenos Aires Youth Olympic Games—and, more generally, the more than century-old involvement of this region with and in the Olympic Movement—suggest that this is an apt time to systematically study the Latin American and Caribbean Olympic Movement: its origins, characteristics, and impact locally and beyond. This is the overall aim of this book, which also aspires to fill an important gap in the scholarly literature on the Latin American and Caribbean Olympic experience, broadly understood.

By "making Latin America and the Caribbean," we mean—in line with

Benedict Anderson's insights into nation formation—the human exercise of imagining, creating, shaping, and contesting the building blocks of societies that see themselves as sharing common bonds.[30] Here, "to make" denotes a dynamic process of invention and constant reinvention, fragmented but comprehensive, multileveled but constant, ideological but concrete. This process of making societies covers all angles of life, including the political, cultural, social, religious, economic, and intellectual. In this regard, the concepts and realities of "Latin America" and "the Caribbean" are not natural and static, but have been and are debated, challenged, and legitimized by agents from different walks of life, ideologies, and aspirations. While aware of these debates, challenges, and legitimizations, here "Latin America" refers to the typical designation that includes the countries of the western hemisphere that gained independence from Spain and Portugal, including the Spanish-speaking Caribbean. This designation emphasizes historical, linguistic, social, and cultural similarities, differentiating Spanish- and Portuguese-speaking countries south of the United States, including those in the Caribbean, from the rest of the western hemisphere.[31] Limitations, omissions, and fragmentations notwithstanding, it is worth mentioning in this context that Coubertin understood the western hemisphere in those terms and even saw a clear distinction between the "Latin" and the "Anglo" conceptualizations of sport.[32]

As noted above, Latin America and the Caribbean have been in the making—a process that features prominently their imagining and reimagining—for quite a long time. This book explores the variegated ways in which Latin American and Caribbean societies have been made through their participation in the Olympic Movement since its beginning late in the nineteenth century. Special attention is paid to this making process in the twentieth century, but the book extends to the dawn of the twenty-first century. As already mentioned, societies in Latin America and the Caribbean share some similarities, historical, linguistic, and cultural. However, they also possess important unique characteristics, nationally and even regionally. They have diverse political traditions and systems, ideologies, economies, and cultures that can be seen as either complementary or contradictory. One element that binds them together today is the discussion of (as well as whether and to what extent they embrace) the idea of Latin America and the Caribbean that also shapes a field of study of international proportions. Another element is the region's consequential levels of *mestizaje*, a process in the making for half a millennium in which diverse worldviews, including but surpassing racial and ethnic mixing, have come together to influence all spheres of life. This has led to a story of a struggle over power, representation, and diverse and often clashing modes of civilization to a degree not seen in other parts of the world.[33]

By exploring the Olympic experience in Latin America and the Caribbean and its role in the making of their societies, both as a whole unit but also as individual countries, this book depicts their similarities and differences through the lens of this powerful international sporting phenomenon. In doing so, it provides potent vistas of the varied ways in which the Olympic Movement has played a significant role in broader social, political, and cultural processes in these societies, and occasionally beyond them. Leaving the Olympic Movement outside the study of Latin America and the Caribbean, in its inextricable interconnections, jeopardizes a compelling and major dynamic in the making of these societies. Similarly, it allows us to observe and evaluate Latin American and Caribbean influences on the Olympic Movement, as well as the agents, rationales, and forces at play.

Although the chapters in the book are structured historically, they are richly interdisciplinary in nature, covering fields such as anthropology, geography, literature, management, and philosophy. This approach seems not only appropriate but also essential to analyze such a multifaceted phenomenon as the Olympic Movement, as well as the multifaceted regions of Latin America and the Caribbean. The chapters of the book are largely organized chronologically; approximately half of them cover the first six decades or so of Olympic history while the other half covers the mid-twentieth century to the present. As a whole, they reveal that the participation of Latin America and the Caribbean in the Olympic Movement has been a preferred terrain for political experimentation, struggles, and clashes; contestation of various social hierarchies; attempts of insertion in an increasingly globalized world; and both inward and outward articulations and projections of identity.

Shunsuke Matsuo opens the book with a chapter that examines the incorporation of Uruguay into the Olympic Movement in the first two decades of the twentieth century. Matsuo uncovers the depth and dynamism of the early Olympic history in this country and also argues that local actors were not passive recipients of external influences but rather active agents in the global expansion of the Olympic Movement. As a result, we can see the intricate ways in which Uruguayan sport leaders contributed to the consolidation of their own national institutions as well as to the Olympic Movement overall. The second chapter, by Thomas F. Carter, offers an overview of the ways in which the evolving understanding of Olympism informed and shaped Cuban nationalism from the celebration of the inaugural Olympic Games in 1896 to the last edition in 2016. In this analysis, Carter makes us reflect on the ever-present political, nationalistic, and even revolutionary uses of the Olympic Movement, despite claims to the contrary. Carter ends his overview speculating about the future of the Olympic Movement in Cuba in light of recent developments on the island.

In the third chapter, Keith Brewster and Claire Brewster analyze the diplomatic role that the Mexican Olympic Movement played in post-revolutionary Mexico's goal of strengthening relations with its neighbors. The chapter covers the fifty years that followed the end of the Mexican Revolution in 1920 and maintains that the country's involvement in the Olympic Movement, including hosting the Olympic Games in Mexico City in 1968, helped build and project a better image of Mexico and its people. Moving beyond an isolated view of the 1968 Olympics, Brewster and Brewster study the longer history of the Olympic Movement in Mexico, demonstrating the diplomatic imperatives that the Olympic Movement has had for Mexicans. The last chapter of the book's first half, by Antonio Sotomayor, examines the process by which Puerto Rican nationalists engaged with the Olympic Movement in their struggle for decolonization. Sotomayor shows not only shifting meanings of colonial Olympic sport for nationalists, but, more generally, that the Olympic Movement has been used and serves as a platform to negotiate nationalism and decolonization. Thus, this chapter displays the intricacies of colonialism, nonsovereign nationalism, and decolonization struggles within the Olympic Movement in the Caribbean.

The second half of the book opens with a chapter by Fabio Peres and Victor Andrade de Melo that studies the Olympic success of Brazilian triple jumper Adhemar Ferreira da Silva during the 1950s, as portrayed in the press of Rio de Janeiro and São Paulo. Peres and Melo illustrate that da Silva's performances embodied Brazilian expectations for a renewed nation and also reveal a need for national redemption, as well as the search for national racial harmony, in the wake of Brazil's loss to Uruguay in the 1950 Football World Cup (known as the *maracanaço*), which allowed Uruguay to win the tournament. Going beyond the usual focus on Brazilian football, Peres and Melo demonstrate the richness of Brazilian sport and the profound role of the wider Olympic Movement in the configuration of the Brazilian nation. In the chapter that follows, Cesar R. Torres explores the process and impacts of the de-Peronization of the Olympic Movement in Argentina from 1955, when a coup d'état overthrew the government of Juan Domingo Perón, to 1960, when it was believed that Argentine sport had been freed from the vices of Peronism. Torres argues that the reforms implemented by the new Olympic leadership severely weakened Argentine sport, locally and internationally, and shows the inescapable and complex relation of politics and sport. In this sense, much like in the previous chapter, Torres also demonstrates the relevance of sport and the wider Olympic Movement in attempts to configure the nation and in the transition from one political regime to another.

The third chapter in the second half of the book, by April Yoder, discusses the strategic uses of sport by Joaquín Balaguer from 1966 to 1978, and especially the hosting of the 1974 Central American and Caribbean Games, as a way to showcase a "Third Way" of development in a new era of democracy in the Dominican Republic. Yoder reveals that, through sport in general and the event in particular, the government boosted the narrative of opportunity while maintaining authoritarianism and inequality, in addition to redefining a new type of paternalism that sought to keep women in traditional gender roles. Along with the chapters on Cuba and Puerto Rico, by Carter and Sotomayor, respectively, Yoder closes the circle of the Spanish Caribbean experiences in the Olympic Movement, providing insights related to the Cold War and gender that carry broader implications. In the book's penultimate chapter, Chloe Rutter-Jensen explores the way that enfleshed bodies with disabilities help us to perceive issues of national identity, in addition to notions of gender, race, social class, and place in Colombia. Examining the case of Paralympian Fabio Torres, Rutter-Jensen looks at inclusions and exclusions within the Colombian Olympic Movement in order to illustrate the dilemmas of the national "other." This chapter also contributes to a much-needed reflection on sport and disability, which can provide a critical angle to study the construction of the nation.

In the last chapter of the book, Lamartine Pereira DaCosta places in a comparative lens the geopolitical stakes in and significances of the process of bidding and hosting different Olympic festivals for Argentina, Brazil, and Mexico. Moreover, in studying the past experiences of these three countries' involvement with and in the Olympic Movement, DaCosta also reflects on what might be in store for the future of this global phenomenon in Latin America and the Caribbean. This chapter ignites a conversation related to the particular insights that can be gained from comparative methodologies in Olympic studies and, more specifically, in the Latin American and Caribbean expression of and engagement with the Olympic Movement. The book concludes with a nuanced and thought-provoking commentary by Christopher Gaffney that takes an overall view of the preceding chapters and the issues they analyze. Gaffney's conclusion contemplates each chapter in a sustained analysis of "crisis" in the past and current Olympic Movement.

A single book cannot cover all topics related to the relationship between the Olympic Movement and Latin America and the Caribbean. This seems expected, as the chapters in the book exemplify, given the intricate ways in which the Olympic Movement and its multiple manifestations have contributed to the making of this region, as well as this region's intricate contributions to the making of the Olympic Movement and its multiple manifestations. As the chapters in the book collectively demonstrate, regardless of similarities and differences, the making of Latin America and the Caribbean can be powerfully illuminated through the study of the region's relationship to the Olympic Movement. While not able to cover all topics, this book is the first of its kind, and we hope we have offered novel approaches, interpretations, and significances. We also aim to stimulate more scholars to turn their attention to this fascinating and, to a large extent, understudied process that involves the interrelation between Latin America and the Caribbean and the Olympic Movement. Hopefully, readers will learn from and enjoy the book as much as we did in working on it.

We would like to acknowledge several individuals who, in different and valuable ways, contributed to the book's publication. First of all, we thank the authors of the chapters for their contributions, predisposition, and responsiveness. We also appreciate the comments and suggestions of two anonymous reviewers that helped improved the book. We are grateful to Fausto Amaro, Camila Augusta Alves Pereira, Linda W. Hacker, and Molly Zientek for their assistance, and to David M. K. Sheinin for his advice. We thank the staff at the University of Arkansas Press for their work and dedication. David K. Wiggins, editor of the press's series *Sport, Culture, and Society,* deserves special thanks for his enthusiastic encouragement. We also acknowledge the Research and Publication Committee of the University of Illinois at Urbana–Champaign Library, which provided support for the completion of the book. Finally, we express our deep and loving gratitude to our families.

CHAPTER 1

Sport Policy, the YMCA, and the Early History of Olympism in Uruguay

SHUNSUKE MATSUO[1]

In June 1924, an unknown country from South America made a name for itself at the Olympic Stadium of Colombes: the Uruguayan national team won the football tournament of the Paris Olympics. The performance was sensational; Uruguay won all five games played, scoring twenty goals and conceding only two. After a 3–0 win at the final against Switzerland, the triumphant eleven walked around the pitch to greet curious European spectators, giving birth to the ritual known today in South American football as *vuelta olímpica* (lap of honor). This victory, along with subsequent successes at the 1928 Amsterdam Olympics and the first FIFA World Cup in 1930, is proudly recorded in every account of the history of sport in Uruguay.

However, the repute of this achievement has hidden rather than revealed the complex nature and earlier expressions of Olympism in Uruguay. While much has been written about the country's successes in Olympic football, virtually no research has examined how this tiny country tucked away between Argentina and Brazil became involved in the modern global Olympic Movement.

Regarding the early history of Olympism in the region, Cesar R. Torres has advanced the thesis of the so-called Latin American "Olympic explosion" in the 1920s. Drawing on a wide range of primary sources, he convincingly argues that an alliance formed in 1920 between the International Olympic Committee (IOC) and the Young Men's Christian Association (YMCA) was crucial to the incorporation of Latin American

DOI: https://doi.org/10.34053/scs2019.0.1

nations in the Olympic Movement. He describes how these two institutions collaborated to organize the South American Games of 1922 in Rio de Janeiro, which led to both the foundation of several National Olympic Committees and a significant increase in Latin American participation in subsequent Olympic Games.[2]

At a glance, this framework seems to best apply to the Uruguayan case. Both the YMCA spokesman Elwood Brown and the IOC representative Henri de Baillet-Latour visited Montevideo as part of their South American tours in 1920 and 1922, respectively. Uruguay participated in the 1922 South American Games, and the following year the Uruguayan Olympic Committee (Comité Olímpico Uruguayo, or COU) was officially constituted for the first time. Consequently, Uruguay made its first appearance at the Olympic Games in the 1924 Paris Olympics, where it achieved the memorable success mentioned above.

However, a more thorough analysis reveals that a simple application of this explanatory model, which regards the emergence of Olympism as a "consequence of" or "response to" the IOC-YMCA partnership, is not sufficient to illustrate the depth and dynamism of early Olympic history in Uruguay. One of the notable characteristics of Uruguayan sport during the first decades of the twentieth century is that a government agency—with its concomitant objectives, missions, and resources—reigned over different sport federations and hence acted as a national authority in Uruguay's earliest relationship with the Olympic Movement.[3] In 1911, the government founded the National Committee of Physical Education (Comisión Nacional de Educación Física, or CNEF) as the official organization in charge of national policy related to sport and physical education, which played a key role in the consolidation and institutionalization of modern sport in Uruguay. Indeed, during the 1910s, the CNEF already maintained contact with the IOC and Pierre de Coubertin. Similarly, and no less important, the CNEF also established a uniquely close connection with the YMCA through the formulation of sport policy in this period. Thus, a fuller analysis of Uruguay's Olympic involvement during the early twentieth century should also incorporate the "national" perspective of the CNEF, around which the "global" dynamism of the IOC-YMCA alliance revolved. In other words, this chapter examines the process of Uruguay's incorporation into the modern Olympic Movement from Uruguay's own point of view, considering it primarily as part of the CNEF's sport policy development, which shared a common goal with the global stimulus.

For this purpose, this chapter first explores the development of

Uruguay's national sport policy and reveals the CNEF's relationships to the IOC and the YMCA during the 1910s. On the basis of these antecedents, it then analyzes in detail how the IOC-YMCA partnership operated in Uruguay in the early 1920s.

Uruguayan Politics and the CNEF in the 1910s

Without doubt, the 1910s was a decisive decade in the political history of Uruguay. From its independence in the 1820s to the turn of the century, Uruguay was afflicted by continual armed conflict between two political parties, the Colorado and the Blanco (or National), which fueled political, economic, and social disorder and underdevelopment. However, during the first three decades of the twentieth century, Uruguay succeeded not only in consolidating state power and enforcing the rule of law, but also in becoming one of the most progressive democracies in the region. This comprehensive remodeling of many aspects of the nation-state was engineered by a radical group from the Colorado Party, captained by José Batlle y Ordóñez. Twice president of Uruguay (1903–7, 1911–15), Batlle promoted a series of reforms that included the substitution of the president with a council of plural members, establishment of a fair and democratic electoral system, strict separation of church and state, implementation of eight-hour working days, and state intervention in different areas of industry and infrastructure—from railroads and electricity to insurance and alcohol—that counteracted the drain of wealth by foreign capitals, provided Uruguayan citizens with a wide range of social services, and led the way to the country's industrialization.[4] Although many of these reforms met with fierce opposition inside and outside the Colorado Party, which culminated in the coup d'état of 1933 that installed a dictatorial regime and undermined the *batllista* supremacy, the political proposals, discussions, and outcomes of this period left an enduring imprint on Uruguay's democratic culture and institutions.[5]

Among these reformist measures taken by *batllista* Uruguay was the creation of the CNEF, a governmental institution that undertook the promotion of sport and physical education. Established at the beginning of Batlle's second presidency, the CNEF was made up of seven members designated every two years by the executive, as well as the chairs of four related public institutions. These eleven members gathered once a week to discuss and implement any national policy related to sport and physical education.[6]

Originally founded as an experimental pilot project,[7] the CNEF optimistically extended its sphere of action and consolidated as part of the rapidly expanding state bureaucracy. Particularly, from 1915 to 1923, when many of the seven seats were occupied by prominent politicians close to Batlle—including Batlle himself from 1915 to 1919—the CNEF developed into a genuinely national institution that orchestrated the diffusion and promotion of diverse physical activities throughout the country. Among these *batllista* political appointees, Francisco Ghigliani, a young physician and one of Batlle's right-hand men, was an indisputably central figure (Image 1.1).[8] Chosen as a CNEF member in 1914, the thirty-one-year-old *batllista* militant soon became a driving force behind Uruguay's progressive sport policy.[9]

Perhaps the CNEF's most renowned project was the construction of public sport grounds, or *plazas de deportes*. Inspired by the North American playground movement, these plazas were typically equipped with a playing field, gymnasium, and shower room, and physical education teachers provided direction for and supervision of activities among boys, girls, and adults from the neighborhood at no charge. The first plaza was established in 1913, and, during the following years, plazas multiplied throughout the country, from seven in 1916 to forty-five in 1923.[10] CNEF's action plan from 1922 ambitiously called for setting up a plaza in every town with a population of more than five hundred.[11]

Another pillar of the CNEF, hand in hand with the *plazas de deportes* project, was the professional training of physical education teachers, although this took more time to be implemented. During the 1910s, there was much discussion in the CNEF about the benefits of founding a school for those who wished to be trained as physical education teachers, but the estimated high costs of such a school hindered its realization.[12] It was in 1921 that the CNEF provided a concrete solution to the lack of qualified teachers when it proposed the creation of a summer course instead of a permanent institute. This intensive course started to be offered regularly in 1923.[13]

The third principal project, though largely ignored in the existing literature, was the organization of sport institutions. In 1911, none of the sports played in Uruguay had national governing bodies that exercised control over different clubs, except for football, which had been led by the Liga Uruguaya de Football (Uruguayan Football League) since 1900. Because bureaucratic organization was essential for the development of modern sport, this absence of federations represented for the CNEF

Image 1.1. Francisco Ghigliani. *El Día* (Montevideo), November 15, 1919.

one of the most significant indications of the perceived "backwardness" of the Uruguayan sport culture.[14] In February 1915, at the proposal of Ghigliani, the CNEF called for all sport clubs in the country to hold meetings and constitute national federations for each sport.[15] Sportsmen responded quickly: during the following months, one sport after another established national federations, and delegates from twelve federations met up in August 1915 to found the Federación Deportiva del Uruguay (Sport Federation of Uruguay, or FDU), a representative body that functioned under the supervision of the CNEF. Ghigliani became the chair of this new institution.[16] However, this so-called "bicameral" system of sport administration, consisting of the CNEF and the FDU, did not last long. Having completed its mission of institutionalizing national sports, and increasingly hampered by internal conflict between different federations, the FDU was dissolved in 1918. Instead, the CNEF conferred official recognition directly on the federations, ratifying the autonomy of each sport.[17] Regardless of the legal framework, the CNEF provided sport federations with generous aid, both financial and technical, all through-out during the 1910s.

The CNEF and the Olympic Movement in the 1910s

The official constitution of the Uruguayan Olympic Committee in 1923 and the country's brilliant debut at the 1924 Paris Olympics by no means suggest the absence of interest in and connection to the Olympic Movement among Uruguayans during the 1910s. Yet most authors have dismissed Uruguay's possible relationship with the Olympic Movement during this period.[18] However, a careful analysis of primary sources suggests that Olympism always provided the CNEF with a reference and an authority of no minor importance.

In May 1912, José Zamora proposed in a CNEF session to send an officer to the Olympic Games to be held in Stockholm that year. The purpose was as modest as it was realistic: "It is convenient for the young and inexperienced countries, like ours, to know the classical way in which the Olympic Games are held in Europe."[19] Zamora expected that to study the organization of the Olympic Games would "bring a number of data and experiences invaluable for the future of our physical education."[20] For him, Uruguay's peripheral status in the world was self-evident, and, for this reason, the CNEF had to establish a solid link to the worldwide Olympic Movement that was expected to set the course of its policy. However, this motion was voted down by other members due to lack of time, the considerable cost of a mission to Europe, and the supposed dubious legality of expenditure abroad.[21]

The following year, the CNEF published a booklet entitled *Stadium Nacional de Montevideo* (Montevideo National Stadium), which described a blueprint for a stadium to be constructed in Montevideo as well as a detailed project of sport competitions at national, *interplatense* (between Uruguay and Argentina), South American, and international levels that the CNEF proposed to hold regularly there.[22] In January 1914, the chairman of the CNEF, Juan Smith, sent this publication to Coubertin, in the hope that the founder of the modern Olympic Games would provide valuable advice on Uruguay's incipient sport policy.[23] However, Coubertin's response was a furious one; what angered him was the denomination of the sport events to be held in Montevideo as Juegos Olímpicos (Olympic Games), a label that he carefully reserved for the Olympic Movement he presided over. Embarrassed by Coubertin's unexpected indignation about the "usurpation of name," Smith sent a letter of apology and clarification with José Destombes, who, along with the Uruguayan Minister in France, Rafael de Miero, participated in the 1914 Paris Olympic Congress.[24] This was the first time that Uruguay made an appearance at an Olympic event.

As the CNEF spectacularly expanded its scope of activities under the stable *batllista* political patronage and Ghigliani's cogent leadership during the second half of the 1910s, the Uruguayans' ambitions for Olympic involvement soared to an unprecedented height. At the end of 1916, the CNEF decided to commission physician and former vice chairman of the Uruguayan Football League Ángel Colombo to research the situation of physical education in France and Italy. Once in Paris, Colombo was introduced by the country's legation to Coubertin. This time, Coubertin expressed his genuine sympathy.[25] According to the report Colombo presented to the CNEF in February 1918, "the auspicious awakening of our physical culture expressed in the meritorious work [of the CNEF]" drummed up the IOC president's avid interest in diffusing Olympism in South America. In view of the upcoming 1920 Olympic Games, Coubertin proposed the organization of a South American International Olympic Committee to strengthen the ties between the IOC and South America.[26] "That is why," Colombo wrote, "we had to accept the opportunity for our country to obtain the IOC's assurance of the real and positive sporting value we have, which ought to be translated into the desire to become one of the candidates to be considered for the future Olympic bid."[27] While Colombo's words were cautious and roundabout, the Uruguayan Minister in Paris, Juan Carlos Blanco, who accompanied Colombo to the interview with Coubertin, confirmed in a separate letter that the IOC president had "accepted, in principle, the suggestion that the Olympic Games of 1920—analogous to the ones held in Athens and Stockholm—be held in Montevideo."[28] Although it is admittedly possible that Blanco exaggerated Coubertin's sympathy to urge the government to take quick action, the historical conjuncture of these years suggests the IOC president's seriousness in bringing the 1920 Olympics to South America. The outbreak of World War I cancelled the 1916 Berlin Olympics and postponed every decision regarding the 1920 Olympic Games. With war still prevailing in Europe, it was not unrealistic that Coubertin found the South American proposal a viable alternative to celebrate the 1920 Olympic Games.[29]

Upon receipt of Colombo's report, the CNEF consulted the Ministry of Public Instruction, since "for its official and international character as well as its importance, it [was] impossible to resolve on this matter by the sole authority of the CNEF."[30] The sources consulted so far do not provide further information on the consequences of this bid. It appears, however, that the bid was only verbal, and that the CNEF, unable to secure financial backup from the government, gave up the idea of hosting the Olympic Games in Uruguay. Shortly after, the Armistice of November 1918 turned Coubertin's attention back to Europe; at the IOC Session of April 1919, Antwerp was officially selected as the host city of the 1920 Olympics.

This proposal to host the Olympic Games in Montevideo, however informal it was, certainly left an impact on Uruguayan sportsmen and contributed to stimulating their interest in Olympic matters. Inspired by this bid, an Uruguayan diplomat published a detailed project of "Pan-American Olympics" to be held in Montevideo.[31] In 1920, then-president Baltasar Brum sent a message to Coubertin that "he longs for the day when his country, by reason of its athletic standards and administration, will deserve to have the Olympic Games held in Montevideo."[32]

These early contacts with the Olympic Movement denote the CNEF's high aspiration—admittedly Eurocentric in nature—to bring the country's sport culture up to European standards, and to play a meaningful role in international sporting relations. These continuous efforts certainly paved the way for Uruguay's "Olympic explosion" in the 1920s.

The CNEF and the YMCA in the 1910s

In contrast to the relative ignorance about Uruguay's early relationship with the Olympic Movement, the influence that the YMCA had on the making of Uruguay's sport and physical education policy at the beginning of the twentieth century is commonly recognized.[33] Nonetheless, few authors base their arguments on thorough primary source research, or understand this peculiar connection as part of the wider global historical context of the North American YMCA's international enterprise.

Beginning at the end of the nineteenth century, the International Committee, the governing body of the YMCAs in the United States and Canada, was eagerly engaged in extending its movement overseas through its Foreign Department. Based in New York, directed by eventual Nobel Peace Prize laureate John R. Mott, and supported by US philanthropists such as the Rockefeller family, the International Committee sent out a number of secretaries (officers in charge of the general organization of YMCAs) and physical directors (experts in sport and physical education), typically educated at its own training school in Springfield, Massachusetts, to Asia, Latin America, and certain parts of Europe during the first three decades of the twentieth century. These missionaries were expected to enter local communities, cultivate religious and cultural activities among youth, and create "self-supporting, self-governing, self-propagating" YMCAs. Given that one of the distinctive features of the North American YMCA movement was its emphasis on sport and physical education programs, this missionary project influenced, to varying degrees, the diffusion and development of modern sport in peripheral regions.[34]

The beginning of the YMCA's missionary work in South America dates to the late nineteenth century. One of the first three secretaries sent overseas by the International Committee was Myron Clark, who arrived in Brazil in 1891.[35] In 1900, he traveled to Montevideo, Buenos Aires, and Rosario to assess the possibility of extending the YMCA movement down to the River Plate region. In Montevideo he was introduced to Eduardo Monteverde, a university mathematics professor, retired politician of the National Party, and member of the Methodist Church, who would become a key contact. His brilliant professional and political career, as well as his radiant and spirited personality, had made him extremely well connected among Montevideo's political, social, and intellectual elites.[36] He was also a promoter of Protestant youth gatherings, somewhat in line with YMCA activities.

In response to Clark's favorable report, the International Committee first sent several officers to Buenos Aires.[37] One of them, Philip Conard, was relocated at the end of 1908 to the other side of the River Plate, where Monteverde and other local Protestants had launched in 1907 the Club Protestante (Protestant Club), whose "character and tendency . . . were entirely analogous to those of the YMCAs."[38] After negotiating with Conard, the leaders of the Club Protestante agreed to change its name to Asociación Cristiana de Jóvenes, or YMCA Montevideo, thus identifying it explicitly with the international movement. By the end of 1909, the membership of the YMCA Montevideo had already increased to almost two hundred.[39]

In 1911, the YMCA Montevideo leaders were informed of the government's intention to create the CNEF. Because sport and physical education were among the YMCA's areas of specialization, these leaders found this governmental initiative a good opportunity to expand their influence. Conard hastily urged the International Committee to send a physical director, while his Uruguayan colleagues, foreseeing New York's possible reluctance, collected funds to independently employ him. Monteverde won an opportunity to interview his old friend Batlle. He described the YMCA's physical education programs to the president and explained their applicability to Uruguay's sport policy. Despite Batlle's general suspicion of foreigners, this lobbying was successful—Batlle appointed the chairman of the YMCA Montevideo, Pedro Towers, as one of the founding members of the CNEF. [40]

In 1912, the International Committee selected a man to be sent to Montevideo: Jess Hopkins, an Iowa-born graduate of Springfield College, who had already worked in YMCAs in the United States, Canada, and the Panama Canal Zone. The CNEF quickly recognized Hopkins for his organizational ability and profound knowledge of physical education, which was unrivaled in the country. In February 1913, the CNEF resolved to employ Hopkins as the director of the first *plaza de deportes* to be inaugurated the same year. Instead of paying him a salary, the CNEF signed an agreement with the YMCA Montevideo to grant the association a subsidy in exchange for Hopkins's services. [41] His contribution was so efficient that Hopkins was later "loaned" to the CNEF on a full-time basis as its technical director, a position from which he supervised the technical aspects of Uruguay's sport policy.

Particularly, it was in the *plazas de deportes* that Hopkins's expertise was most appreciated, since no one else in Uruguay had experience in organizing North American–style playgrounds. The *plazas de deportes* also became a vehicle through which US sports such as basketball, volleyball, and baseball were introduced to Uruguayans. Hopkins's contributions were also crucial for the professional training of physical education teachers. Because the CNEF delayed launching its own institute of physical education, Hopkins sent several Uruguayans to Springfield College so that they could bring professional expertise back to the country and play leading roles among the technical staff of the CNEF. [42] Hopkins's influence in the formative years of Uruguay's sport and physical education policy were so decisive that Conard proudly stated: "It is just once in the life-time of a nation that the privilege is given to determine its type of Physical Education, and it is especially gratifying to know that that education in Uruguay will carry the mark of the North American Young Men's Christian Associations, adapted to meet the local conditions but following those highest principles." [43]

Uruguay and the IOC-YMCA Partnership in the Early 1920s

In 1919, after two years on furlough in the United States, Hopkins returned to Uruguay, this time employed by the North American YMCA's International Committee as the physical director of the South American Federation of YMCAs, a continental organization launched in 1914, with its office in Montevideo. He also continued his service to the CNEF on an honorary basis. Soon after, he was informed of the upcoming 1920 Olympics. He enthusiastically wrote to New York: "I want to attend these games by all means. I am sure that you will appreciate the value of such an experience and contact for me in relation to our continental work. . . . The thing I lack most in my work down here is the prestige which would come from some European experience."[44] However, his personal ambition was not the only reason for his excitement:

> There is a rumour that the World's Olympic Committee is going to district the globe, naming sub-committees in each section of the world who will be responsible for the detailed organisation of continental or regional championships . . . it would be a great thing for us, and I think the logical thing too, for the Association, because of its international character on this continent, to be represented on this committee.[45]

Hopkins seems to have been somehow aware of the negotiations under way. During 1919, IOC president Coubertin and the physical director of the YMCA International Committee, Elwood Brown, communicated intensely to settle a scheme in which the two institutions would cooperate to spread their common goals. The basic proposal Brown envisioned was to make use of the YMCA's worldwide network to organize, under official recognition of the IOC, several regional sport competitions, analogous to the Far Eastern Games that Brown had founded in 1913 when he was the physical director of the YMCA Manila.[46] Most likely, Hopkins, having overheard this idea, felt responsible for ensuring that South America was involved in the new global conjuncture.

Hopkins's anxiety was assuaged when he was informed that Brown was about to visit South America. Since Brown already had connections in North America, Asia, and Europe,[47] this trip was expected to further strengthen his international prestige before the official presentation of the IOC-YMCA partnership, which was scheduled for the 1920 IOC Session.[48] From March to May 1920, Brown toured Peru, Chile, Argentina,

Uruguay, and Brazil and interviewed several governmental and sport authorities. According to the report he submitted to New York, Brown assessed three items in each country: the existence of a national organization controlling different sports; the possibility of participation in the first South American Games, projected to take place in 1922 in Brazil; and the willingness to join in the constitution of a South American International Athletic Federation, an umbrella organization of national governing bodies, which would organize the South American Games in collaboration with the IOC.[49] Hopkins accompanied Brown through most of the journey, and they forged an intimate friendship.[50]

On May 6, Brown was introduced at a CNEF session. Hopkins explained briefly the circumstances surrounding the negotiation between Brown and Coubertin. Brown expressed that his mission was entrusted by the IOC, who wished each South American country to have a national institution representing all sports, which would act as each country's intermediaries before the IOC in Olympic matters. Additionally, he invited Uruguay to "the constitution of a South American Olympic Committee (*Comité Olímpico Sudamericano*), which the International [Olympic Committee] considers convenient to be instituted."[51]

In response to this exposition, Ghigliani summarized the history of the institutionalization of sport in Uruguay, including the foundation and dissolution of the FDU in the 1910s. Ghigliani mentioned that if "the IOC wants to treat with one body for each country, the CNEF would be able to serve as an intermediary," but "this is not entirely correct because the IOC wants to treat with institutions *representative* of the sports, and this is not the case of the CNEF in which the sports associations do not have representation."[52] He went on to affirm that he could present a bill in the Chamber of Deputies, of which he was a member, modifying the law to nominate some representatives of sport federations as CNEF members to ensure that the CNEF would have a representative character. "Otherwise," he continued, "it would be necessary to embark on the constitution of a National Olympic Committee."[53] Other CNEF members supported Ghigliani's assessment.

Satisfied with this explanation, Brown said that the IOC wanted to designate a delegate in each country and asked for the CNEF's opinion as to the most appropriate person in Uruguay to assume that role. Everybody present agreed that it was Ghigliani, the driving spirit of the national sport policy.[54] Before closing the session, the CNEF formally resolved that it would proceed in accordance with Ghigliani's formula and contribute to the creation of a South American Olympic Committee.[55] The follow-ing year, Ghigliani submitted the announced bill to reform the CNEF. After extended and intense debates, however, this proposal was not able to obtain a definitive sanction.[56]

Having finished a long journey through South America, Brown headed for Antwerp to present the IOC-YMCA partnership plan at the IOC Session. Hopkins sent him encouraging words: "The whole matter of the Federation hinges on the meeting you will have with the International Olympic Committee in Antwerp. If we are given some official recogni-tion, there is no question in my mind but that we can bring about the organization of a South American Athletic Federation along the lines we desire."[57] Brown accomplished his task; the IOC accepted the proposal unanimously, and the IOC-YMCA partnership was officially endorsed. Brown and Hopkins set out to undertake their next venture: the 1922 South American Games in Rio de Janeiro.

The preparation of this event, intended as part of Brazil's centenary festival, was plagued by difficulties, one of the principal problems being an economic crisis that was severely affecting Brazil.[58] Throughout 1921 and early 1922, Brown, Hopkins, and Brazilian sport officials stayed in close touch, while little moved forward. Hopkins was inclined to give up holding the event in 1922 and proposed more than once to organize the first regional competition under the IOC patronage more decently in Montevideo in the following year. He secured a verbal promise from the CNEF that Uruguay could host the Games in 1923 if the event in Rio de Janeiro eventually fell through.[59] Brown, less pessimistic, stuck to the original idea.

While preparation for the South American Games was reaching a deadlock, Ghigliani was designated officially as an IOC member at the IOC Session held in June 1921 in Lausanne.[60] This news was particularly pleasant for the YMCA because, according to Brown, this was the first time the IOC had selected a member solely on the recommendation of a third party, a fact that was believed to enhance the prestige of the YMCA in the Olympic Movement.[61] Coubertin also dispatched to Brown, quite generously, seven credentials that certified the holder as a representa-tive of the IOC in all technical questions regarding the regional games, with the name of the bearer left blank. These credentials were forwarded to Hopkins, who could designate anyone suitable in South American countries.[62]

Despite the announced disposition of the CNEF to collaborate with the South American Games, it was not until May 1922 that the CNEF started preparing to send a national team, after a report from Hopkins assured that the event was definitely going to take place. As the schedule was too tight to obtain financial support from the government by way of a legislative process, the CNEF decided to cover the traveling expenses with its own budget.[63] In August, the CNEF approved a national delegation to be sent to Rio de Janeiro consisting of sixty-three athletes and six staff members for track and field, boxing, fencing, shooting, basketball, and rowing.[64]

In September 1922, the first regional competition under the IOC-YMCA partnership was held in Rio de Janeiro. The event itself was as troublesome as its preparation. Soon after arriving in Brazil, Uruguayan athletes raised objections to a series of organizational problems: sources of dissatisfaction ranged from the lack of sufficient water to maintain the tidiness of the lavatories to the repeated modification of the competitive schedule and disputes over interpretations of the rules. Unable to stand the complaints from sportsmen and the organizers' laxity in fixing the issues, the Uruguayan *chef de mission* Héctor Gómez abandoned his post in the middle of the event.[65]

Despite widespread discontent, Uruguayan sport officials embraced the noble cause of the regional "Olympics." After the closing of the event, the CNEF sent a detailed questionnaire to Brown concerning the way in which future international competitions should be organized, which indicates the Uruguayans' willingness to host the next South American Games. "Should the CNEF," Ghigliani argued ardently, "wish to take up the organization of the International Games to be held in 1925 . . . it would be able to demonstrate to the whole world how an official authority is capable of realizing the international games better than any sport institution."[66]

In October 1922, Henri de Baillet-Latour, who represented the IOC at the South American Games in place of Coubertin, visited Montevideo, where he started his Latin American tour, which lasted more than six months.[67] When invited to a CNEF session, Baillet-Latour expressed his "immense satisfaction to know personally his beloved colleague Dr. Ghigliani," and he lauded the CNEF's "indefatigable and efficient work" that had brought about the "considerable advance . . . in comparison with the other countries, in matters of physical education," which he was able to verify during his short stay in Montevideo.[68] He underlined an excessive nationalist sentiment that South Americans tended to express in sport fields as the gravest problem that surfaced in Rio de Janeiro, and he enumerated several requirements that needed to be considered so that future South American Games could be held under the IOC flag.[69]

Upon his return to Europe, Baillet-Latour presented a report on his Latin American mission at the IOC Session held in Rome. Notwithstanding his criticism of the organization of the South American Games, Baillet-Latour showed that his admiration for the CNEF was not mere diplomatic flattery: "I dare to say that the physical education in Uruguay, under the skillful direction of Mr. Jess Hopkins, backed by our eminent colleague Deputy Ghigliani, surpasses that of almost all the countries of the world."[70] Referring to the *plazas de deportes*, he praised the CNEF's plan "to have someday one playground in every town."[71] Baillet-Latour even recommended the CNEF to be a candidate for the *Coupe Olympique* (Olympic Cup), a prize awarded by the IOC every year in recognition of institutions that contributed to the development of sport and Olympism around the world (Image 1.2). This honor was ultimately bestowed in 1925, in the wake of Uruguay's football triumph at the 1924 Paris Olympics.[72]

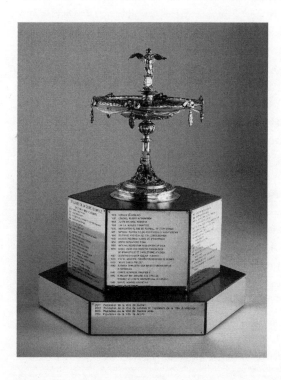

Image 1.2. Olympic Cup. *Courtesy of the International Olympic Committee.*

The IOC-YMCA-CNEF Triangle and Its Collapse

In retrospect, Baillet-Latour's applause for the Uruguayan sport policy at the heart of the Olympic Movement was a culmination of the harmonious relationship that was being cultivated between the IOC, the YMCA, and the CNEF. If the CNEF had already forged more or less substantial connections with the IOC and the YMCA during the 1910s, the IOC-YMCA partnership signed in 1920 intensified these existing connections, effectively triangulating these three sport institutions.

One principle that linked these institutions was a strong belief that the ultimate goal of large-scale sport competitions was not the formation of a handful of elite athletes, but the diffusion and establishment of healthy sporting habits among the masses, thus contributing to raising the physical and moral standards of all citizens. The magnificent performance of elite athletes in Olympic arenas was meaningful as long as it emerged as a consequence of the development of a wider sporting culture. If Coubertin summarized this principle in 1919 as "all sports for all people," the YMCA had "play for everybody" as an emblem of its global strategy for sport diffusion.[73] These mottos—which, for Brown, were identical to each other—were fully embraced by the CNEF, whose policy, as best exemplified in the *plazas de deportes* project, was oriented toward the formation of a democratic, participative, and inclusive sporting culture since its foundation in 1911.[74]

However, the IOC-YMCA-CNEF triangle, shaped through the effort of Coubertin, Brown, Hopkins, and Ghigliani and united by similar sporting ideals, was tragically ephemeral. The first rupture came between the IOC and the CNEF. Since 1919, the appointment of CNEF members had been in the hands of the National Council of Administration, a plural executive branch composed of nine members that took up most of the functions previously assumed by the president. This council turned into a highly contested stage of intricate political maneuvers that characterized Uruguayan politics. Particularly significant were the deepening splits within the Colorado Party between the reformist *batllistas* and other more moderate sectors.[75] This political situation directly affected the CNEF's path.

In August 1923, the Nationalist and the non-*batllista* Colorado councillors banded together to make up a majority against the *batllistas* in the National Council of Administration and to vote for the replacement of all the appointed members of the CNEF, unquestionably in an attempt to kick the *batllista* dominance out from the nucleus of national sport policy. Among the newly nominated CNEF members were Nationalist deputies and nonorthodox Colorados, but no core *batllista* politicians were included.[76] Removed from the CNEF, Ghigliani founded the COU in October.[77] This was as much a procedure he had announced in front of Brown in 1920 and a legitimate exercise of his authority endorsed by the IOC as a tactical measure to counteract the CNEF, which was now controlled by his political rivals. A conflict emerged between the CNEF and the COU regarding the participation in the 1924 Paris Olympics, particularly concerning football, which had split up by then, at least partly, due to the same political antagonism. This conflict eventually led to the dissolution of the COU by the decision of Ghigliani himself.[78]

In 1925, once tensions within the Colorado Party eased, Ghigliani was brought back to the CNEF.[79] Two years later, however, in protest against the betrayal of a Colorado councillor who had joined with the Nationalists on an important issue, the *batllista* sector decided to oblige its members to decline all public positions designated by the current National Council of Administration.[80] Ghigliani, as a faithful party politician, left the CNEF, to his bitter regret, never to return.[81]

Kept away from sport policy-making and increasingly bothered by day-to-day political struggles, it is reasonable to assume that Ghigliani lost his initial interest in Olympic matters, although he remained an IOC member until his death in 1936. Ghigliani refounded the COU in 1927, but sporadic references suggest that there was no consensus between the CNEF, the COU, and national sport federations as to who was responsible for organizing the Olympic delegation for the 1928 and 1932 Olympic Games.[82] Indeed, none of them was willing to take a strong initiative. In the 1928 Amsterdam Olympics, the football team sent independently by the Asociación Uruguaya de Football (Uruguayan Football Association) constituted the entire national delegation.[83] In 1932, only one rower represented Uruguay in Los Angeles. The Olympic fever seems to have lost its momentum in Uruguayan sport as well as in the CNEF's agenda.

The IOC-YMCA partnership did not last long either. The unexpected death of Elwood Brown in 1924 considerably damaged its fluid and productive cooperation. The idea of organizing regional games across the world—the core of the alliance scheme—did not flourish. Despite Hopkins's attempts to continue the effort of his late friend in the mid-1920s, the second South American Games never came into being. One of the principal obstacles appears to have been the reluctance of South American sport federations, which preferred holding continental championships separately.[84]

Finally, the last piece of the triangle collapsed in 1928, when Hopkins decided to step down from his sixteen-year-long work in South America. During the 1920s, the YMCA's International Committee suffered from a serious financial deficit, which led to the philanthropists' growing pressure to "rationalize" its missionary work abroad.[85] The drastic budget cut imposed by New York compelled Hopkins to withdraw, in order to save the South American Federation of YMCAs from a financial crisis, since he recognized the high cost of retaining him, his wife, and their seven children in Uruguay.[86] Even though the CNEF maintained a degree of connection through its technical personnel with the YMCA Montevideo, the direct and efficient contact with North America was broken off after the departure of Hopkins.

Conclusion

From the Uruguayan viewpoint, the Olympic participation in the 1920s was an expected consequence of the efforts that the CNEF had invested since 1911 in establishing a link with European and North American sporting cultures, which were supposed to provide an indisputable reference that would guide Uruguay's sport policy. This perspective sheds light on the role of local actors not as passive recipients of external influence but as active vehicles of the global Olympic expansion in peripheral regions.

Another interesting fact that the Uruguayan experience reveals is the existence of a prototype of the ideal known today as "sport for all" as a catalyst of these connections between the IOC, the YMCA, and the CNEF. In this sense, the CNEF's status as a governmental agency created by the democratic, welfare-oriented regime facilitated the embracement of this sporting ideal and contributed to Uruguay's successful incorporation into the Olympic Movement. At the same time, however, the political nature of the CNEF also turned sport and Olympic matters into a field of intense political struggles. The award of the Olympic Cup in 1925 was certainly belated, but it testifies to the time when the CNEF's sport policy and the global Olympic diffusion created a harmonic resonance with each other.

CHAPTER 2

Enthusiastic Yet Awkward Dance Partners

Olympism and Cuban Nationalism

THOMAS F. CARTER

For over a hundred years, the choreography between Olympism and Cuban nationalism evolved with the changing political tunes within Cuba and among international actors. The idea of Olympism has not remained static over the past twelve decades. The coherence found in the twenty-first century Olympic Charter was nowhere to be found in Olympism's original articulations. Initially, Olympism was promoted as a movement designed for the betterment of civilization, embodied through white men of a specific social class through what broadly can be considered as a form of humanism. In no way has Olympism played a part in the populist expressions of *cubanidad*, nor has the Olympic Movement played a significant part in the ongoing struggles over how the Cuban nation should be defined. Yet Cuban leaders constantly linked nationhood to Olympism to maintain and justify their acts and positions in Cuba and the world. The dance steps of Cuban nationalism and *cubanidad*—that is, the idea of being Cuban—rumba-ed their way through their own complex set of melodies over several centuries.[1] Olympism provided some new notes for Cuban elites to lead the dance of the Cuban nation. Cuban elites harmonized Olympism and nationalism to espouse a particular version of *cubanidad* to maintain their advantageous political and economic position in Cuban society.

This chapter provides a preliminary overview of the ways in which Cuban elites embraced Olympism to inform and shape Cuban nationalism. As a result, this chapter is broken into five distinct Olympic periods

DOI: https://doi.org/10.34053/scs2019.o.2

based on an earlier Cuban analysis of Olympic history. Manuel González García, the president of the Cuban National Olympic Committee from 1963 until 1993, defined the first four of these Olympic periods in 1991.[2] González García identified each of these periods as distinct in the evolution of Olympism—not as specific to Cuban Olympism per se, but more generically to Olympism overall. The fifth Olympic period is one I have added, to cover the most recent twenty-year period. Consequently, it is also the purpose of this chapter to make some initial analysis of Cuba's engagement with and relationship to Olympism as an evolving ideology of sporting modernity. The summary discussion of the main themes that emerged during these epochs that characterize the relationships between Olympism and Cuban nationalism is preceded by a concise review of the principle tenets of Olympism and their evolution in International Olympic Committee (IOC) practice, and an even more terse summary of the emergence and shifting currents of Cuban nationalism. In each Olympic period that follows this discussion, the importance of Olympism to the Cuban nation is relayed through a recounting of both Cuba's athletic participation in various Olympic Games and the Comité Olímpico Cubano's (Cuban Olympic Committee, COC) various interactions with the IOC in its various iterations.

Olympism and Cuban Nationalism

The establishment of the International Olympic Committee in 1894 coincided with an increasing number of a broad range of newly formed international organizations, such as the International Red Cross and the International Council of Women, that all shared humanistic and universal values. These organizations were products of late nineteenth-century liberalism, which emphasized values of equality, fairness, justice, respect for individual persons, rationality, international understanding, peace, autonomy, and excellence. Coubertin's contribution was to embed these values in the milieu of sport.[3] Consistently throughout the ensuing twelve decades, the one standard value is that of humanism. Olympic leaders and dominant Olympic institutions claim that "Olympism is Humanism."[4] This core, unchanging aspect of Olympism is what made it so readily easy for socialist societies to link Olympism with their own state-based ideologies. Even after the demise of the Soviet bloc, Olympism became readily linked to neoliberal ideals of individualism and market forces as humanistic in the form of a neo-Olympism that still asserted a humanistic core linked to consumption. At the end of both world wars, Olympism was readily incorporated into the ideological position of the victors, allowing the dehumanization and exclusion of the defeated even within a humanistic rhetoric. Quite simply, Olympism is a flexible ideological tool that allows for its adoption under a range of political ideologies.[5]

While Olympism is promoted and performed broadly through the Olympic Games, the actual ethos of Olympism extends beyond the Olympic Games themselves into other international sporting events, such as the Central American and Caribbean Games and the Pan-American Games. Although these events are not usually understood in the popular imagination to be affiliated with the Olympic Games, a clear and strong association of Olympism is made in the historiography of late twentieth-century and twenty-first-century Cuban sport history. Consequently, Cuban involvement in all of these international sporting events is salient to the inculcation of Olympism into the project of building the Cuban nation.

Nation building is widely considered to be a relatively recent phenomenon characteristic of modernity.[6] Late twentieth-century academics' concentration on national identities certainly increased as greater attention was paid to identity politics in Latin America. Scholarship on Cuba and Cuban nationalism was a clear part of this focus, particularly in terms of understanding how Cuban nationalism historically inspired, fed into, and sustained the revolution. The dilemmas and struggles of Cuban nation building extending from the late nineteenth century through the entirety of the twentieth form the core of this scholarship.[7] Beginning with the writings of Félix Varela and José Martí, then ranging from Jorge Mañach's *choteo*, Fernando Ortiz's *ajiaco*, Manuel Moreno Fraginals's sugarmill, Gustavo Pérez-Firmat's hyphen, and Ruth Behar's bridges, *cubanidad* has remained fluid, focused more on structures of feeling and social relations than on a geographically fixed notion of being Cuban.[8] At first glance, this approach could be attributed to the transnational position of the abovementioned writers: all of them spent at least part of their lives outside Cuba. However, Cold War–era scholarship often "froze" the fluidity of *cubanidad* into reified political stances that depended upon which side of the Florida Straits one wrote. Nevertheless, to dismiss debates over the Cuban nation as simply blinkered Cold War ideologies is a facile, and thus inadequate, explanation for the distinct histories espoused about Cuban nation building. Instead, they are part of the continuous process of (re)defining and refining national identity. All of these studies, irrespective of political ideology, reinforce the sentiment that nations are discretely modern formations of identity.

However conceived, the emergence of nineteenth- and twentieth-century nations as recognizable entities is inextricably linked to the expansive European colonial systems and industrial capitalism. These imperial systems both informed and limited the construction of social existence. Such systems and identities where culturally specific institutional and representational forms are produced include the way certain powers classify the world, how these classifications change over time, and how, where, and when such notions emerge.[9] For instance, "when the colonized respond in the genre of rational debate—at least as defined in European terms—the hegemony of the colonizing culture may well be on its way to instilling itself in its new subjects."[10] Given that the earliest manifestations of national imaginaries were in the Caribbean colonies,[11] the very concept of "nation," although part of the triumph of a European modernity that entailed a wholesale revolution—a revolution in the way the world was categorized, producing a framework of knowledge that proclaims its own universality and validity independent of local social hierarchies—emanated and originated from colonial elites seeking greater autonomy and independence from imperial centers.[12]

It is in this context that the Olympic Movement, the IOC, and the ideology of Olympism should be understood, particularly in relation to the nascent postcolonial nations of Latin America, including Cuba, at the end of the nineteenth century. Sport certainly plays a role in nation building, and it most definitely did so in Cuba's case. Sport was primarily for the wealthy as a diversionary entertainment, whatever the sport might have been, but most especially the ones used as symbols of a modern Cuban national identity, such as baseball.[13] Participation in and certainly control of sport was mostly restricted to the urban elite of Havana and the wealthy Cuban diaspora from the mid-nineteenth century well into the twentieth century.[14] The use of sport was part of the continuous process of building a Cuban nation in a specifically modern "European" image. Olympism played a clear part in the shaping of Cuban national identity, particularly in the early part of the twentieth century, even though popular sports in Cuba, such as baseball and boxing, were in no way affiliated with Olympism (boxing has been contested in Olympic Games since 1904). The latter part of the twentieth century saw a more conflicted relationship between Olympism and Cuban national identity. As the Olympic breadth of sports expanded, several Cuban popular sports became part of the late twentieth-century Olympic Games. It is striking how the various histories written about the Cuban Revolution and the longevity of the Fidel Castro regime do not give any substantial attention to sport despite Castro's clear passion for and value of sport as a mechanism for nation building and international politics. Throughout Cuba's nominal and actual independence, Olympism, even though certain Olympic sports may not have been widely practiced in Cuba, has played a role in shaping how the Cuban nation was imagined.

Cuban scholar Pedro Pablo Rodríguez insists that national identity is a process that is constantly transforming in historical and social terms.[15] Rodríguez recognizes that although identities are constructed, the processes of their formation are ongoing and indeterminate, as the relations that they represent and their content are continuously evolving. Cubans are acutely aware that national identity is not immutable and fixed but contested—rife with conflicted, contradictory, and incoherent representations—precisely because the very history of the Cuban nation has been one of ongoing and continuous struggle for existence, recognition, independence, and sovereignty.[16] Therefore, the Cuban nation has been undergoing and continues to undergo a constant process of construction and deconstruction as it adjusts to and reconciles world events alongside Cubans' own perceptions of their changing needs. Yet it can be argued that non-European nations are emergent forms of modern identity partially determined by the historical circumstance of European empires. This is certainly the way in which Cubans engaged with Olympism, and if this view is accepted, then any consideration of those national struggles and nation-building exercises must take into account not only the domestic political contexts but reach beyond those imperially defined borders. Thus, the question of Olympism as it exists in relation to the Cuban nation is especially pertinent, and the particular approach of this chapter aims to excavate the core, intertwined threads of Olympism and Cuban nationalism even as each underwent its own separate evolution.

1896–1912:
Emergence of Olympism and
Nascent Cuban Independence

Cuba at the turn of the twentieth century had gained and lost independence in one fell swoop. After a brutal campaign against the Spanish at the end of the nineteenth century, Cuban forces found themselves sidelined by invading US military might, transforming their conflict from a Cuban war of independence into a US war of foreign conquest. The United States occupied Cuba in 1899 and over the next few years enforced its will by directing the nominally independent Cuban state's constitution. In it, the Cubans were forced to include the 1902 Platt Amendment, named after the US ambassador to Cuba in 1900, which stated that the United States had the sovereign right to intervene in Cuba's domestic affairs if, at any time, the United States felt its own interests were at threat.[17]

Cuba's elite expressed early and considerable commitment to the Olympic venture as Olympism began. Cuba's explicit announcement of Olympism's presence in the country was formalized with the founding of a nominal Comité Olímpico Cubano (as in existing in name only) in 1896, making it one of the first Latin American countries to form such a body, even though it was not part of the Olympic Movement. Rather, the earliest engagements with the Olympic Movement were individual efforts that had nothing to do with that nominal COC. Nonetheless, some Cuban elites attempted to forge strong links between Olympism and nascent Cuban national identity. This was done through individual participation in early Olympic Games and an attempt to bring the Olympic Games to Havana in 1920.

Cuba's participation in the first five Olympic Games (1896–1912) comprised a limited handful of athletes (the majority of whom came from the upper echelons of Cuban society) in the 1900 and 1904 Games. Cuba did not participate in the 1908 or 1912 Games. The most well-known and Cuba's first medalist was Ramón Fonst; he was also the first Latin American athlete ever to win Olympic gold. Fonst was a wealthy Cuban who did not even live in Cuba; he moved to Paris at the age of ten in 1893. As a teenager he competed in European competitions in target shooting with the pistol and revolver, finishing first forty-four times. He also boxed, winning trophies and titles among the prestigious sporting societies of Paris, London, and Brussels. He also won first-place trophies in cycling against some of the best cyclists in Europe, all before 1899, when he then dedicated himself to fencing, winning the world's championship in épée. Fonst won gold in fencing in épée at the 1900 Olympics in Paris and then gold in foil and épée at the 1904 Olympics in St. Louis, respectively. He was not the only Cuban to win gold in St. Louis. Manuel Dioniso Díaz won gold at sabre, which meant that Cuba swept the individual golds in fencing. Those two, along with Albertson Van Zo Post, who represented the United States in individual competition and then joined the Cubans to form a "Cuba" team, won the team foil competition, defeating the US team 7–2.[18]

The exception to the gentleman athlete that epitomized early Cuban national sporting self-imaginings was Félix "El Andarín" Carvajal Soto, a Cuban Olympian who continues to symbolize the Cuban attitude toward sport and the Olympics. A controversial sporting figure at that time, he was a professional walker who competed in long-distance endurance events in Cuba at a time when the 1895–98 War of Independence against Spain was raging. He ran the marathon at the 1904 Olympics in St. Louis. Carvajal was either a postman or a doorman—it is not entirely clear—but what is agreed upon is that Caravajal was not part of the Cuban elite and used his own funds and popular donations to finance his trip to and participation in the Olympic Games.[19] His trip to St. Louis was not smooth sailing, however. He allegedly lost all his money in a game of dice on the boat to New Orleans, arriving with no way to pay for the rest of his journey, food, or hotels. He stepped up to the starting line in St. Louis wearing long trousers and high walking boots. He had no money, no coach, no appropriate shoes or clothing for such a race. A North American sportsman spotted him at the starting line and gave him some shorts that reached to his knees to wear instead of his trousers. To the spectators' great surprise, Carvajal led after thirty kilometers (a marathon is 42.195 kms), but suffering from hunger and not having any coaches to assist him, he picked a green apple from a tree along the route. This fruit gave him extreme stomach cramps, ultimately leading to him being overtaken and finishing in fourth place.[20] Carvajal's efforts epitomized the Cuban spirit, reflected in his embodiment of "coger botella" by dealing with his setbacks and refusing to be denied—values that continued in later nationalist struggles and revolutions in the twentieth century.[21]

It was not just in the fields of competition that Cuban Olympism was expressed and aspired to as an indicator of Cuba's existence as a modern nation. Cuban elites also expressed a dedicated interest in hosting the 1920 Olympics. Dignitaries of Havana, some who were Cuban and others who were not, wrote to the IOC several times throughout 1914–16 requesting more information and demonstrating the support of the country's political and economic leadership, including formal letters direct from the mayor of Havana, Freyre de Andrade, and secretary to the president, Rafael Montero, confirming the backing of the president of the Republic, Mario Menocal.[22] Commitments from leading businesspeople in Havana amounting to a total of a million US dollars "to cover the expenses and required publicity campaign" with another half a million dollars committed for the construction of a stadium, in which "the ground will cost nothing," were promised as inducements for naming Havana as Olympic host.[23] In related correspondence, Cuba's economic situation was highlighted as being able to afford hosting the event: "Last year Cuba sold over $240,000,000.00 worth of sugar besides tobacco, fruit, and minerals. Her customs revenues were $28,000,000.00 so you can see how well she is fixed to successfully 'stage' the Games."[24] Further, it was claimed that the Cubans would cover the transport costs of all European athletes and the King of Belgium's expenses to travel to Havana for the 1920 Olympics. Cuba at this time was experiencing the beginnings of "the Dance of the Millions," an economic boom based on sugar exports that was directly linked to the hostilities in Europe.[25] The benevolent offer of hosting the 1920 Olympics might be seen as a jaded political move, since Antwerp was supposed to host the 1916 Games. It was clear to everyone that World War I would not end by then. Several cities from around the world contacted the IOC to see if they might serve as a viable host for the 1920 Games, even as informed political opinion was divided among European members of the International Olympic Committee in 1916 as to whether World War I would have ceased by 1920. Nonetheless, Cuba was willing to host regardless of the situation in Europe as "a way to assuage the wounds and devastation of Belgium and the rest of Europe" in which "the people of the City and the Republic are willing to go to almost any expense to get you here in order to show off their beautiful country and city."[26]

1920–1936:
Modernist Olympism and Neocolonial Cuba

The offer to host the 1920 Games was curious given that the IOC had not yet recognized the Cuban Olympic Committee (COC) as a fully fledged, proper National Olympic Committee. Nevertheless, Cuban leaders, including the COC, expressly linked Cuban nationalism with the emergence of a modernist Olympism by noting that the signs of modernity—progress, civilization, and technological sophistication—that would be evident in any such international sporting spectacle would thereby demonstrate Cuba's status as a "modern, civilized" country. It was not until 1926 that the Cubans finalized the organization of their NOC and had it recognized by the IOC. While the attempt to bring the 1920 Olympics to Havana was not successful, other Olympic-style events did come to Havana as part of the regional sporting nationalism that Cuba advocated as a clear demonstration of those modern qualities that all nations aspired to and espoused.

Havana hosted the second Central American Games in 1930, in which nine countries in total took part. While these Games invoked the spirit of modernity and hinted at Olympism, they were not part of the Olympic Movement at this time. There are two notable aspects of these Games. One, Jamaica was the first Anglophone country in the history of the event to take part; the other eight countries in the 1930 Central American Games were all Hispanophone. nations.[27] The other item of note was the participation of women, with six Cuban women taking part in the tennis tournament. In the end, Cuba topped the medal table, winning more medals (and more gold medals) than all the other countries combined.[28]

Beyond hosting the 1930 Central American Games, Cuba sent athletes to the then-renamed Central American and Caribbean Games in El Salvador in 1935, again winning more medals than any other participating nation.[29] Cuba also did well at the Central American and Caribbean Games in Panama in 1938, although it slipped to third in the total medals table behind Mexico and Panama, respectively, before again topping the total medals table in Barranquilla, Colombia, in 1946.[30]

While Cuba did send contingents to these regional international sporting events, attending the Olympic Games themselves was much more problematic. Having lost out on hosting the 1920 Olympics, Cuba also did not send any athletes to Antwerp for the Seventh Olympic Games held in 1920. Actual participation in the Olympic Games by Cuban athletes did not resume until 1924, in Paris, where, as in the previous era, Cuba's presence was limited to a handful of wealthy individuals, including Ramón Fonst, competing in two events: fencing and yachting. However, these were the first Olympic Games in which Cuba was recognized as an official delegation, taking part in the opening ceremonies, in which Fonst was the flag bearer. Cuba did not send an official delegation again until after World War II; however, Cuban athletes did compete in some of the ensuing Olympic Games. From those nine in 1920, only one Cuban competed in the 1928 Olympics in Amsterdam. José Barrientos, known as El Relámpago del Caribe (Caribbean Lightning), competed in the 100 meters sprint but did not make the finals. Barrientos, like Fonst and other athletes, did not specialize in sport in the manner that is now the norm in the twenty-first century.[31] Barrientos also rowed and played intercollegiate US-American football while a student at the University of Havana.[32] Cubans did not compete in the 1932 Los Angeles Olympics or the 1936 Berlin Olympics, though some Cubans were part of a contingent of Cuban athlete-artists that participated in the cultural Olympiad in Los Angeles.[33]

1948–1968:
High Modern Olympism and Postcolonial Cuba

Cuba's Olympic presence truly begin to expand at the so-called Austerity Olympics of 1948 in London. This era of modernization and development entangled Cuba, along with many other Latin American countries, in the burgeoning international tensions of the Cold War between the United States and the Soviet Union. At the same time, Cuba itself was embroiled in its own political struggles throughout these years as growing frustration with US domination of all aspects of Cuban life seethed underneath a growing connection between US-led consumerism and the ongoing attempts of national identity to demonstrate both how alike and distinct Cubans were from their North American counterparts at the same time.[34] The 1948 London Olympics saw Cubans compete in more sports than in any previous Olympic Games and would remain the broadest level of competition until the 1968 Mexico City Olympics, which occurred after the 1959 Cuban Revolution. Throughout these two decades there was no attempt to bring the Olympic Games to Cuba, primarily because Cubans were caught up in their own neocolonial nationalist struggles. While the 1936 Berlin Olympics were a clearly nationalist, ideology-based politicization of the Olympic Games, further politicization of the Olympics continued at the London Olympics, as neither the defeated Axis powers nor the Soviet Union and its Eastern European bloc allies were allowed to participate. Throughout this Olympic period, nationalism played a major role, if not the major role, as two competing ideologies used the Olympic Games as the stage to symbolically prove which was the more vital, strong, and vibrant way of life politically, economically, and socially. The inclusion of the Soviet bloc nations starting in 1952 led to inherent tensions within the Games as the Olympics themselves became a dramatic kind of "war minus the shooting."[35]

Throughout the 1950s, Cubans were more focused on their own nationalist struggles, and this was reflected in the decreasing numbers from the high at the 1948 London Olympics back down to a handful (single digits) of athletes participating in the 1956 and 1960 Olympics.[36] During that time of neocolonial nationalist struggle, one of the battlegrounds was the Cuban Olympic Committee. The Fulgencio Batista government attempted to co-opt the COC by forming its own committee. At this time, a political struggle ensued in which the president of the independent COC, Miguel Moenck, wrote to Avery Brundage, then-president of the IOC, about the political pressure Cuba's national sporting federations were facing from the Batista dictatorship.[37] Brundage had a long, fruitful friendship with Moenck, and Moenck's trouble with Batista was emblematic of a larger IOC challenge in which many of the existing NOCs only existed at the behest and funding of their respective governments—a direct threat to the intent of Olympism as being removed from political persuasions and thus a direct threat to the sovereign independence of the IOC itself. Moenck was Brundage's trusted advisor on all things related to Latin America and Olympism.[38] After a protracted struggle, the Batista government failed to fully subsume the COC into its orbit because, although Batista, like all dictators, sought to control all aspects of political and economic life, there was a distinct lack of ideological fortitude within his regime.[39]

Things would not be the same when the Castro-led 1959 Revolution took over. Throwing off neocolonial US domination, the revolution heralded the beginning of a postcolonial Cuba. Echoing the Olympic Spirit—though not necessarily in the same vein, given the strong national and anticolonial sentiments of the revolutionary ethos in the 1960s—Castro explained Cuban Olympism:

> Someday it will be so—Olympiads where the people participate, all the people with the same sporting spirit, with the main spirit of competition and in reality, as it should be and as it will be someday: the day when there are no contrary interests against the people. When nobody will go there with anti-sporting and political ends.[40]

The terminology here is illuminating. Castro's use of "Olympiad" was a broader incorporation of the Olympic ethos, applied to any and all international sporting events. Thus, for the new revolutionary Cuba, Olympism is precisely that which Coubertin espoused: a form of humanism embedded in sport. Nonetheless, Castro recognized the Cold War ideological pretext that underpins any such event, clearly linking politics and sport despite Brundage's insistence that Olympic sport is sacrosanct and removed from international politics. Thus, Castro argued,

> we cannot remove ourselves from the reality that our team is the team most feared in these Olympiads and also it is going to be the most hated in the Olympiads. The ideal would be that everyone goes to compete with real sporting spirit, as we are going. But the enemies of our country and our Revolution, are not going with this spirit. They are going with political spirit, with politicians' spirit in these Olympiads.[41]

Therefore, Olympism for revolutionary leaders in the 1960s was a humanistic ethos of sport that had clear links to the ethos of the revolution in terms of amateurism, anticommercialism, and the intrinsic worth of athletic endeavors as a means of betterment of humanity—all values that Brundage espoused as well.

Olympism, though, was a highly contested symbol throughout the decade as Cuban exiles in Miami under the auspices of the Unión Deportiva de Cuba Libre (Sporting Union of Free Cuba) maintained a constant barrage of correspondence with Brundage, calling attention to the explicit politicization of sport by Cuban officials and the "professional" athletes of Cuban sport in international competition.[42] At this time, Brundage was loath to recognize the revolution's incarnation of Cuba's NOC even as allies of the Unión Deportiva de Cuba Libre asserted that they spoke for the "real" COC, whose members were now in exile or imprisoned on the island, including Brundage's close associate Moenck.[43] Ultimately, though Brundage had to acknowledge the Cuban Revolution's NOC as the legitimate COC since the precedent of recognizing other communist countries' National Olympic Committees had been set, despite the clear links between those committees and government ministries.

1972–1992:
Cold War Politics and the
Golden Era of Cuban Olympism

The golden era of Cuban sport announced itself at the 1972 Munich Olympics, in which Cuban boxers, athletes, and basketball players won medals. Throughout this period, Cuban Olympians became legends, such as heavyweight boxer Teófilo Stevenson and athletes Alberto Juantorena and Javier Sotomayor, who were lauded as exemplary revolutionary heroes and fed the embodied ethos and nationalist rhetoric of revolutionary values. This same period of Cuban success coincides with Cold War tensions dominating the Olympic Games. International politics, usually publicly asserted to be outside or beyond Olympism, were all too brutally introduced to a worldwide audience when Palestinians snuck into the Olympic Village and killed and took members of the Israeli Olympic contingent hostage in Munich at the 1972 Olympics. Live television coverage of these violent events demonstrated all too clearly that the Olympic Games were not sacrosanct and removed from world events and international politics, despite the ideological rhetoric espoused by the IOC's leaders. That reality was reinforced throughout the ensuing Olympiads as international boycotts of the 1976, 1980, and 1984 Olympics hampered the vision and message of Olympism as a unifying humanitarian movement.

Cuba used the IOC as a means to facilitate its own agenda amid tense international political situations. At times successful and at other times not, Cuba's relations during this period in particular ranged from outright hostility to a warm embrace of Olympism as a global political project. The Cuban government used the IOC when other means of communication between it and foreign governments were not producing desired results.

For example, Cuban officials became gravely concerned about the reports coming out of Chile regarding the arrest and treatment of Salvador Allende's supporters in the immediate aftermath of the Chilean coup d'état on September 11, 1973, because there were Cuban personnel in Chile. Cuba had been unable to obtain any information about or communication with their citizens in Chile and were receiving no response from the newly installed Augusto Pinochet regime to their official queries. A week after Pinochet's coup d'état, Cuban authorities beseeched the IOC to locate Cuban sport personnel in Chile, as they were gravely concerned about these technicians that were part of Cuba's support for the now-deposed Allende government.[44] The director of the IOC, Monique Berlioux, wrote to the Cubans on November 1 of that year that the president of the IOC, Lord Killanin, did send formal requests for information about the Cuban contingent and received reassurances of their well-being and that they would be repatriated soon. The Cubans did return to Cuba in late November that year.[45]

For the rest of the 1970s, Cuban Olympism maintained its victorious results in athletic competition, but the 1980s, in which Olympism no longer reflected Cuban aspirations, proved to be highly contentious. During this time, the Cubans positioned it as an obstacle to the Cuban

Revolution. Cuba became heavily involved in the behind-the-scenes Olympic politics in the 1980s precisely because of its initial solidarity with the Soviet boycott of the 1984 Los Angeles Olympics. That absence led to a dispute in the Pan-American Sports Organization's (PASO) allocation of the 1987 Pan-American Games. Initially awarded to Santiago, Chile, the Pinochet regime's outright political oppression and human rights violations resulted in the PASO's removal of the event from Santiago to Quito and Guayaquil, Ecuador, in 1983. However, the Ecuadorian government informed PASO that it too would be unable to host the 1987 Pan-American Games due to its own economic stresses. Aware of this situation, the Cubans made it publicly known in early 1984 that they were interested in hosting the 1987 Pan-American Games. Mario Vázquez Raña, then-president of the Mexican NOC and president of PASO, held a hastily convened meeting, unbeknownst to the Cuban representatives, in Mexico in November 1984 in which Indianapolis, Indiana, was chosen to host the 1987 Pan-American Games.

The Cubans were incensed at Vázquez Raña's actions, claiming it was all a conspiracy against them, and appealed to Juan Antonio Samaranch as the president of the IOC, which was the authoritative organization that oversaw the regional Games' governing bodies, including PASO.[46] Samaranch, however, denied any such authority, stating that each regional governing body was independent of the IOC Executive Board and as such he could not intervene in the decision. Both Vázquez Raña and the United States Olympic Committee secretary general, George Miller, independently communicated with their Cuban counterpart, Manuel González García, in an attempt to mollify the Cubans, by insisting that there was no desire to disenfranchise the Cubans or prevent them from ever hosting the Pan-American Games.[47] Miller's concern was sufficient to warrant a visit to Havana to meet with Castro, González García, and the COC president, José Ramón Fernández, on June 3, 1986.[48] Miller's concerns over Cuba's anger made them anxious about Cuba's participation in the 1987 Pan-American Games and the 1988 Seoul Olympics.

Practically simultaneously as the conflict over the Pan-American Games was occurring, the IOC itself was facing a new challenge. When Seoul was announced as the host city for the 1988 Olympics on September 30, 1981, the Democratic People's Republic of Korea (PRK) through its NOC began a vast international protest campaign, which was considerably increased immediately after the end of the 1984 Los Angeles Olympics. A number of National Olympic Committees gave their support to the PRK, including Italy and Yemen. The last thing the IOC desired was yet another Olympic Games riven by international politics. Given that the last three Olympics in Montreal, Moscow, and Los Angeles all suffered from some major international boycott consisting of at least twenty-seven countries, the fear was that the Olympic Movement was in danger of falling apart due to international tensions. Seeking to avoid just such a division, President Samaranch sought to resolve the pending Korea Olympic crisis at the behest of the IOC Executive Board.

A complicated, tangled dance ensued as Samaranch sought to nullify this potential threat through numerous communications with all the parties concerned during 1984 and 1985. Three tripartite meetings brought together the National Olympic Committee delegations of the Republic of Korea (ROK) and the PRK and an IOC delegation composed of the three vice presidents, the president of the Olympic Council of Asia, and the IOC's managing director, assisted by IOC legal advisors. These took place in Lausanne on October 8 and 9, 1985; January, 8 and 9, 1986; and June 10 and 11, 1986. Samaranch himself chaired these meetings. After the third, the NOC of the ROK gave swift written consent without any conditions to the proposed compromise in which two sports' events would be held in Pyongyang if North Korea agreed to open the militarized border between the two Koreas and allow free movement. The NOC of the PRK agreed in principle with the caveat that more sports (how many were unspecified) should be held in Pyongyang and that the name of the 1988 Olympics should be Pyongyang and Seoul—a dual host Olympiad, something that had and has never been done for an Olympiad. Throughout the rest of 1986, the IOC and the North Korean NOC went back and forth over their positions without either side actually changing their stances.[49]

The Korean situation was firmly linked to Cuba's PASO dispute by the Cubans both publicly and in diplomatic back channels. Publicly, Castro attacked the IOC. Other Cuban officials suggested that the IOC itself was an anachronism of colonialism.[50] The president of the National Institute of Sports, Physical Education, and Recreation (Instituto Nacional de Deportes, Educación Física y Recreación, INDER), Conrado Martínez, called for a radical reorganization of international sport at the July 1986 II Meeting of Physical Education Coordinators and Sport in Non-Aligned Countries to be led by the NOCs of the Non-Aligned countries in alliance in order to democratize and decolonize the IOC.[51] As part of that call, Martínez called for a boycott of the 1988 Seoul Olympics. This caused considerable consternation among the IOC Executive Board members:

they feared a boycott by the Non-Aligned Movement nations would put the Soviets in an untenable position, possibly leading to the Soviets also withdrawing from the event.

Gravely concerned with this Korean impasse in the summer of 1986 and the calls for reform and potential fourth consecutive boycott, Samaranch flew to Havana in September 1986 to meet with Castro, who was considered to have significant influence with the North Korean leaders. At the same time, the IOC was determined that Castro and Cuba would receive no public credit for its part in this dispute, especially since the intransigence of the North Korean position appeared to have been bolstered by Castro. Samaranch reported that the conversation started with a surprising turn:

> President Castro expressed his ideas on the structure and organisation of the International Olympic Committee, reiterating that it reminds him of a bygone era based on the domination of the world by a small number of countries and, above all, on colonialism. He insisted that I am the man to bring about true change, converting the International Olympic Committee into an international organisation with a truly democratic basis.[52]

In the two years prior to this meeting, Castro caustically condemned the IOC Executive Board's ethos, called the IOC a "band of Mafiosos," among other pejoratives, and insinuated outright corruption.[53] This canny political change of tune appears to have caught Samaranch off guard.

In total, Castro and Samaranch met twice in two days. After the first meeting Samaranch felt that

> the IOC, with its proposal, had already gone a long way, and that I considered that the proposal was very important as it was unprecedented in the history of the IOC and it had been very difficult to persuade South Korea to agree to give up part of the Olympic programme [sic].[54]

Samaranch reiterated to Castro that he was not prepared to call a fourth meeting between the two Koreas until North Korea accepted the IOC proposal unconditionally, yet acknowledged that the IOC was prepared to listen to the various points of view at the negotiating table.

In turn, Castro claimed that Cuba "convinced North Korea to maintain its initial position, namely total opposition to the Olympic Games in Seoul" unless a greater accommodation could be reached, insisting that North Korea was serious and wanted to arrive at a solution. Castro averred that North Korea was not inflexible, but something more must be offered. He suggested to Samaranch that

> North Korea is not at all disposed to accept only the organisation of two complete disciplines and part of two others. Perhaps the distribution of sports in proportion to the population of each of the two Koreas would be fairer. That would represent 2/3 in South Korea and 1/3 in North Korea.[55]

That first day did not appear to lead to any movement on either side, but the next morning Samaranch appeared to have a change of heart and made an offer that seemed to surprise and please Castro. Samaranch offered parts of both the men's and women's volleyball events to North Korea as well. Castro immediately accepted and averred that the North Koreans truly wanted a solution to this dilemma. Samaranch believed that Castro was seeking a way out of his untenable position of solidarity with North Korea; after all, other major socialist countries had not supported the North Koreans objections to the Seoul Games, especially since Havana had been awarded the 1991 Pan-American Games a few months earlier. Samaranch was acutely aware of the high value Castro placed on international sport and thus believed that Castro had no desire for Cuba to remain isolated internationally, which is what Samaranch speculated would happen if the Cubans did not participate in Seoul.

It appears that Castro was playing a canny game of cat and mouse with the IOC: heavily criticizing it on the one hand while working as an advocate of Olympism by positioning himself as a power broker on the other. The two disputes—one between Cuba and PASO and the other revolving around the South Korean city of Seoul as Olympic host city for the 1988 Olympics—were firmly linked in Cuba's efforts to influence international events, expand its own soft power (particularly among the postcolonial Non-Aligned Movement states), and demonstrate how the revolution's ethos and morality were clearly part of Olympism, through the hosting of events and brokering agreements. Ultimately, the Cubans were only partially successful in reaching their goals. Cuba was awarded the right to host the 1991 Pan-American Games in 1987. That success led many in the IOC and US circles to believe that Castro would be mollified and Cuba would attend the 1988 Seoul Olympics in fear of losing the Pan-American Games. They were deluded. Castro continued to insist that Cuba would not attend unless a compromise including the North Koreans as host was reached and continued to call for a boycott. While the dispute over the two Koreas continued into 1987, the IOC was concerned that Cuba, and Castro in particular, should not be seen to have played any part in the reaching of an agreement between the ROK and the PRK.[56]

Ultimately, the IOC offered Pyongyang five events for the Seoul Games, but not the name change. North Korea never did agree to open its border with the Republic of Korea. Cuba followed through on its boycott threat, but Castro's aspiration of being a leading broker of world politics largely fell flat. Only four NOCs—Albania (which had boycotted the past four Olympiads), Ethiopia, Madagascar, and the Seychelles—heeded Castro's call. Nicaragua also refused to participate because of US support of the Contras fighting the socialist Sandinista government and not because of solidarity with revolutionary Cuba.

Cuba did host the 1991 Pan-American Games. Those Games proved absolutely essential to Cuba at the time of their performance. The Soviet Union had collapsed in 1989, and Cuba's economy was rapidly disintegrating as the former Soviet trading bloc countries reneged on their international trade agreements with Cuba, forcing the Cuban government to renegotiate foreign trade deals at much worse rates than the favorable ones under the auspices of the bloc. In many places around the world, the dissolution of the European socialist states suggested to various experts that the Cuban state would be the next to vanish and that there were plenty of Cubans in Miami ready to sweep in any such power vacuum. Hosting the 1991 Pan-American Games was absolutely timely and crucial, for they provided an opportunity for Cuba to renew its existing relations and reopen relations with other Latin American countries. Internationally, the 1991 Pan-American Games were a success, for they provided concrete evidence that Cuba would abide by its international agreements even in the face of severe adversity.[57] That adversity would not directly impact Cuban Olympism until several years later.

1996–2016:
Neoliberal Olympism and Post-Soviet Cuba

The end of the United States-Soviet Union Cold War, along with the triumphalist neoliberal globalist rhetoric, reduced Cuba's prominence in international politics. For Cuba, though, globalization was the emperor's new clothes that shrouded US imperialism. Globalization was a form of neoimperialism that threatened Cuba as much as US neocolonialism had threatened and dominated Cuba for most of the twentieth century.[58] Cold War rhetoric easily shifted tone to globalization positions on the basis of the dehumanizing aspects of global capital. At the same time, the IOC enthusiastically embraced this global neoliberal capitalist ethos, resulting in stratospheric rise of Olympic influence on the global stage. Through its leading role in the production of the commodities we so readily recognize as "global sport" via Olympic commercialization in the 1980s and 1990s and Olympic professionalization in the 1990s and 2000s, Olympism became a leading façade of global neoliberal capitalism, in which the IOC's actions did not match its avowed philosophy. It is only now, with the sudden refusal of city leaders to commit their populations to the economic drain of hosting an Olympic festival, that the IOC has begun to address the excesses of this particular neoliberal Olympic era.

While the Olympic star was in ascendancy, Cuban sport officials reluctantly yet pragmatically engaged with these antithetical aspects of neo-Olympism because of their own domestic economic woes. The Cuban government simply did not have the resources to continue to fully support Cuba's elite programs. They contracted transnational sporting goods corporations to augment and support their international sporting ambitions, signing contracts with a number of European and Asian brands (Adidas, Mizuno, and Yaohan). Cuba branded teams and some replica uniforms became available products, but only outside of Cuba.[59] Yet, during this period, the Cubans so previously concerned with the increasing commercialism of the Olympic Games also made two bids to host the event despite the enormous economic difficulties in which the country was immersed. The COC submitted Havana as a candidate host city for the 2008 Olympics in 2000 and the 2012 Olympics in 2003.[60] The Cuban public remained largely unaware of these bids, which had no realistic chance of success, given the internal politics of the IOC, the international political context of China's ascendancy, and the dominance of neoliberal capitalist principles driving the siting of sporting mega-events like the Olympic Games. Neither bid made the finalist list, yet the symbolism of the bids themselves reflected the continued belief of Olympism's resonance with the revolution's own humanistic ethos even as the Olympic Movement appeared to diverge from it.

Cuban athletic success in the 1996 Atlanta Olympics and 2000 Sydney Olympics continued the golden era of Olympic success, and that level of medal winning continued until the 2008 Beijing Olympics when Cuba fell out of the top ten down to twenty-eight on the medal table. Cuban heroes included Félix Savón, who repeated Teófilo Stevenson's incredible feat in the heavyweight division of winning three successive gold medals, Ana Fidelia Quirot and others also won medals as Cuba experienced success across a range of sports. The economic crisis suffered throughout the 1990s after the collapse of the Soviet-led socialist trading bloc decimated the Cuban economy so thoroughly that the aftereffects were still reverberating throughout the country at the 2012 London Olympics. Although the economy improved in the 2000s, its medal count had significantly shrunk, and its overall performance had diminished considerably from the heights of the 1990s by the 2016 Rio de Janeiro Olympics. It should be noted, though, that Cuba still excels in comparison to other countries in similar global economic conditions, yet it is unlikely that Cuba will place in the top ten nations in the world as it did at the end of the twentieth century.

Conclusion:
Whither Cuban Olympism?

The death of Fidel Castro may detrimentally affect Cuban Olympism. Castro was a passionate advocate of sport, but other Cuban leaders, including Raúl Castro, are not so emphatic about the importance of sport in Cuba's revolution. Given the decline of Cuban Olympic performances from their heights in the 1990s and the continuing economic pressures on the Cuban government, how much the state will continue to support sporting activities is a question that will persist over the next decade or so. The exodus of elite athletes over the past twenty years has also detrimentally affected many of Cuba's programs; it would appear that this pillar of the revolution is rapidly being eroded. The challenge is that the humanism at the core of Olympism is also a core element of the revolutionary ethos, and thus sport would appear to be one way to continue to maintain the legitimacy of the Cuban government even as it struggles to meet the nation's demands for greater liberties and consumer goods. This, however, is a significant challenge for the continued stability of the Cuban nation. The mutually entwined discourses of Olympism and Cuban nationalism are founded on an idealistic notion that does not provide any succor to the Cuban populace. It has served Cuban leaders in establishing their position as leaders of an aspirant nation to reach greater heights, but the practical everyday realities do not match such rhetoric today, and that disjuncture is what threatens Cuban leaders' legitimacy.

Such a conclusion is seen in the ways in which Cuban leaders deployed the coherence of Olympism and Cuban nationalism, particularly on the international stage, for their benefit, but not necessarily for the benefit of the nation itself. The various instances discussed in this chapter demonstrates that much work remains to be done on the nexus of Cuban Olympism, and this chapter provides a potential starting point for further investigation. Each of the five periods could, in and of themselves, have been a full chapter, but that would not have provided the sense of how Olympism and Cuban nationalism have danced together over the past 120 years. Cubans would not necessarily separate and define their own engagement with Olympism into these periods; rather, these time periods are framed around Olympism broadly understood instead of a specific history of Cuba. Nonetheless, the erstwhile partners leading Cuban nationalism and Olympism have changed and the rhythm of their steps has altered, but Olympism and Cuban nationalism continue to move in tandem, each responding to the other's steps in a dance of mutual interest and benefit that continues to exclude the majority of the Cuban populace.

CHAPTER 3

Olympic Diplomacy and National Redemption in Post-revolutionary Mexico

KEITH BREWSTER AND CLAIRE BREWSTER

In 2004, during a ceremony to launch the United Nations' International Year of Sport and Physical Recreation, Secretary-General Kofi Annan proclaimed, "Sport is a universal language. At its best it can bring people together, no matter what their origin, background, religious beliefs or economic status."[1] Such a claim is not remarkable. After all, politicians and sport administrators have been saying something similar for over a century. What is remarkable is the longevity of the notion. Despite occasions when international sporting events have been blighted by racism, boycotts, corruption, or drug scandals, an unswerving faith in the capacity of sport to temporarily override underlying tensions between nations and peoples remains intact. In this chapter, we analyze this enduring conviction within the context of twentieth-century inter-American relations. More specifically, we focus on the part sport played in post-revolutionary Mexico's broader objective of strengthening relations with its neighbors despite challenging and changing international politics.

We begin by adopting an inclusive definition of cultural diplomacy that recognizes how the exchange of ideas, values, traditions, and other aspects of culture are deployed to strengthen relations, enhance socio-cultural cooperation, and/or promote national interest. In her study of sport as a form of diplomacy, Brenda Elsey points out the limitations of such an approach. While cultural diplomacy might assume equality among nations and argues that mutual understanding can defuse tensions between nations, beneath the platitudes of fraternity often lie less

DOI: https://doi.org/10.34053/scs2019.0.3

altruistic sentiments.[2] To understand Mexico's use of cultural diplomacy, therefore, we need to acknowledge the environment within which it took place. The "loss" of Cuba and Puerto Rico in 1898 ended Spain's colonial presence in the Americas and heralded US economic and political dominance. Secured by periodic US military interventions, much of Central America was converted into a region led by compliant regimes that satisfied an insatiable US appetite for raw materials. For some, the arrival of US influence was viewed as a positive contribution to national development; others perceived it as a threat to long-held social values and national integrity.[3] As José Martí underlined, "Our America's greatest danger is the scorn of our formidable neighbor; one who does not know us. . . . Our neighbor needs to become acquainted with us as a matter of urgency, so that he ceases to look upon us with disdain."[4] It is within this imperative that sport and diplomacy were situated in Central America.

During the twentieth century there was no shortage of cultural diplomatic initiatives designed to improve mutual understanding within the Americas. Yet an elite narrative linking modernity with national development meant that Latin American contributions were often framed within parameters set by the developed world. Evidence of indigenous cultures, for example, tended to be decontextualized and exhibited in museums and galleries—edifices that validated Western values. Furthermore, while Elsey correctly suggests that the Cold War significantly politicized transnational cultural events across the Americas, this was nothing new. Indeed, the cultural renaissance in US-Latin American relations during the "Good Neighbor" policies of President Franklin D. Roosevelt (1933–45) was highly politicized and aimed at keeping Latin America onside as the United States battled to repel threats to its hemispherical control.

In the case of Mexico, cultural diplomacy was complicated by specific political issues. Emerging from a decade of violent civil war, the 1920s heralded a period of national redemption designed to convince the world that Mexico's turbulent past had ended. In terms of foreign policy, Mexico adopted a rhetorical stance that remained throughout the rest of the twentieth century: that of peaceful coexistence, the upholding of democratic principles, nonintervention, and national self-determination. While sentiments of commonality and fraternity added to the diplomatic rhetoric in Mexico's engagement with its Latin American neighbors, in practice these ties were frequently stretched. Mexico's assumed left-wing political sympathies, such as its willingness to offer asylum to republicans during the Spanish Civil War and its support for Fidel Castro's regime in Cuba, often placed it at odds with other countries.

Within Central America, tensions were further complicated by geopolitics. Mexico's brief and disastrous attempt to incorporate the region within a Mexican empire under Agustín de Iturbide (1822–23) starkly underlined an asymmetrical relationship in which Mexico saw itself as the dominant partner in the region. It is, perhaps, too strong to assert that Mexico viewed Central America with paternalism, but Mexico might justifiably believe that its prominent position within regional international affairs allowed it to set an example for other Central American countries. Pedro González Olvera suggests that these dynamics in Central American relations have fostered an intangible, yet nonetheless real, sense of nationalism among Central American countries in their dealings with Mexico. He argues that the most obvious manifestation of this sentiment is through sport. It matters less, for example, if a Central American national team fails to qualify for the football World Cup finals provided it beats Mexico along the way.[5] Alejandro Estivill concurs, proposing that this antagonism is exacerbated by a form of Mexican sporting nationalism that includes a lack of recognition and, sometimes, respect for the sporting capacity of its southern neighbors.[6]

If these observations are accurate, then sport would not appear to be a promising genre through which to analyze Mexican diplomacy. Yet there are examples in which sport has been deployed to calm troubled waters between more belligerent rivals: for instance, during the early 1970s the United States engaged in ping-pong diplomacy with the Chinese, and in baseball diplomacy with Castro's Cuba. The extent to which either of these initiatives produced long-term progress is hard to identify, and it is similarly difficult to measure the beneficial consequences of Mexico's sporting contact with its neighbors. The purpose of the present chapter assumes a different analytical perspective. What interests us is the correlation between the underlying ethos of the Olympic Movement and the professed values that guided Mexico's international relationships, particularly within Latin America. Specifically, we analyze how its presence at multisport international events was commensurate with how Mexico wished to be seen.

Mexico's staging of the 1968 Olympics was, of course, the pinnacle of the nation's sporting diplomacy. Yet, in the same way as suggested by Antonio Sotomayor in the case of Puerto Rico, Mexico's achievement underlined a much longer process of engagement in the Olympic Movement.[7] When, in October 1963, Mexico City was elected to stage the Olympic Games, the country was euphoric. One journalist claimed this was the culmination of efforts that had begun at the 1924 Paris Olympics. Since then Mexico had participated in every Olympic Games; it had been instrumental in the foundation of the Central American Games and had hosted the inaugural event in 1926 and again in 1954. It also staged the second Pan-American Games in 1955.[8] Outlining a clear trajectory from the aftermath of its Revolution (1910–17) to a period of political and economic stability, Mexico's hosting of major sport events appeared to mirror a process of national regeneration and growing confidence on the international stage. This chapter proposes that the rhetorical flavor accompanying Mexico's most prestigious sporting event, the 1968 Olympics, was consistent with its previous forays into sporting diplomacy. Moreover, we argue that the very nature of the Olympic Movement's ethos of friendly competition free from racism, religion, and political influence perfectly suited a nation that wished to project itself as a stable, independent country determined to overcome periodic differences with its regional neighbors in the pursuit of broader international respect.

Redemption through Sporting Competition

While the cessation of hostilities in 1917 may have heralded an end to the Mexican Revolution, it was not easy to convince international opinion that the country had regained stability. For many, the brutality of the revolution confirmed stereotypical images of an unruly, "barbarous" Mexico, while "antiforeign" clauses within the revolutionary Constitution exacerbated fears abroad that Mexico was not a country to be trusted. The delicate negotiations that eventually led to US diplomatic recognition in 1923 may have relieved overriding economic concerns, but they did little to diminish Mexico's reputation for social and political instability. While the Álvaro Obregón and Plutarco Elías Calles administrations (1920–24 and 1924–28, respectively) were acutely aware of the need to improve Mexico's reputation overseas, Richard V. McGehee correctly contends that sporting diplomacy was not an obvious priority in achieving this objective.[9] Indeed, international sporting events were still very much in their infancy in the Americas, and while individual countries were waking up to the potential that sport offered in aiding domestic social programs, this rarely extended to overseas competitions.

It should not be assumed, however, that Mexican sport was in as moribund a state as the country's international reputation. The interest in modern sport that emerged prior to the revolution continued to take place throughout the years of violence. Indeed, one significant aspect of cultural diplomacy during the immediate post-revolutionary period was the Mexican government's willingness to continue supporting US initiatives such as the ones led by the Young Men's Christian Association. During the 1920s, this organization was seen as a useful tool in the dual task of luring Mexican youths from the clutches of the Catholic Church while simultaneously furthering revolutionary ambitions "to improve the race" through healthy physical pursuits.[10]

As relative stability returned, therefore, there was an appetite to place Mexican sport on a more organized and regulated footing. In January 1923, Count Henri de Baillet-Latour, vice president of the International Olympic Committee (IOC), visited Mexico as part of a goodwill tour of Latin America to promote the establishment of national sporting federations, national Olympic committees, and regional games. The subsequent formation of the Mexican Olympic Committee and Mexico's presence at the 1924 Paris Olympics paved the way for the country's first steps into international sport. While enthusiasm was not initially mirrored by Mexican government officials, McGehee notes that the Mexican press was quick to recognize the opportunity "to gain prestige and political benefits through sports participation."[11] After Mexico's daily newspapers *Excélsior* and *El Universal* launched a successful campaign to fund Mexican participation in the Paris Olympics, President Obregón eventually authorized government financing of the team's expenses. As Mark Dyreson notes, their failure to win honors led to Mexico's participants being portrayed as a "national disgrace" in the Mexican press.[12] From the very early days of international competition, the potential for sport to bring national prestige or discredit was acknowledged, and a link between sporting excellence and post-revolutionary nationalism was forged.

During the Paris Olympics, Baillet-Latour gained the agreement of representatives from Mexico, Guatemala, El Salvador, Costa Rica, and Panama to stage a multisport Central American Games, with the first meeting to be held in Mexico City in 1926.[13] To host an IOC-sanctioned event at this time was certainly an ambitious undertaking for a nation still emerging from years of bitter conflict. Indeed, only a few months earlier, Mexican forces had quelled a military revolt that almost toppled the incumbent government. McGehee links Mexico's willingness to host the

Games to its wish to become rehabilitated in the arena of international opinion.[14] A decade of negativity associated with revolutionary violence, Mexico's impending appropriation of foreign-owned properties, and the considerable hesitancy in US diplomatic recognition, needed to be countered with tangible evidence of Mexico's deliverance from violence and its ability to reassert its position as a leader of the Central American region.

As the Games approached, the rhetorical tide of goodwill that would become a customary companion to hosting sporting events was taken up by the Mexican press. *Excélsior* published photographs of the Cuban team outside Mexico City's prestigious Hotel Regis and anticipated forthcoming days of "fraternal competition."[15] The newspaper's coverage of the Guatemalan team's arrival continued in the same manner. At a meeting with the director of the Casa del Estudiante Indígena (House of the Indigenous Student), the Guatemalan ambassador sent a message of "brotherly love" from the Guatemalan indigenous to their Mexican counterparts. A basketball match between indigenous players from Guatemala and Mexico was preceded by a hearty rendition of both national anthems that "set nationalist passions alight, projecting a vision of a new America that will march forward, confident in reaching the highest accolades of life."[16] In welcoming members of visiting teams to the National Palace, President Calles stressed that "Latin Americans must not view Mexico as a foreign country. People from Hispanic nations of this continent should view our country as an extension of their own and must feel at home."[17]

Another *Excélsior* reporter, using the pseudonym Fray Gerundio, underlined that Mexico was far more strongly committed to sport than other countries. He regretted that the Central American Games would be a much smaller meeting than anticipated: Nicaragua, Honduras, Venezuela, Colombia, Panama, Costa Rica, Jamaica, Puerto Rico, and Santo Domingo had all accepted their invitations. "Then the excuses came pouring in: lack of funds, poor economic climate, and a lack of sporting preparations" left just Mexico, Guatemala, and Cuba. Although evidently disappointed, Gerundio concluded on a positive note:

> The seeds sown by the Mexican National Committee will bear fruit in 1930 in the second Central American Games in Havana. We must remember that only 14 of the 40 countries invited to the 1896 Athens Olympics actually turned up.... The Games begin tomorrow and will serve as an opportunity for competing countries to show their advances in sports and above all to bring a new physical and spiritual intimacy between nations.[18]

Sport commentator Rafael Cardona emphasized the importance of the Olympic spirit. In an optimistic mood, he celebrated Mexico's achievements on the sporting field and beyond and took heart from notable advances elsewhere:

> Central Americans have also realized the significance of sporting success. In the five republics of the Centre there are laudable trainers and associations that have recently achieved unforgettable accolades. . . . The forthcoming Games will be a startling revelation, especially for Mexico. The value of sporting victory lies in its ability to set good examples and to change the habits of a people: even politics can adopt qualities found on the Olympic track where the most capable triumph, and where one learns to win or lose with a smile on one's face.[19]

Such sentiments matched contemporary political rhetoric of fraternal respect and unity among neighboring countries. When President Calles inaugurated the Games on October 12 he proclaimed that they were taking place "for the good of Hispanic American youth." Reflecting Cardona's sentiments, *Excélsior* implored its readers to display sportsmanship: "We will fight with passion during the Olympiad, but the winners, whomsoever they may be and particularly if they are foreigners, should always receive enthusiastic, sincere praise." Only then, it concluded, "shall we be worthy of calling ourselves civilized and generous."[20] During the contests, spectator magnanimity was rarely put to the test. Mexico's team, twice the size of its competitors, won all the events apart from baseball and fencing, in which it came second to Cuba. Demonstrating that contemporary newspapers were well aware of the diplomatic value of sporting events, *El Universal* proclaimed that the Games "had shown visitors that Mexico did not deserve its reputation as a nation of near-naked savages cutting off heads left and right."[21]

An interesting concurrent development was the staging of two baseball charity matches, with the proceeds dedicated to help victims of a recent cyclone in Havana.[22] While more "traditional" sports, such as bullfighting, had long since supported charitable events, these baseball matches represented one of the first times that a "modern" sport event had been used to exemplify Mexico's altruism toward a neighboring country in a time of need.[23] Sporting diplomacy between the two countries was again displayed a year later when a Mexico City sport club proposed an annual tennis tournament against Cuba to further fraternal relations. In recognition of the two countries' struggles for independence from Spain, the club asked President Calles to supply a trophy for the women's competition, which would be called the [José] Martí Cup. The Cuban president, Gerardo Machado, would donate the [Miguel] Hidalgo Cup for the men.[24] Mexico's commitment to sporting ties with Cuba was reaffirmed with its significant presence at the second Central American Games in Havana in 1930. According to Marco Antonio Maldonado and Rubén Amador Zamora, the friendly rivalry in boxing, baseball, football, and volleyball that Mexico and Cuba maintained throughout the 1930s could be directly connected to the Central American Games.[25] The perpetuation of sporting ties was all the more impressive given the political instability in Cuba: Machado's fall from grace, the 1933 Revolution, and the rise to power of General Fulgencio Batista. What these links reflected was a degree of mutual respect between two countries that were at the forefront of regional sporting achievement. Cubans had long been admired for their prowess in baseball and had frequently made exhibition tours to Mexico during the preceding three decades. As Mexico became more engaged in the sporting world, Cuba represented a worthy competitor against which to measure its development.

More generally, the period following the 1926 Central American Games heralded a new opportunity in dealings between Mexico and other American countries. At a time when the US president, Franklin D. Roosevelt, was adopting a "good neighborly" approach toward the continent, Mexico moved to strengthen its own diplomatic ties. Friedrich Schuler argues that the Calles presidency had already adopted a firm stance against US gunboat diplomacy in Central America, with diplomatic initiatives in Nicaragua and Guatemala in 1926.[26] The fact that Roosevelt's move away from interventionism coincided with Mexico's actions strengthened Mexican diplomatic credentials. In 1933, relations resumed between Mexico and Venezuela, as they did with Nicaragua, albeit through Mexico's envoy based in neighboring El Salvador.[27] Replying to an address by the Peruvian president in November 1933, Mexico's foreign minister, José Manuel Puig Casauranc, specifically referred to Roosevelt's Good Neighbor initiative. While recognizing that many Latin American countries still viewed the United States with suspicion, he stated that this was a new era in Pan-American fraternity, and that with "cooperation, love, and spiritual union" the continent could be optimistic about the future.[28] That sport could reflect this conviction was increasingly acknowledged. In 1931, the Mexican embassy in Costa Rica highlighted the exceptional hospitality that had accompanied a Mexican football team's recent tour of the country.[29] Mexico had every reason to eagerly anticipate the third regional sport competition in El Salvador in 1934. Renamed the Central American and Caribbean Games to reflect the region's increasing participation, these Games offered an opportunity to gain prestige by demonstrating Mexico's sporting prowess. As the influential sport columnist Fray Nano underlined, while the priority in the Olympics Games may be to take part, "we truly compete" in the Central American and Caribbean Games.[30] When a severe cyclone in El Salvador postponed the Games, Mexico's sport bodies were fully supportive of plans to reschedule for the following year.

Yet the postponement provoked a degree of tension within Mexico that severely tested the relationship between sporting performance, national duty, and international fraternity. One sporting newspaper reported concerns about Mexican competitors' ability to retain the "magnificent condition" they had attained in preparation for the Games.[31] Indeed, many athletes voiced hesitation about competing in El Salvador in the rearranged Games. The football confederation claimed Mexico's team was insufficiently prepared. Of five possible women tennis players, only one agreed to go.[32] When the basketball team also showed signs of reluctance to attend, there seemed a distinct possibility that Mexico might be absent from the Games. What remains unclear is the extent to which unwillingness to compete was due to matters of physical fitness or whether these Games were less of a priority than the forthcoming 1936 Berlin Olympics. Their rationale notwithstanding, the hesitancy of Mexico's foremost athletes to travel to El Salvador provoked harsh criticism in the sporting press. Fray Nano emphasized Mexico's moral obligation to attend: "It is criminal not to cooperate in the Central American Games. . . . It is a poor sportsman who refuses to play for his country."[33] Days later his colleague Fray Kempis joined Nano's crusade and urged players to train hard for "our sister republic's" Games.[34] To these commentators at least, the imperative to support a neighboring country's endeavors was as important as gaining medals. Mexican athletes did go and performed well in the Games, either winning or coming runner-up to Cuba in each of their participating events.[35]

The sense of fraternity outlined by politicians and journalists was placed under specific scrutiny in the following years. Sebastiaan Faber claims that the 1930s saw Mexico City become the "undisputed cultural center of the Spanish-speaking world" as Pan-Americanism was boosted by the Good Neighbor policy, impending war in Europe, and the arrival of Spanish exiles in Mexico.[36] Yet Mexico's overt sympathy for Republican Spain was in stark contrast to the more conservative responses from other Latin American countries. When President Lázaro Cárdenas (1934–40) expropriated foreign oil installations in 1938, admiration in some Latin American quarters for this act of defiance was tempered elsewhere by fears that such a move would embolden left-wing movements throughout the continent. The message Mexico sought to disseminate to the Americas at this time is exemplified in two speeches on foreign policy. The first was Cárdenas's address to the Cuban people, in which he reiterated his faith in the unity of Hispano-American nations and their right to self-determination and national integrity. He pointed out that Mexico's oil expropriation was merely one example of what Latin American nations could do in pursuit of social equality. The second was by the foreign minister, General Eduardo Hay, in a speech at the National Center for Sciences and Arts on Americas Day in April 1938. Underlining Mexico's policy of nonintervention and the spirit of Pan-Americanism that bound all nations of the Americas together, Hay nonetheless affirmed, "The countries to our south are, first and foremost, our brothers. The great country to our north remains foremost among our friends."[37] While US oil companies might have disagreed, the Roosevelt administration's broader foreign policy priorities elicited a more benign response. As Dennis Merrill outlines, although the oil issue severely strained relations, it could not derail a process that had begun in the 1920s and picked up momentum in the 1930s: a US cultural diplomacy offensive aimed at Latin America and Mexico in particular. US gunboat diplomacy had been replaced by a charm offensive in which US businesses and individuals were encouraged to invest in or to visit Mexico with the aim of improving mutual understanding.[38]

As Cesar R. Torres points out, sport played a part within this broader rapprochement between American nations. The notion of hemispherical sporting events gathered momentum, not only in the United States but in other countries keen to test themselves in the international arena. Avery Brundage, president of the US national Olympic committee and member of the IOC, acted as a conduit for the various ideas emanating from Latin America, viewing regional and hemispherical sporting competitions as a crucial means of developing the Olympic Movement as a whole. Correspondence between Brundage, US politicians, and various sport administrators emphasizes that sport was seen as a useful tool of cultural diplomacy; moreover, if handled sensitively, it could act as the most effective means of consolidating the spirit of the Good Neighbor policy.[39]

For its part, Mexico's Foreign Office pursued its own cultural diplomacy with its "northern friends" and "southern brothers," which included a continuation of sporting exchanges. In October 1934 a Mexican polo team toured the United States and, although it suffered defeats, the monthly sporting paper *La Afición* reported that the players' sportsmanship and chivalry was of great diplomatic value to Mexico's relationship with the United States.[40] In 1939 a Mexican team won a shooting competition in California with a world-record score. This, the organizers informed Cárdenas, had "honored the name of our country abroad" and brought much admiration from the hosts.[41] In 1938, a series of sporting events took place in Guatemala designed to build on the fraternal friendship between Mexico and Guatemala.[42] Two years later, Ignacio Beteta (a former equestrian, and minister of education, and incumbent director of Mexican physical education) led a team of five hundred Mexican diplomats, soldiers, athletes, and artists on a goodwill tour to Chile, Panama, Ecuador, Peru, and Colombia. Reports from each country's embassy suggest that the visit was a complete success.[43]

When, in 1942, Mexico followed the United States in declaring war on Germany and Japan, the nation made a dramatic gesture in its professed friendship toward its northern neighbor. While several Central American countries preempted Mexico's declaration of allegiance to the Allies, Mexico was one of only two Latin American countries (the other being Brazil) that committed troops to armed combat. Any previous ambiguity regarding Mexico's sympathies in the conflict were definitively settled. While Mexico's policy of nonintervention may have been compromised, its often-expressed solidarity with the American continent was assured.

Consolidation through Sporting Competition

Following the end of World War II, Mexico embarked on a project designed to boost its economic sector through a program of import substitution backed by growing oil revenues. Thus began two decades of uninterrupted growth, the so-called "economic miracle" that promised to deliver Mexico the long-sought prize of respect among developed countries. The sense of national confidence accompanying this economic growth can be seen as the nucleus of the nation's aim to place itself on the world's sporting map by hosting the Olympic Games. Yet, in seeking this objective, Mexico's leaders had to embark upon an entirely different form of sporting diplomacy: one that focused on leaders of world sport as well as leaders of nations.

Early indications did not augur well for Mexico's ambitions. Its bid to host the Central American and Caribbean Games for a second time in 1954 was met with little enthusiasm. Indeed, Central American delegates voted by eight to four for the venue of the next Games to be "anywhere but Mexico." Reflecting González Olvera's observation regarding underlying resentment within Central America (see above), one reason given was that Mexico City's altitude favored home athletes who were already dominating events. Mexico had indeed performed well at the 1950 Central American and Caribbean Games in Guatemala, winning almost 50 percent of the gold medals—far more than its nearest rival, Cuba.[44] Despite a written protest from the Mexican delegation, Panama triumphed in its bid to host the 1954 Games. When Panama announced its inability to fulfil its commitment in 1952, however, Mexico quickly stepped in to save the day.[45]

In his speech at the opening ceremony, President Adolfo Ruiz Cortines (1952–58) reiterated an increasingly routine eulogy regarding the benefits of international sport competition. Without any overt trace of irony regarding Mexico City's altitude he expressed hope that

> the atmosphere of friendship and affection that one breathes here will bestow confidence within you and stimulate you to victory; and when you return to your homes you will reflect that in this tournament there were no losers, we were all victorious as victory belongs to this new world of America, the continent of brotherhood and hope.[46]

In order to further enhance such fraternity, Mexican radio broadcasted a series of "chats" in which Central American diplomats focused on the symbolism of the Games for the region.[47] An editorial in *Excélsior* encapsulated the spirit Mexico wanted to project:

> The importance of these periodic competitions is obvious. . . . They are as important as any international reunion between brother countries, and sporting competition can do nothing other than affirm the political, social and popular goodwill between neighboring countries. Records and scores may indicate the level of development that nations have achieved, but they also bring a more intimate understanding between participating countries.[48]

The extent to which this was wishful thinking depended on the country involved. The backdrop to the Games was an ongoing operation by the

Central Intelligence Agency to undermine the government of President Jacobo Arbenz in Guatemala. As *El Universal* indicated in its coverage of the opening ceremony, the Central American and Caribbean Games could not have taken place at a less auspicious moment. When Arbenz was toppled three months later, Mexico offered him asylum, placing the country at odds with Guatemala's new military rulers. Violent border incidents in 1959 led to a break in diplomatic relations and, although they resumed a year later, border tensions marred relations throughout the 1960s.[49]

Mexico's willingness to relieve Panama of hosting the 1954 Games was indicative of its increasing influence in sport administration. From the outset, decisions relating to the Central American and Caribbean Games were taken by delegates, comprising two national Olympic committee members from each country, and their respective IOC members. Following meetings held during the 1954 Games, Mexico's IOC representatives, Marte Gómez and José de Jesús Clark Flores, played an important role in modifying the Fundamental Charter of the Central American and Caribbean Games. Conveying the IOC's provisional approval of the charter in 1957, Brundage expressed indebtedness to Marte Gómez's "effective work in keeping these regional Games in conformity with Olympic regulations." When delegates agreed to form the Central American and Caribbean Sports Organization in 1960, Clark Flores was made honorary president in recognition of the way he had used his influence within the IOC to consolidate and develop sport in the region.[50]

Through their active involvement in IOC-endorsed sporting events, Mexico's sporting administrators built strong links with influential members of the IOC Executive Board—none more so than Avery Brundage, who became president of the IOC in 1952. In a press conference held during the 1954 Games, Brundage may have been alluding to the growing crisis in Guatemala when he expressed relief that politics had been kept out of the event. He went on to praise Mexico's hospitality and organizing capacity, which he judged to augur well for Mexico's staging of the Pan-American Games the following year.[51] That Mexico had been selected to host the 1955 Pan-American Games was in no small measure due to the tenacity of its representatives within Pan-American sport.

As David J. Wysocki Quiros notes, since the 1930s Mexican sport administrators had viewed themselves as stalwart advocates of Pan-Americanism and had been decidedly peeved by the decision to stage the first continental mega–sport event in Argentina in 1942.[52] While wartime disruption brought a postponement of the inaugural Pan-American

Games in Buenos Aires until 1951, Mexicans continued to take a leading role in the administration of regional Games. With Clark Flores as secretary general and later president of the Permanent Commission of the Pan-American Sports Committee, and the administrative center of the Pan-American Sports Committee located in Mexico City, the Pan-American Games could be seen as a physical manifestation of the country's commitment to the sporting ethos promoted by the Olympic Movement. As with other regional and global sport events under the auspices of the IOC, the statutes of the Pan-American Sports Committee expressed an apolitical, nonreligious, and antiracist stance. Furthermore, the Games were specifically designed "to strengthen and tighten the bonds of union and friendship among the peoples of the Americas."[53] Such sentiments were consistent with an increasingly coherent policy in Mexico's dealing with its regional neighbors. A fitting example of Mexican diplomacy occurred when General Fulgencio Batista reconstituted the Cuban Olympic Committee in a way that contravened the IOC rule regarding political interference. With a real threat that Cuba would be excluded from the Pan-American Games, Clark Flores and Gómez wrote to Brundage in November 1954 asking for patience while their emissaries went to Cuba to seek a solution: "Sometimes," they explained, "in Latin American quarrels, the important thing is not the decision to be taken, but the way on [sic] which you need look for honorable ways to save face when in error."[54] The dispute was eventually resolved, and the Cubans athletes who traveled to Mexico were warmly welcomed by the public and diplomats alike.

In 1954, a Mexican sporting mission toured twelve Central, South American, and Caribbean countries "to make the bond of friendship even closer among Mexican diplomats and sporting officials of each country so that working in accord, they might co-operate with the Organizing Committee in the worthy task undertaken by the Organizers." They also aimed to address the public of each country through press, radio, and television interviews, and by broadcasting an athletics musical program.[55] While the "worthy task" itself was severely hampered by internal political strife within the organizing committee and other sport bodies, the Games did take place, and in June 1955 Mexico's efforts were officially recognized when the country was awarded the Olympic Cup for its staging of the 1954 Central American Games and the 1955 Pan-American Games.[56] While this was an achievement in itself, there is little doubt that for Mexico, hosting regional games was merely a stepping stone to the ultimate prize: one that would cement the nation's place as a leading sport destination in the Americas. As the author and political journalist Elena Poniatowska later reflected, "No other country wanted [the Olympic Games] as much as we did. It was the culmination of Mexican politicians' efforts and of the rising economic development."[57]

Validation through Sporting Competition

Mexico's interest in staging the Olympic Games can be seen as a continuation of a longer process of raising the nation's international profile through the medium of sport. In his report on the 1948 London Olympics, the Mexican team's *chef de mission*, Ignacio Beteta, confirmed he had forwarded Mexico's proposal to host the 1952 Olympics, but noted that the Games had already been awarded to Finland. "However," Beteta confidently added, "we are now in the hat with Argentina, Brazil and five US cities to host future Olympic Games."[58] Although Mexico's bid never gained momentum, it did register Mexico's intentions as an increasingly confident nation and was in keeping with its ongoing efforts to secure both the Pan-American and Central American and Caribbean Games. Seven months later President Miguel Alemán (1946–52) established an "invitation committee" with the responsibility of securing the 1956 Olympics for Mexico City.[59] Although fighting to secure Mexico's bid, Gómez did not anticipate success.[60] Nor, it would seem, did the Mexican press: in reporting that Melbourne had won the bid, *Excélsior* remarked, "It was a surprise that Mexico received nine votes in the first round."[61]

Gómez prepared a detailed report on why Mexico's bid had failed. What is clear is that, although Alemán's administration viewed hosting the Olympic Games as recognition of Mexico's emerging economy, the nation had much to learn about the dynamics of Olympic diplomacy. Gómez stressed that Mexico's altitude presented "a serious obstacle," but identified what Mexico should do to secure the Games:

> We must promote Mexico more emphatically: Melbourne's success was partly due to its strenuous efforts to promote the young nation's beauty. Although we did this, our embassies have not yet formed sufficiently strong social links with members of the IOC. We must produce translated, photographic publications that promote our archaeology, ethnography, popular arts, etc. We must network, by attending IOC functions without becoming embroiled in the many controversial issues that are discussed. IOC members need

to become familiar with Mexico to break prejudices. We must invite members of the 1960 Olympic Games jury to Mexico. They would then see the beauty of our city, the sweet climate, and the wonderful hospitality for which we are famous.[62]

Here, Gómez was calling for a change in the relationship between sport and Mexican diplomacy. If throughout our analysis we have been careful not to overemphasize the role of sporting diplomacy, this report suggests that, rather than sport being an addendum of foreign policy, hosting the Olympic Games should become an objective in itself. Diplomats, businessmen, and sport functionaries were asked to deploy their diplomatic skills to deliver the Olympics to Mexico. Both Gómez and Clark Flores remained crucial to this endeavor. As Wysocki Quiros points out, they had established a close friendship with Brundage, building up his knowledge of, and confidence in, their country.[63] A demonstrable example of such faith was when Brundage, as recently elected president of the IOC, used his influence to select Mexico City as host for the organization's forty-eighth session, as well as its Executive Board and National Olympic Committee meetings. This was the first time any such meetings had taken place in Latin America. Diplomatic pressure was matched by government commitments to improve Mexico's stadia and infrastructure. At the same time, Clark Flores and Gómez reiterated their conviction that Mexico should again bid for the Olympics.[64] The rest of the world, however, was slow to appreciate Mexico's efforts and ambitions. In 1955, Mexico City's bid was eliminated in the first round with six votes in a contest that saw the 1960 Games go to Rome.[65]

That Mexico did not bid for the 1964 Olympics suggests that the country had experienced a blow to its self-confidence and/or national pride. Correspondence shows, however, that Brundage was keen to keep Mexico's ambitions alive.[66] As we have discussed elsewhere, Brundage's encouragement was not entirely in recognition of Mexico's advances in recent decades. It had much to do with the IOC's need to be seen to embrace more fully its member countries in the developing world.[67] Within that context, Mexico's successful hosting of regional sporting events and the close links between Clark Flores, Gómez, and the IOC Executive Board made Mexico the most obvious venue for Latin America's first Olympic Games. Furthermore, the enthusiastic support of the incumbent president, Adolfo López Mateos (1958–64), ensured that the Mexican bid was based upon solid foundations. So it was that in

October 1963 members at the IOC session at Baden-Baden voted over-whelmingly in support of Mexico City's fourth Olympic bid.

Mexico's hosting of the 1968 Olympic was to be the pinnacle of its endeavors to use sport as a platform to further its international profile. Ever since Mexico's belated bid to host the Olympic Games in 1948, a successful hosting of the Games was seen as an opportunity to prove that the nation was worthy of inclusion in the international circle of developed nations. Within that world, however, enduring negative stereotypes of Latin America as a continent of military dictators, banditry, and incompetence forced the Mexican organizers to reconsider their stance. Mexico quickly adopted the posture of using the 1968 Games as a showpiece, not just of its own capacity, but of that of all competing nations from the Third World and, more pertinent to our present analysis, Latin America.[68]

The five years between Mexico being awarded the Games and hosting them were filled with the same type of diplomatic rhetoric and activity that had accompanied their previous staging of sporting events. Despite ongoing border tensions between Mexico and Guatemala, Mexico's president, Gustavo Díaz Ordaz (1964–70), accepted an invitation made by the governments of all Central American countries to visit the region in 1965.[69] Indeed, 1965–66 was declared the "Year of Mexican-Central American Friendship" and was sealed by the president's tour.[70] During it, Díaz Ordaz was at pains to stress that his main purpose was not to promote Mexican trade but to reaffirm the friendship that, despite occasional setbacks, had long existed between Mexico and other nations. He pointed to a series of agreements in which Mexico offered technical expertise and cultural exchanges, and he extended invitations for Central American presidents to visit Mexico.[71] Mexico responded swiftly to El Salvador's appeal for humanitarian aid following a destructive series of earthquakes, and, in the year leading up to the Olympic Games, Mexico provided diverse material and technical help to several Central American countries.[72]

A controversy that threatened to jeopardize Mexico's Olympic preparation concerned the 1966 Central American and Caribbean Games in Puerto Rico. Citing a fear that the presence of Cuban athletes might ignite tensions with the many Cuban exiles residing on the island, the Puerto Rican organizing committee banned Cuban delegates from attending the Games. That Clark Flores played a pivotal role in rescinding the ban underlines the degree of diplomatic influence he then enjoyed within the sporting world.[73] More generally, the Mexican government reinforced its message of fraternity by offering training facilities and financial support to help less-wealthy Central American countries prepare and compete in Mexico's Games.[74]

The way in which the organizing committee positioned Mexico in the lead-up to the Games also reflected rhetorical patterns that stretched back to the beginning of the country's endeavors to host international sporting competitions. As the committee's chairman, Pedro Ramírez Vázquez, pointed out in 1967:

> Our responsibility in hosting the Olympic Games is one we share with Latin America and the entire Spanish-speaking world, because we know that the rest of the world will judge the Spanish-speaking world by how the Olympic Games proceed. But with the full cooperation that we are receiving from all Mexicans, we are confident that we will be able to meet our great responsibility.[75]

Mirroring a tactic deployed in the 1954 Central American and Caribbean Games, the committee used the mass media to convey these aspirations to a Latin American audience. In June 1968, the first of a series of radio "chats" was launched:

> Mexico's commitment is, in reality, a commitment made by all countries who speak Spanish, especially those in Latin America. That is why the committee wants as many Americans as possible to give a demonstration of what they can do through Mexico. Hence, the Olympic committee wants American radio stations to take a few minutes to inform their listeners about what is happening in Mexico and thus demonstrate the organizing efficiency and capacity of Latin Americans.[76]

Mexico's hosting of the 1968 Olympics succeeded in undermining all those who had doubted Mexicans' organizing capacity. Fears of half-built stadia and installations proved unfounded. Similarly, concerns that competitors and visitors might fall victim to random acts of violence also proved unfounded. It was a matter of bitter irony, therefore, that the two-week celebration of youthful vigor was fundamentally poisoned by the killing of up to five hundred student protesters by government forces just ten days before the opening ceremony. The tragic events in a Mexico City square in Tlatelolco brought a violent end to a summer of rising tensions between students and government authorities. With it, a fundamental flaw was exposed in Mexico's projection of itself as a stable country, at peace with itself and its place in the community of nation states. Rather than cancel the Games, as some foreign voices demanded, Brundage's determination that the show must go on helped to bring sporting competition once more to the center of international focus. In a sense, the diplomatic value of sport was reconfirmed as attention switched to Mexico's role as host rather than as a brutal oppressor of its own people.

Reflecting on the ambitious task facing the organizing committee, Ramírez Vázquez stated that it had had to reconcile "sovereignty with non-intervention, nationalism with universality, international coexistence with peace, economic development with social justice, material well-being with education and culture, modernity with tradition."[77] While it is, of course, impossible to measure the degree to which any form of diplomacy materially affects one nation's relationship with another, in this case Ramírez Vázquez was arguably overplaying the diplomatic importance of the Olympic Games. In an environment in which politics, ideology, religion, and economics take center stage, diplomacy remains in the wings of international relations. Yet, while recognizing the limitations of diplomacy, the influence of subjectivity should not be overlooked. Foreign perceptions of a nation and its people are stubbornly resistant to change and can prejudice judgments of reliability and confidence. The role of diplomacy, perhaps, is to enter this subjective world with the aim of making incremental changes that will, over time, modify opinions for the better.

Such difficulties reflect Mexico's international relations in the fifty years following the end of its revolution. Economic and political issues dominated the way that Mexico was viewed during this period and gave rise to admiration and suspicion in equal measures. Mexico's nonintervention, national self-determination, and rhetorical stance in foreign affairs of upholding democratic principles would appear to be noncontroversial. Yet, in practice, many of its neighbors went through periods in which democracy was challenged by military regimes, neighboring countries engaged in armed conflict, and US interests jeopardized a nation's right to determine its own path. Indeed, Mexico's own domestic political climate quite often ran contrary to its professed democratic principles. Within such an environment, however, the maintenance of diplomatic relations acted to sustain a degree of consistency.

In the world of international sport, the fifty years after Mexico's revolution can justifiably be seen as exceptional. The country rose from obscurity to become a driving force in hemispherical sport, and, while it lacked sporting prowess, it excelled in organizational ability. While many might question such credentials, Mexico was repeatedly chosen to host prestigious sporting events and, in the cases of the 1954 Central American and Caribbean Games and the 1986 Men's Football World Cup, stepped in when the original hosts defaulted on their responsibilities. Mexico's eventual presence at the heart of the Olympic Movement meant that, despite its many critics both within and beyond the country, it not only gained the prize of hosting the world's most prestigious event, but added a significant building block in its attempt to construct a better image of the nation and its people.

The Nationalist Movement and the Struggle for Freedom in Puerto Rico's Olympic Sport

ANTONIO SOTOMAYOR

"I think I united a nation . . . I just love where I come from," said Mónica Puig after winning Puerto Rico's first-ever Olympic gold medal at the 2016 Olympics in Rio de Janeiro, Brazil. Puig indeed had united the masses throughout the island as shopping centers, pharmacies, gas stations, hospitals, schools, churches, government offices, and even Senate offices paralyzed activities to watch the tennis matches.[1] Ranked thirty-fourth by the World Tennis Association, Puig beat the second-ranked and reigning Australian Champion Angelique Kerber after beating a two-time Wimbledon champion (Petra Kvitová) and a French Open champion (Garbiñe Muguruza) on her way to Olympic gold. Her #PicaPower war cry became the top global Twitter trend as celebrities including Ricky Martin, Lin-Manuel Miranda, and Yasiel Puig and tennis legends Chris Evert, Martina Navratilova, and Billie Jean King, among many more, sent congratulatory messages.[2] Alejandro García Padilla, then-governor of the Commonwealth of Puerto Rico, led the welcoming reception and massive popular parade, saying that August 13, 2016, had become a key date in the history of Puerto Rico because that day Puerto Rico's anthem had played at the Olympics and the "flag was hoisted at the highest flagpole."[3]

Despite this prominent and positive embrace of national identity, earlier in the year all three branches of the US government officially ratified Puerto Rican political subordination to the plenary powers of the US Congress. This left no doubt of Puerto Rican colonialism,[4] while

DOI: https://doi.org/10.34053/scs2019.o.4

up-and-coming politicians called for independence or sovereignty.[5] Calls for decolonization and/or independence have existed in Puerto Rico under both Spanish and US regimes since the nineteenth century.[6] Under the United States, a new feature in Puerto Rico's struggle for self-determination and independence has been the power of sport, the Olympic Movement in particular. The Olympic Movement has given Puerto Ricans a powerful platform to foster national identity and nationalism, given that only sovereign nation-states can participate at the Olympic Games. For Latin Americans, in the discussion of the Olympic Movement Puerto Rico occupies a special place, because it is the only Latin American nation that does not have political sovereignty. Puerto Ricans, as Latin Americans/Caribbeans with US citizenship, have found their political and cultural intricacies intertwined in the Olympic Movement. For Puerto Ricans, the Olympic Movement has been a special platform to not only display their nationhood, but also to challenge colonialism and strive for national independence.

Explaining why Puerto Ricans have such strong nationalist feelings while not traditionally opting for independence is not easy. One point of view might be that Puerto Ricans have opted for an "intermediate nationalism" that allowed those who favor autonomy to satisfy nationalist feelings while maintaining close ties with the imperial metropolis.[7] This seems to go in line with the idea that Puerto Ricans have nurtured cultural nationalism more than political nationalism.[8] While political nationalists sought independence, cultural nationalists sought political autonomy that allowed for the strengthening of a national culture, without the need of independence from the metropolis. For the current study, the generic term "nationalists" encompasses those who believe in a Puerto Rican national identity, either for cultural or political purposes. Instead, the proper noun "Nationalists" refers to those who belonged or sympathized with Puerto Rico's Partido Nacionalista (PN). Lastly, independentistas are all of those nationalists and Nationalists who believe in and seek Puerto Rican independence.

As the president of Puerto Rico's PN, Pedro Albizu Campos spearheaded a radical and sometimes violent movement for Puerto Rican independence throughout the 1930s, 1940s, and 1950s. The Nationalists' relation to Olympic sport since 1930 was not as supportive as some might think. This was because Puerto Ricans actually represented the United States during the 1930s, 1940s, and early 1950s. Since then, a complicated negotiation over colonialism, Olympic sport, and national identity began and endured in a process called colonial Olympism.[9] As I show elsewhere, Puerto Rico's Olympic sport was adopted by the autonomist movement, rather than by independentistas, as a way to showcase cultural nationalism and autonomy and engage in international politics.[10] An unanswered question, then, remained: How was Olympic sport viewed by Puerto Rican Nationalists and independentistas? To what extent, if at all, did the Nationalists and independentistas utilize Olympic sport in their struggle for freedom?

In this chapter, I show the different ways in which Puerto Rican Nationalists and independentistas viewed or utilized the Olympic Movement in their struggles for independence. I argue that when Puerto Rico entered the Olympic Movement representing the United States, the Nationalist leadership refrained from incorporating Puerto Rico's Olympic participation in their official arsenal for decolonization. On the contrary, during the 1930s, 1940s, and early 1950s Albizu Campos and other top-ranking nationalists viewed Puerto Rico's delegation as a US tool for Americanization and inherently anti-Puerto Rican. Yet, for others, especially patriotic athletes, the Olympic delegation constituted the best scenario to display and celebrate the nation. A turning point occurred in the late 1950s: in 1959 a new independentista coalition, the Movimiento Pro Independencia (MPI), was established by Juan Mari Bras. Under the MPI, sport and the Olympic delegation gradually became accepted by independence leaders as an expression of the nation. Recognizing the diplomatic and symbolic power of the Olympic Movement, many athletes and their followers viewed Puerto Rico's national Olympic delegation not only as the embodiment of the nation, but also as a vehicle in the fight for decolonization.

The chapter begins with an overview of how sport served to negotiate the terms of US imperialism and Americanization during the first decades of the twentieth century. Following this I will discuss the ideological tenets of the nationalists, including the PN. Next, I analyze how Puerto Rican Nationalists' view of the Olympic delegation changed with the establishment of the Commonwealth in 1952 and the rise of the MPI in 1959. The independentistas' use of Olympic sport in their struggle for independence reached a climax during the 1979 Pan-American Games in San Juan, when the pro–US statehood governor proposed the use of both the US and Puerto Rican flags throughout the tournament.

Sport, Americanization, and Nationalism

When the United States took possession of Puerto Rico in 1898 it embarked on an aggressive Americanization agenda that sought to transform Puerto Ricans' Spanish Caribbean traditions into Anglo-American ones. This transformation occurred under a colonial framework that stated that "Puerto Rico belonged to, but was not part of, the United States," and that the US Congress held "plenary powers" over the island.[11] The Foraker Act of 1900 established a civilian government that included a governor appointed by the US president and an executive council with legislative and judiciary powers (composed of six US-Americans and five Puerto Ricans), which was charged to carry out the Americanization project, and a locally elected House of Representatives.[12] Americanization included having English as the language of instruction in all schools, celebration of US patriots and historical figures, patriotic songs, holidays, and the US national anthem.[13] Together, these were the symbols of US progress and the new culture locals were expected to make their own. Sport also arrived with this same purpose. Baseball, viewed under Spain as foreign and threatening, was now accepted and supported by US authorities and their loyal Puerto Rican allies.[14] Other US sports made their way into Puerto Rico as part of Americanization and to aid a US imperial agenda of worldwide expansion, including basketball, volleyball, athletics, and boxing, among others.[15] The development of Puerto Rican nationalism and Olympic sport occurred not only under this colonial context, but also under broader Latin American and Caribbean nationalist processes.[16]

Puerto Ricans' nationalist activities can be traced back to the late nineteenth century. On September 23, 1868, a group of Puerto Ricans declared the island's secession from Spain by establishing the Republic of Puerto Rico. The "Grito de Lares" was led by Ramón Emeterio Betances and Segundo Ruiz Belvis, but the uprising did not garner enough popular support and was quickly crushed by the Spanish authorities. Instead, Puerto Ricans opted for an autonomous solution to their colonial relation with Spain. Autonomy from Spain was granted in 1897, only to be dismantled in 1898 by the invading US forces. Under the new regime, the existing political factions continued under new names and in shifting alliances. Those who advocated for complete independence, both from Spain or the United States, persisted and resisted the new empire, just as they had done under Spain.

In sport, we see the same celebration of the Puerto Rican nation in the early twentieth century. However, scholars so far have not addressed the ways in which nationalism and sport interact in Puerto Rico.[17] Different Puerto Rican athletes expressed their nationalism at different venues and in different ways since at least the 1910s. Perhaps the most vocal of the early Nationalist athletes was Nicasio Olmo, a marathon runner from the town of Arecibo. Olmo won the New York Bronx Marathon in 1911 and 1912. For his 1912 victory he wore a jersey with the Puerto Rican flag. Under the US occupation, this flag was not recognized, becoming instead a nationalist symbol. As a result of Law #53, otherwise known as "Ley de la Mordaza" (Gag Law, 1948–56), which criminalized any actions or association to groups that advocated for Puerto Rico's independence, the flag became more visibly associated with the Nationalists. While the flag was eventually adopted under the Commonwealth status in 1952, repression against nationalists continued. The organizers prohibited Olmo from running with the Puerto Rican flag in 1912 and threatened him with expulsion if he used it. Olmo used it and quit his association with the New York Club, returning to Puerto Rico to open his own athletic club.[18]

Nicasio Olmo was not the only athlete to express nationalist conviction during the Americanization years. We see similar nationalist acts in international football (soccer). On July 25, 1914, the Argentine battleship Rivadavia visited San Juan, and a group of sailors played the local San Juan FC. After the game they had lunch at "La Mallorquina," where they celebrated and toasted Argentina, Puerto Rico, and Spain. Later that night, the Argentines were hosted at the Casino Español, which was decorated with the Puerto Rican, Argentine and Spanish flags, bypassing the US flag, Puerto Rico's official flag at the time.[19]

Founded in 1922, the PN became the most radical of the pro-independence groups, with José Coll y Cuchí serving as its first president.[20] His 1923 book *El Nacionalismo en Puerto Rico* advocated for a peaceful and diplomatic approach to national freedom:

> We long to be a sovereign people without holding hostile resentment to the United States. We love our soil, our race, our language, and our right to absolute freedom. Those are precisely the feelings that characterize the most pure nationalism . . . If the United States pretend to have in this island a group of servants, they are mistaken. We will keep firmly fighting for our ideal, for our flag, for our beloved freedom.[21]

As president of the PN, José Coll y Cuchí was the premier voice of Puerto Rican nationalists. Coll y Cuchí was a renowned fencer serving also as field judge. He helped to teach the sport—and, along the way, a love of sport—to a generation of Puerto Ricans.[22] However, it should be underscored that Coll y Cuchí's main sport was fencing. While fencing was popular in many countries, it was one of the sports that the Catholic Spanish monarchy celebrated in their sporting sphere. Fencing was one of the most popular sports during the Spanish regime and was considered the sport of the nobles and gentlemen, oftentimes used to "defend the honor."[23] As we will see later, given the significant Catholic and Hispanic component of Puerto Rican nationalism US sports were rejected by the Nationalists as hegemonic tools of the US empire.

Nationalists got a strong advocate with the arrival of Pedro Albizu Campos in 1924. A graduate of Harvard University, Albizu Campos became Puerto Rico's leading Nationalist and remains today one of the most salient symbols of Puerto Rican nationalism. Albizu Campos was elected president of the PN in 1930, the same year Puerto Rico sent its first delegation to the Second Central American and Caribbean Games (CACG) in Havana, Cuba. In an era of ascending nationalism and growing use of Olympic sport to display national might, one might think that Albizu Campos and the PN would have celebrated Puerto Rico's participation in these Games. But this was not the case. The PN did not acknowledge Puerto Rico's participation in the CACG of 1930, 1935, or 1938, despite the delegation proving highly successful. The fact that the Puerto Rican delegation actually represented the United States, and not Puerto Rico, was an obstacle to the Nationalists. Indeed, the PN never used Puerto Rico's Olympic delegation as an expression of national might (as other countries did) or in their fight for freedom. In the course of Puerto Rican participation in Olympic-patronized tournaments such as the CACG, Pan-American Games (PAG), and Olympic Games, the Nationalist Party mostly ignored Puerto Rico's delegation.

The Puerto Rican Olympic delegation throughout the twentieth century was actually used for different colonial political and imperial diplomatic purposes.[24] The invitation to attend the 1930 CACG came from the US ambassador to Havana, Harry Guggenheim, and the delegation carried the US flag. Under these circumstances, Albizu Campos was not willing to celebrate a colonial delegation that actually represented the imperial oppressor. Indeed, their official platform for the 1932 elections said that "nationalism repudiates alliances, understandings, pacts, etc., with government factions because it considers a moral impossibility the union between separatism that fights for the immediate establishment of the republic and the organized claudication that supports the present irresponsible government, deferring with subterfuges the proclamation of independence."[25] In this regard, Puerto Rico's Olympic delegation was not only dismissed by the Nationalist Party, but—while not saying so publicly—was also considered an impediment for independence.

The reluctance by the PN leadership to recognize Puerto Rico's Olympic delegation contrasts with the feeling of many athletes and even their followers. The best example of a Nationalist athlete was Juan Juarbe Juarbe. Born on March 30, 1910, in Isabela, Puerto Rico, Juarbe Juarbe was one of Puerto Rico's best basketball players during the 1920s. He belonged to the Isabela's Gallitos team from 1922 to 1925, and while studying at the University of Puerto Rico (UPR) belonged to the 1929 champion team Floral Park. Also in 1929, he represented the UPR at insular athletic tournaments in track and field, winning the high jump, 100 and 200 meters, the 440 meters hurdles, and the 4 by 400 meters race, a performance that placed him among the best athletes of this time.[26] As a result of this, he was asked to join the Puerto Rican delegation for the 1930 CACG in Havana.

While his participation with the delegation was brief, Juarbe Juarbe became an integral component of the Nationalist struggle for independence. His participation at the 1930 CACG demonstrates why the PN considered supporting Puerto Rico's delegation an impossibility. Juarbe Juarbe was selected to be the flag bearer for the 1930 Games and paraded with the US flag during the opening procession. However, in an interview years later Juarbe Juarbe confessed to being utterly depressed by the situation. While considering being flagbearer an honor, he desired more than anything to carry the Puerto Rican flag. As a compromise, he paraded with the US flag, but did so barefoot.[27] For the Nationalists, carrying the US flag at this ceremony was a direct affront because the local US colonial state, diplomatic representatives abroad, and the Puerto Rican officials collaborating with the United States portrayed Puerto Ricans as US-Americans, in effect denying Puerto Rican nationhood. When Juarbe Juarbe returned to Puerto Rico from Havana he met Pedro Albizu Campos and quickly won his trust, becoming his personal assistant and retiring from international competition. Soon after, he was expelled from the UPR due to his political activism,[28] and in 1936 he was accused of conspiring to overthrow the US government in Puerto Rico, although he was eventually absolved.[29] From 1936 to the 1980s, Juarbe Juarbe became the PN's foreign affairs secretary and lived in exile. Nonetheless, although his main objective was to denounce US imperialism in Puerto Rico and promote bonds of solidarity throughout Latin America, he stayed abreast of Puerto Rican sport and managed also to utilize the Olympic scenario to denounce colonialism.[30]

The 1930s was a highly unstable and politically volatile decade. The Great Depression of 1930 hit Puerto Rico particularly hard. High unemployment, dire social conditions, and overall despair produced numerous strikes and confrontations. Despite the United States's interest in fostering the Good Neighbor policy, repression was the governing attitude toward Puerto Rican Nationalists. Violence climaxed during what became known as the Ponce Massacre, when the colonial police opened fire on a peaceful Nationalist parade that commemorated the abolition of slavery and protested Albizu Campos's political imprisonment on March 21, 1937. The result was twenty people killed and over two hundred wounded, with most of the victims shot in their backs.[31]

Two years before this dreadful incident, Puerto Rico attended the third CACG in San Salvador in 1935. During the opening parade, Nationalist Manuel Luciano carried the Puerto Rican flag, in open defiance of the colonial mandates and in a clear act to display the national emblem (Image 4.1). Puerto Rican trainer, Cosme Beitía, provided the Puerto Rican flag to organizers every time a Puerto Rican athlete won a medal, and in an example of Latin American solidarity the Salvadorian band played the Salvadorian anthem instead of the US anthem for Puerto Rico. The solidarity with Puerto Rican independence reached the Salvadorian press when Nicaraguan journalist Juan Ramón Avilés wrote for *La Prensa*, "Olympically speaking, in San Salvador we have witnessed the birth of a nation: Puerto Rico."[32]

Puerto Ricans returned to the island on April 22, 1935, to a heroes' welcome. Hundreds filled the streets in San Juan as a private plane flew over the sea of people towing a Puerto Rican flag. "La Borinqueña," a song that eventually became Puerto Rico's anthem, and Rafael Hernández's patriotic music played through loudspeakers. Reporter Arturo Gigante captured for the newspaper *El Mundo* the people's perspective and emotional attachments to the Puerto Rican delegation: "That's Puerto Rico absent, overflowing with the hearts of its sons, that against drawbacks and vicissitudes have managed to have the name of our small island be repeated with admiration and respect by all the nations, which, forming an enormous heart on the map, are the nucleus of the Hispanic republics, spine and marrow of our race."[33] These expressions are particularly special given the turbulent times of the 1930s. In a decade of heightened

Image 4.1. The Puerto Rican delegation parading at the open ceremonies at the 1935 Central American and Caribbean Games in San Salvador, El Salvador. *Courtesy of Carlos Uriarte González.*

nationalism and state repression, Olympic sport became both a cultural and political battlefield between nation and colonialism.

Although Pierre de Coubertin envisioned the Olympic Games as a manly affair, Puerto Rican female athletes have also contributed to the celebration of the nation at international sporting events. Rebekah Colberg, a pioneer of Puerto Rican Olympic sport, became the first Puerto Rican woman ever to win a medal (gold) at the 1938 CACG in Panama City. Only twenty years of age, Colberg, dressed in black and white (PN flag colors; Image 4.2) stood at the winners' podium listening to the US anthem, which played every time Puerto Rico won gold. However, when the US anthem ended she stood there in the same platform and began singing "La Borinqueña." Seconds after hearing Colberg sing, other Puerto Ricans present at the ceremony joined her singing.[34] Colberg inspired countless other women to play sport and represent the nation abroad. Both the municipal stadium in her native Cabo Rojo and a multisport complex in San Juan bear her name.

Rebekah Colberg, though an independentista, was willing to collaborate with the authorities in order to continue representing Puerto Rico abroad, eventually becoming a physician. Juarbe Juarbe, as a Nationalist,

Image 4.2. Rebekah Colberg at the 1938 Central American and Caribbean Games. *Courtesy of Jerjes Medina Albino, Wikimedia Commons.*

was not willing to collaborate. His exile began in 1936 as he embarked on a Latin American and Caribbean journey advocating for Puerto Rico's freedom in countries such as Argentina, Chile, Peru, Venezuela, Mexico, Cuba, Colombia, Brazil, and Guatemala, among others. His first stop was representing the "movement" at the Populist Parties of the Americas Congress of 1936 in Buenos Aires. Over there, he stated that Puerto Rico was the only American nation occupied by another American nation, while calling attention to the fact that, with 2.2 million inhabitants, a population larger than six Latin American nations, Puerto Rico's case urged action.[35] Two years later, in 1938, he gave a talk before the Federation of University Students of Cuba, condemning Fulgencio Batista. While in Cuba in 1950, Juarbe Juarbe met Fidel Castro and quickly adopted the Cuban struggle as his own.[36] While living in Mexico in 1954, he gave hospice to other Latin American revolutionaries such as Argentine Ernesto "Che" Guevara and Peruvian Luis de la Puente. Once the Cuban Revolution was successful he was granted Cuban citizenship and was a member of revolutionary Cuba's first delegation to the United Nations.[37]

While Juarbe Juarbe's commitment to the Cuban Revolution was unquestionable, his first mission was Puerto Rico's freedom. In 1948, he attended the Ninth International Americas Conference in Bogota, Colombia, and gave a talk entitled "Independencia de Puerto Rico." Stating that the "Puerto Rican nation has been militarily occupied by the United States of America since July 25, 1898," he urged the international body to call on the United States to adhere to its promises of liberty and democracy and to sponsor the speedy establishment of the Republic of Puerto Rico via a Constitutional Convention.[38] By the 1940s and 1950s, Juarbe Juarbe was mainly an international advocate of Puerto Rico's independence, yet later in life he confessed that he always followed Puerto Rican sport, be it on radio, television, or in the press.[39] He took advantage of any opportunity to denounce US imperialism in Puerto Rico, including the platforms provided by the Olympic Movement. Once again, at the 1950 Central American and Caribbean Games in Guatemala, Puerto Rico paraded with the US flag. Juarbe Juarbe was in Cuba, where he met a contingent of Guatemalans who had come in solidarity with Cuban revolutionaries. It didn't take long for him to conspire with the Guatemalans to go back and sabotage the opening ceremonies. Two Sandinista Nicaraguans, Dr. Carlos Castillo Ibarra and Professor Edelberto Torres, joined other young revolutionaries and together managed to hoist the Puerto Rican flag, play Puerto Rico's anthem "La Borinqueña," and throw twenty thousand flyers in the air with independentista propaganda at the time Puerto Rico paraded during the opening parade.[40] When the Guatemalan band played "La Borinqueña" (instead of the US anthem), Juarbe Juarbe exclaimed through the loudspeakers that "Guatemala does not recognize a colony, we are against colonialism in America!"[41] This incident angered the US ambassador to Guatemala, Richard Patterson, who was present and left the stadium threatening to introduce an official complaint. Juarbe Juarbe's tactic was successful in bringing attention to Puerto Rico's colonial problem, as the incident was covered in the US press by newspapers such as the *New York Times*, the *New York Herald Tribune*, and the *Chicago Tribune*.[42]

Despite Juarbe Juarbe's Nationalist and anticolonial demonstration at the 1950 Games in Guatemala, the PN again failed to recognize the delegation. Instead, it denounced it. Pedro Albizu Campos openly rejected the Puerto Rican delegation as colonial, saying that "we have to summon those bastards that go abroad using Puerto Rican money to carry the [US] flag and claim to have an anthem in their country," saying further that the delegation was "an exhibition of slaves."[43] Like Albizu Campos, José Enamorado Cuesta, former Nationalist military trainer,[44] also accused Puerto Rican sportsmen, especially those associated with US Major League Baseball, as yankophile traitors.[45] Even when the Puerto Rican delegation at the opening procession at the III CACG in San Salvador carried the Puerto Rican flag, the PN did not use that act as an example of nationalism through sport. Cuesta did acknowledge this and other similar *individual* expressions of nationalism that "have been demonstrated abroad by athletes who have resented their categorization as Yankees and insisting [instead] on being recognized as Puerto Rican nationals."[46] But, as an institution, the PN rejected Puerto Rico's delegation.

The Nationalists did have a reason to associate Puerto Rico's delegation with colonial leadership. Puerto Rico's Olympic Committee (COPR) was established within the structures and by the colonial administration. During the 1940s, COPR was led by Julio Enrique Monagas, a loyal ally of the Partido Popular Democrático (PPD), the party that led the political reforms that culminated in the Commonwealth in 1952. As such, COPR and Julio Enrique Monagas, by providing a platform to celebrate the nation and doing it so under an "autonomous" relation with the United States, were integral in the preservation of colonialism. As the Puerto Rican flag became the official flag of the delegation, Nationalists began to understand the power of the Olympic Movement for nationalism and its potential uses for political freedom.

Nationalism, Independence, and the Commonwealth of Puerto Rico

The Nationalists' quest for independence reached a climax in the 1950s. On November 30, 1950, members of the PN staged an armed insurrection in several municipalities in the island, attacking Blair House in Washington, DC, where President Truman was staying temporarily, as well. In October 1954, four Nationalists opened fire in the US Congress, calling for Puerto Rico's freedom and denouncing the new Commonwealth status as a colonial farce. During the 1950 uprising, Nationalists took the town of Jayuya and declared the Republic of Puerto Rico.[47] However, the uprising was quickly tamed by the well-armed and well-trained local National Guard. The National Guard used ten US P-47 Thunderbolt fighter planes dropping 500-pound bombs and spraying several towns with .50-caliber armor-piercing machine guns with a capacity to release 1,200 rounds per minute. Four thousand soldiers from the 296th Regiment took possession of a town of 12,000, arresting anyone in the streets.[48] The insurrection was in reaction to the political negotiations in Congress. Puerto Ricans, with congressional sponsorship and approval, moved toward establishing the Commonwealth of Puerto Rico, in a process that started in the late 1940s.[49] However, this Commonwealth, although providing a US-approved Puerto Rican Constitution, did not alter the core colonial statutes as established in the Jones Act of 1917. Luis Muñoz Marín's PPD led the colonial reforms that sought a limited degree of autonomy. While the Nationalists by now used armed resistance to claim independence, another pro-independence party committed to pacific strategies entered the political scene. The Partido Independentista Puertorriqueño (PIP) was established by former PN activists who chose a peaceful path toward independence and PPD followers disaffected by the PPD's abandonment of its independence platform.[50] Gilberto Concepción de Gracia, a former Nationalist, spearheaded the PIP and managed to amass significant electoral support, obtaining 19 percent of the votes in the 1952 elections, positioning the PIP as the PPD's premier opposition party.[51] However, internal party struggles, anti-independence repression, and the solidification of US hegemony led to the PIP's rapid decline.[52]

Independentista activism contrasts with how the Puerto Rican delegation was presented in international competition. Puerto Rico participated at the Fifth CACG in Barranquilla, Colombia, in 1946, using the US flag throughout the events, including the opening and closing ceremonies. Puerto Rico's first appearance at the Olympic Games occurred in 1948 in London. Since the US delegation participated at these Games, and given that an Olympic nation cannot send two delegations, Puerto Rico was allowed to participate, but carrying a different flag from the United States.[53] For the London Games, Puerto Rico was represented by the coat of arms that was granted to the island in 1511 by the Spanish monarchy and still used officially (Image 4.3). In lieu of a Puerto Rican national flag, and following Puerto Rican pride as a Hispanic people, Puerto Rican

PUERTO RICO

Image 4.3. Puerto Rican flag at the 1948 Olympics in London.
Courtesy of Malarz pl, Wikimedia Commons.

athletes fully embraced the coat of arms as a symbol of Puerto Ricanness during the these decades.[54]

Sport was definitely part of the activities being surveilled as part of the US Federal Bureau of Investigation (FBI) surveillance of independentistas. For example, in 1945, policeman Rafael Correa from the town of Caguas reported to the FBI that in a meeting of the PIP there was a discussion about the shameful colonial experience of Puerto Rican athletes abroad.[55] Gilberto Concepción de Gracia, or the PIP, did not publicly react, either to celebrate or condemn, the Puerto Rican delegation abroad; while Concepción de Gracia was an avid baseball fan,[56] he did not express particular scorn or pride in Puerto Rico's Olympic participation.[57] Concepción de Gracia's silence does not mean that the PIP disregarded sport entirely. The PIP's propaganda and organizational activities during the 1950s included work with trade unions, community associations, newspapers, women's groups, and youth. In 1953, these youth clubs included cultural and entertainment activities and the sponsorship of sport.[58] The fact that the PIP included sport as part of the community organization is indicative of the progressive adoption of sport not only for entertainment, but also to foster a sense of communal unity. This was certainly the point of view of Concepción de Gracia. While not necessarily celebrating the colonial delegation abroad, the PIP did incorporate sport as another tool for community uplifting, and particularly in the recruitment of youth. The PIP's change of attitude toward sport evidences a recognition of the difference between the colonial government's pro-US affinity and the benefits of sport to build the nation from the bottom up and to recruit a new generation of independentistas. In that regard, the PIP distanced itself from the PN, which had condemned the 1950 delegation as "lackeys of the Empire," and moved to incorporate sport into their programs.

The acceptance of Olympic sport by nationalist and independence leaders as a vehicle for Puerto Rican nationalism occurred outside the Partido Nacionalista by a new wave of activists led by Juan Mari Bras after the late 1950s. Frustrated by the increasingly detached and bureaucratic policies of the PIP, Juan Mari Bras and others left the PIP to pursue a new way to organize the independence movement. In 1959, the Movimiento Pro Independencia (MPI) was established under the leadership of Mari Bras in order to unite dispersed pro-independence groups. After the defeat of the 1950 Nationalist insurrection, the systematic repression under the Gag Law that left the population in a constant state of paranoia, and the FBI surveillance program, the pro-independence groups became increasingly unstable. The MPI tried to reorganize and regroup nationalists and independence supporters. Their second point in their political thesis sought to

> stimulate the alliance of the vanguard patriots with the forces of Puerto Rican affirmation aimed at advancing concrete actions in defense of the national patrimony, national rights, and Puerto Rican national culture, pursuing the isolation of the annexation forces and their definite defeat in the different daily spheres.[59]

The MPI proposed the unity of different anticolonial groups to advance the struggle for freedom. They made a clear differentiation between independence unity and anticolonial unity. The first moved toward the unification of all of the forces for independence; the latter sought to mobilize all of the forces that sought decolonization, but, most important, "to advance concrete actions in defense of the patrimony, rights, and national culture." For the MPI, the mobilization of anticolonial unity was critical because they included "all Puerto Ricans that agree in their supreme loyalty to Puerto Rico as their only *patria* and fight against the colonial state."[60] In other words, their focus was to find common ground among all of those that sought a national project to defend Puerto Rican culture and identity and fight against the structures of colonialism. Those who sought decolonization through full annexation to the United States threatened Puerto Rican national culture, and thus were excluded from this alliance. Of particular importance to our case is that the MPI left a clear space for national culture, including sport.

Juan Mari Bras, while not being a particular fan, did play some sports in his youth.[61] Perhaps he was not a public fan of Puerto Rico's Olympic delegation, but he was always supportive of Puerto Rico's Olympic sovereignty. One of Mari Bras and the MPI's most enduring legacies was the 1959 establishment of the newspaper *Claridad*, which became a weekly news source for nationalist struggles. Nationalist Carlos Raquel Rivera, a prominent artist, wrote about sport and politics in one of *Claridad*'s early issues. Noting that Puerto Rico's national anthem "snatches tears from the depths of one's soul," and that the "national flag is not seen, but embraced," Rivera fully endorsed the Olympic Movement as a space to fight for national existence. He denounced those who sought US-federated statehood, since this status would invalidate Puerto Rico's Olympic nationhood. Instead, he urged that an independent Puerto Rico would be the only means to guarantee a truly independent Olympic delegation.[62] Accompanying Carlos Raquel Rivera's article was a drawing that displayed a number of athletes standing proudly behind a flying Puerto Rican flag (Image 4.4). The drawing most probably can be attributed to graphic master and independentista Lorenzo Homar, who served as the artistic director for *Claridad* at that time.

It was through *Claridad* that the MPI tried to reach out to as many people as possible and unite in one voice all of those who believed in the Puerto Rican nation. Despite the PPD's use of Olympic sport to legitimize the autonomous nature of the Commonwealth during the 1950s, it was that same power of sport to legitimize the existence of the nation that attracted this new wave of nationalists and independentistas to cheer the Puerto Rican delegation.[63] In other words, there was no denying that the Olympic delegation was sending a strong message that the Puerto Rican nation existed, despite the colonial nature of the Commonwealth. Notwithstanding achieving Olympic nationhood, colonial censorship still permeated Puerto Rico's delegation. At that time, the delegation was commonly known as Delegación de Puerto Rico, instead of Delegación

Image 4.4. *Claridad* (San Juan), December 21, 1959.

or Equipo *Nacional* de Puerto Rico.[64] Using the term "nacional" was
too closely associated with the *nacionalistas* and could bring political
repercussions.

The increasing acceptance of Olympic sport in Puerto Rico's
struggle for independence after the 1960s has to be placed in the context of the increasing volatility of those decades. From the late 1960s
through the early 1980s, independentistas in Puerto Rico and the diaspora were increasingly active and radical, despite having increasingly
less electoral support. Radical independentista groups formed soon after
the establishment of the Commonwealth, including the Federación de
Universitarios Pro Independencia (FUPI) in 1956.[65] The MPI rebranded
as the Partido Socialista Puertorriqueño (PSP) in 1971, and in 1974 the
Fuerzas Armadas de Liberación Nacional (FALN) was formed in Chicago.
Between 1974 and 1981, the FALN carried out some 120 bombings in the
United States, mostly of governmental offices and offices of multinational
corporations.[66] Back on the island, the Ejército Popular Boricua (a.k.a.
Los Macheteros) was established on July 26, 1976, by Filiberto Ojeda Ríos,

to embark on an armed struggle for Puerto Rico's freedom. In 1979, the Macheteros attacked a US Navy bus, killing two servicemen, while in 1981 another attack destroyed eight fighter planes at the National Guard Air Force Base in San Juan.[67] The Macheteros averaged two incidents per year during their first decade of existence.[68]

Claridad noted the increasing importance of sport in the struggle for Puerto Rican freedom. In 1974, the newspaper launched a steady sport section, first managed by Jaime Córdoba and by Elliott Castro in 1976. In 1978, Castro made it clear to the readership that sport, particularly international, was crucial in the struggle for independence. Castro used the platform of *Claridad* to reiterate the importance of Olympic sport for Puerto Rican nationhood:

> From our part, we hope to enlarge even more our activity and influence in the sport world. CLARIDAD will multiply its sport coverage. We have recruited new personnel, with whom we hope and trust be able to provide more attention and spread of amateur sport. Every day our Party and our newspaper recognize and give more importance to all sporting activity, always keeping in close mind that it is in sport the only area internationally speaking that we are recognized as an independent country, with our own personality, anthem and flag and representation.[69]

By 1979, Puerto Rico had participated in twelve Central American and Caribbean Games, six Pan-American Games, eight Olympiads, and multiple World Championships in various disciplines. There was no doubt that, in international sport, Puerto Rico was a nation. In that year, Puerto Rico hosted its biggest international sport tournament, the Pan-American Games, the second largest multisport event in the world. Yet political controversy marred the event, when Carlos Romero Barceló, the pro–US statehood governor at the time, tried to sabotage Puerto Rican Olympic sovereignty by wanting to use the US flag and anthem next to the Puerto Rican in all ceremonies. A "war of the flags" ensued as a multisectorial coalition and the civil society joined in an effort to repudiate Romero Barceló's plans and affirm Puerto Rico's Olympic nationhood. The coalition urged the PNP administration to respect Puerto Rico's Olympic sovereignty and nationhood by desisting from pressuring the organizers to use both the US and Puerto Rican flags and anthems in representation of Puerto Rico. After much debate and public demonstrations the governor desisted, but still ordered the band to play the US anthem during the opening ceremonies. Reacting to this, the people packed in the Estadio Hiram Bithron collectively booed the governor during his opening remarks, a demonstration dubbed then and still remembered as "La pitada olímpica."[70]

Finally acknowledging the sporting sphere as a battleground, Puerto Rico's Nationalist Party acknowledged and celebrated Puerto Rico's delegation. Through the party's official publication, *Boletín Nacional*, the Nationalists sent a fraternal message to the visiting delegations: "Puerto Rico, the land of the Puerto Ricans, feels profoundly honored with your visit. Our wishes are that you take to your nations the most gratifying memories of the still unredeemed fatherland of Betances and Albizu Campos."[71] Yet, by 1979, the defense of Puerto Rican nationhood no longer rested with the PN. The coalition to defend Puerto Rico's Olympic nationhood at the 1979 Pan-American Games included people from different shades of the independence and autonomy spectrums. Moreover, as seen during the CACG in 1935, 1946, and 1950, showing Puerto Rican national pride was not within any institution's purview, but equally up to athletes and their followers. As former 1960s Olympian Pedro Juan Camacho asserts, Puerto Rican athletes were for the most part patriotic.[72] In 1979, Puerto Rican swimmer Jesse Vassallo, although wanting to represent Puerto Rico, was not allowed to represent his nation due to COPR's rule that an athlete had to reside in Puerto Rico for at least one year before the competition. Representing the United States, Vassallo, who earlier that year broke the 400 meters race at the World Championships in Berlin, won the 400 meters race in San Juan with another record-breaking performance. During the medal ceremony, while the US anthem played, the public in a spontaneous spark of nationalism and overpowering the speakers began singing Puerto Rico's national anthem, "La Borinqueña." Vassallo then raised and waved a small Puerto Rican flag he had brought with him to the podium, triggering a euphoric reaction.[73]

Recognizing the power of sport to exhibit the nation, influence local politics, and move the masses in collective manifestations of nationalism, the independentista leadership also fully embraced Puerto Rico's Olympic sport as a site for national freedom and nationalism. Elected President of the PIP in 1970, Rubén Berríos Martínez was seen as the heir of the independentista leadership after the passing of Gilberto Concepción de Gracia. A lawyer and scholar with degrees from Georgetown University, Yale University, and Oxford University, Berríos Martínez served multiple times as senator and, despite losing his nominations for governor, enjoyed much popular support. Contrary to previous Nationalist and independentista leaders that attacked Puerto Rico's Olympic delegation, by the 1979 Pan-American Games in San Juan Berríos Martínez fully understood the stakes of such delegation and the usefulness, almost imperative, of the Olympic Movement for Puerto Rican nationalism and freedom.

In a lengthy article in Puerto Rico's leading newspaper entitled "Nacionalismo y Bandera," Berríos Martínez attacked Romero Barceló's postures regarding the flags and anthems, arguing instead for the importance of the Puerto Rican flag for the people of Puerto Rico. He said that "a flag is neither an accident nor a colorful rag. A flag is years and years of suffering, sleeplessness, frustrations, heroisms, yearnings, hopes, [and] a common dedication of a people's cause."[74] Regarding the booing at the opening ceremonies, he stated that it "symbolized the people's preference in the struggle taking place in Puerto Rico between the North American and the Puerto Rican and protested the vexations of the last 81 years of domination."[75] He went on to list all of the components of these vexations and their impact on different segments of society, including the "sweat and blood" of sugarcane workers working for US economic interests, the "pleas" of women who saw their sons die in another country's wars, and the "rebelliousness of those fallen in Ponce under police machine gunfire that Palm Sunday."[76] Despite Albizu Campos and the PN's rejection of the delegation, Berríos Martínez now spoke for all nationalists in the full legitimation of the national delegation as redeemer of the nation and its colonized victims:

> That day's gesture demonstrate the existence of a vigorous people, of a strong nationality maintained after 81 years of Americanization, demonstrate the freshness of our Latin American lineage. There are few peoples in the world, that after many years of control by the most powerful country in the world, have sufficient vital energy to reaffirm its nationalism. . . . What happened at these Games is a reflection of the enormous flow of nationalism that beats in the majority of Puerto Ricans and that, like the water streams that spontaneously searches and without apparent direction finds a channel, is conducted now in sports, for being this the option that for now is available.[77]

Rubén Berríos Martínez was able to confidently express the importance of Puerto Rico's Olympic delegation for Puerto Rican nationalism and independence due to its disassociation from the US delegation. No longer was the delegation associated with the United States as it had been in the 1930s, 1940s, and early 1950s. The negotiations that led to Puerto Ricans having their own national delegation had stabilized by the 1970s, though issues of colonialism still persisted. Being able to use the Puerto Rican flag and anthem in such popular sport mega-events was reason enough for Nationalist and independence leaders to jump on the bandwagon of the Olympic Movement. This participation, already embraced by the majority of Puerto Rican athletes and other delegates, was enough to serve as an amplifying showcase—perhaps the best—in the Puerto Rican struggle for independence and national survival. So much so that, two days after Mónica Puig's victory at the 2016 Olympics in Rio de Janeiro, the PN, in addition to congratulating Puig, said that "today we congratulate all athletes that place our banner in the highest. Nationalism is this sense of belonging that blossomed like an explosion with Mónica Puig's triumph, who we hope continues, like yesterday, embracing, forever, our flag."[78]

Conclusion

Much has transpired since nationalist José Enamorado Cuesta lambasted against those Puerto Rican baseball players in the United States and the idea of baseball as an Americanization scheme. In March 2017, Puerto Rico's national baseball team reached the finals of the World Baseball Classic unbeaten, fueling once again nationalist fervor that even made the pro–US statehood governor, Ricardo Rosselló, cheer for the Puerto Rican squad during the final game against the United States.[79] Team manager Edwin Rodríguez openly confessed being heavily influenced by the patriots Pedro Albizu Campos, Ramón Emeterio Betances, and Eugenio María de Hostos, due to their conviction to "[offer] the greatest sacrifice . . . for an ideal they believe is true, and for the benefit of society."[80] The Puerto Rican squad lost to the United States, but not before uniting for two weeks a nation that still received them in San Juan with a heroes' welcome observed by the entire country.[81]

Puerto Rico's Olympic sport tells us much more than the confluences between nationalism and the Olympic Movement in Latin America and the Caribbean. Puerto Rico's unique status as a colony of the United States challenges an easy reading of identity through sport. In Puerto Rico, the Olympic Movement has been used or served as a platform to negotiate the very existence of a national identity that is at risk of being assimilated into another. The discussion over Americanization, Olympic sport, and nationalism is heightened in Puerto Rico, as the politics of colonialism—in effect of colonial Olympism—often create a push and pull between factions seeking particular political goals and advancing different ideologies. As Rubén Berríos Martínez aptly said in 1979, Puerto Ricans have been resisting (I would say negotiating) their identity against the assimilationist policies of the most powerful empire humanity has ever known. This negotiation has resulted in a strong sense of a Latin American and Caribbean identity, which lives and thrives despite Puerto Rico being an unincorporated US territory and its people having US citizenship. Yet the power of the Olympic Movement is such that Puerto Rico's Latin American and Caribbean identity shines through the structures of political constraints.

Puerto Rico's independence leaders, from Juan Juarbe Juarbe to Juan Mari Bras and then Rubén Berríos Martínez, noticed the potential of the Olympic Movement in the struggle for freedom. As the reality of a Puerto Rican Olympic nation cemented locally and internationally, independentistas and Nationalists adopted that reality and made it their own, aligning with most of the athletes who already embraced their patriotism at any sporting event throughout the twentieth century and into the twenty-first. As Puerto Rico's colonial dilemma continues strongly into the present, the Olympic Movement stands as a central piece in the perennial discussion over decolonization and an unwavering element of Puerto Rican nationalism.

CHAPTER 5

Adhemar Fereira da Silva

Representations of the Brazilian Olympic Hero

FABIO DE FARIA PERES
AND VICTOR ANDRADE DE MELO

Introduction

Adhemar Ferreira da Silva stood out in the international Olympic Movement for twice being crowned champion in the triple jump contest (Helsinki 1952 and Melbourne 1956). His achievements had significant repercussions for Brazil's Olympic Movement. In the 1950s, Brazil had gone thirty-two years without winning an Olympic gold medal—since the 1920 Antwerp Olympics, when a Brazilian delegation participated in the event for the first time.

The first Brazilian delegation to participate in the Olympic Games, in 1920, was sent by the Brazilian Sports Confederation. The delegation had athletes participating in shooting, swimming, diving, rowing, and water polo. In addition to the difficulties of organization and travel, knowledge about the philosophy and structure of the Olympic Movement was limited. It must be considered that, even if Olympic sports were already popular and had been consolidating since the nineteenth century, there was still a degree of precariousness in the field, in addition to persisting conflicts among the sport leadership. Nonetheless, the 1920 Brazilian delegation won a gold (Guilherme Paraense, in the revolver event); a silver (Afrânio Costa, in the pistol event); and a bronze medal (in team pistol by Sebastião Wolf, Dario Barbosa, and Fernando Soledade).[1]

The Brazilian Olympic Committee was founded in 1914. However, as a result of various problems, it became functional only in 1935, due to

DOI: https://doi.org/10.34053/scs2019.o.5

the action of important figures from Brazilian society, including Raul do Rio Branco, Arnaldo Guinle, José Ferreira dos Santos, and Antônio Prado Júnior, who were all, at different times, representatives of Brazil on the International Olympic Committee (IOC).[2]

In the 1950s, Brazil attempted to establish itself on the international sport scene, but it had to address the "tragedy" of the 1950 FIFA World Cup, when the Uruguayan team defeated the national team at Maracanã Stadium. In the eyes of the journalist and playwright Nelson Rodrigues, this failure became an ethos that, years later, would ironically be termed as the "underdog complex"—that is, a certain "modesty in self-belief" mixed with "fear of disillusionment." In other words, the so-called *maracanaço* left a feeling of "inferiority in which the Brazilian, voluntarily, places himself compared to the rest of the world."[3]

During the 1950s, the country underwent a period of democratic transition after living for fifteen years under the presidency of one leader (1930–45), Getúlio Vargas, who governed dictatorially for eight years (1937–45) and returned to office in 1951 through a democratic election.[4] Economically, there were steadier steps taken toward industrialization, which changed the national corporate structure. Cities grew enormously, diversifying the profile of their inhabitants. The strengthening of the media contributed both to exposing the identity crisis that affected Brazil and to mobilizing Brazilians around the idea of a nation.[5]

In this context, we should consider that da Silva's profile was typical of a large segment of the Brazilian population: he was black, born in the largest city in Brazil (São Paulo), and a member of a working-class family (son of a worker and a cook) who managed to improve his socio-economic status. He was not the first great athlete to receive attention from the country or the first black sportsman to be recognized (he was preceded, for example, by the notable soccer player Leônidas da Silva). However, he was certainly the athlete who achieved the greatest fame up to that point, foreshadowing the spectacular repercussion that another character would experience from the 1960s onward: the soccer player Edson Arantes do Nascimento, also known as Pelé.

In this chapter, we will discuss the representations of da Silva's victories in the 1952 and 1956 Olympics as published in the press of Rio de Janeiro and São Paulo, the capital of the country and the capital of the largest state, respectively. Our intention is to analyze how the assumptions of the exaltation of the great Brazilian Olympic hero overlap with important national questions as well as with the conflicts and desires of a nation that underwent rapid and intense changes. We believe that the case of da Silva helps us open new perspectives on the history of the relationship between sport and national identity, particularly because it involves the success in track and field at a time when soccer had already become the most popular sport (and mass entertainment) in Brazil.

1952:
The Hero in the Service of the Nation

Shortly before embarking for Helsinki to compete in the 1952 Olympics, part of the Brazilian press placed in da Silva, albeit cautiously, the hope of winning the gold medal that Brazil had not won since the 1920 Antwerp Olympics. At that point, the athlete had already tied the triple jump world record (in 1950) and won the event in the 1951 Pan-American Games and the 1952 South American Track and Field Championship.

Última Hora, a Rio de Janeiro newspaper, used expert opinion to evaluate the "Brazilian representation" that would participate in the Olympic Games. Osvaldo Gonçalves, a professor of athletics at the National School of Physical Education and coach of the team that would go to Helsinki, and who was considered "one of the greatest national coaches," said:

> It is, in fact, the team with the highest values of national athletics. They have performances and technique that rise to the greatness of the Olympic Games. However, going through the two qualifying rounds against the representatives of world athletics to qualify for 6th place in the final is not an easy task or something that is expected to happen by luck or as a simple "chance" offered by mistakes from strong competitors. In the Olympic Games, the biggest champions will participate with the same desires for even a third place medal. Such an honorable qualification requires the athlete's effort, training, physical ability, and a lot of technical difficulties.[6]

According to Gonçalves, it would not be surprising if da Siva did not win a medal. Qualifying for the final was already considered a "great achievement." Regardless, da Silva was quoted by the coach as being one of the likely winners. Gonçalves considered that the Brazilian was on the same level as other athletes already consecrated worldwide:

> There are few contests whose possible winners can be identified. In this case, they are not just champions but super champions. Of the national athletes, Adhemar Ferreira, in the Triple Jump, is in

this class, along with Jim Fuchs, the shot put world record holder at 17.95 meters, and with Zátopek in the 10,000 meters, at 29 minutes 2 seconds.[7]

Despite his analysis, Gonçalves was subsequently more restrained, suggesting that da Silva awaited for an "honorable placement." Prudence was justifiable. Not only did Brazilian amateur athletes face significant obstacles to access quality training, but Brazil had also already suffered the "traumatic" loss of the 1950 FIFA World Cup. Overconfidence and a lack of modesty seemed to be viewed with suspicion by certain members of the athletic community, including journalists and trainers.

Nevertheless, *Última Hora* made a point of exalting the Brazilian competitors, contrasting with the professor's sober-minded style. On the day of departure for Helsinki, the newspaper printed the following headline in bold letters: "THESE ATHLETES WILL DEFEND BRAZIL."[8] The terms used in the article were carefully chosen. Defense and praise of the nation were valued attitudes in the Brazilian context at that time (and that still persist as interpretative keys to history, particularly regarding Brazilian political and economic history).[9]

During the 1950s, the newspapers in fact highlighted the struggle between those who favored "nationalism" and those who were pejoratively called "surrenderers." These were trends that defended, on the one hand, conflicting models of Brazilian development with the use of exclusively national capital and usufruct with state monopoly, and, on the other hand, with the participation of private capital, mainly international, and the exploitation of national "riches" by foreign groups.[10]

In this sense, the discussion of the role that the state should occupy in the "modernization" of the country delineated distinct plans for the nation. Is it worth emphasizing that the president at the time, Getúlio Vargas (1951–54), was elected on a platform that proposed independence and economic sovereignty through the progressive nationalization of industry vis-à-vis overcoming the agro-export model of development.

Therefore, the nature of the discourse in the newspapers about da Silva's victory is not surprising. Almost all of the newspapers printed pictures of the athlete accompanied by texts with a proud tone. The 1952 gold medal conquest in Helsinki was placed above political disputes, with different and even divergent groups seeking to link to da Silva's victory. All of them wanted the country to be internationally legitimated, albeit with distinct interests and appropriations in the construction of the nation's narrative.[11]

However, the representations of da Silva's gold medal conquest seemed to be more in line with the discourses that inflated the value of nationalism to the detriment of possible foreignisms. In fact, Brazilian sport institutions—the Brazilian Sports Confederation (Confederação Brasileira de Desportos, CBD), governed since 1941 by the National Sports Council (Conselho Nacional de Desportos, CND); and the Brazilian Olympic Committee—were directly linked to the state.[12] They were organs of the bureaucratic structure, which, at that moment, defended the "nationalist flag."[13]

Surprisingly, there was no substantial reaction on the part of the Brazilian president in the newspapers. However, according to Maurício Drumond, the Brazilian *Estado Novo* (1937–45) led by Vargas considered sport as a valuable political tool:

> When analysing sport during the government of Vargas, it is easy to see how the political field tried to approach it. . . . It played an important part in the official propaganda, especially in conveying messages of optimism, nationalism, racial democracy and physical enhancement of the Brazilian people. The new image of the Brazilian man had in sport (mainly football) one of its strongest icons. Sporting victories represented the success of the nation, and public celebrations linked the sporting prowess to the new regime.[14]

A different set of political coalitions may explain the difference between the two Vargas governments, including sport. In the context of the 1950s, the same weakness of the political system that permitted his election in 1951 did not allow him to govern as he desired.[15]

Whatever the differences in the Vargas governments, for the press da Silva was a model of the abdication and dedication that characterize national martyrs. One chronicler suggested that the athlete "had promised to do everything, not for the individual projection of his name, but to project even more, in the world sport scene, the name of Brazil."[16] His character and his devotion to the nation acquired a greater dimension, particularly because of the "poor and modest" origins of his parents.[17] Incidentally, the athlete constantly emphasized the difficulties of being an amateur sportsman. In fact, da Silva's trajectory reflected, in part, the tensions present in Brazilian amateurism, particularly for those from the working classes: from the beginning of his career, the athlete had to reconcile several professional occupations with training and travel for competitions, both national and international. One of the most emblematic situations regarding the contradictions of being an amateur athlete occurred when, even having already won his first gold medal in 1952, da Silva had his wages docked for eighteen days for attending the 1953 South American Track and Field Championship. Afterward, he lost the position he occupied in Mayor Jânio Quadros São Paulo's City Hall.[18] At the time, there were protests against the measure. In part, his move from São Paulo to Rio de Janeiro was precisely due to labor and financial issues.[19]

Not infrequently, however, da Silva stressed his main motivation for overcoming these issues—his commitment to the country:

> I trusted in my possibilities, though I recognized that I would find great opponents. But there was also the desire not to disappoint my countrymen. And, thinking of Brazil, only of Brazil, I went to the sand pit where I achieved the greatest result of my entire career.[20]

The feeling of belonging to the nation marked the peak of his experiences. Da Silva clearly expressed this nationalistic sentiment in his speeches: "When they played the Brazilian National Anthem, I felt that I was living the greatest moment of my life."[21] A similar sentiment had been repeated upon arriving at the dining hall of the Olympic Village, when athletes from every Latin American country stood up and shouted "Brazil! Brazil!" cheering da Silva and celebrating his achievement.[22]

In the eyes of many chroniclers, the positive portrayals of da Silva were especially important because they were echoed by international news agencies, which described him as "a tall, long-legged black man" who "received great affection when, after receiving his gold medal, he spontaneously made a turn on the track, greeting the crowd, enchanted by the picturesque manner in which the Brazilian athlete spread his joy."[23] On another occasion, a news agency emphasized the athlete's modesty: "I just did what I could" and "I did not plan to do anything like this," da Silva said.[24]

In the Brazilian press's representation, the surprised foreign eyes confirmed some characteristics of the Brazilian character, such as being peaceful and mixed-race, similar to what had been categorized by Gilberto Freyre, an intellectual whose reflections on race relations in Brazil already enjoyed great prestige at the time.[25]

The famous singer and dancer Josephine Baker, who was in Brazil performing her show when da Silva won gold in Helsinki,[26] affirmed in an interview titled "I want to kiss Adhemar da Silva," that "a victory of a man of color is also mine."[27] To her, it was "very normal" for the Finns to admire da Silva "because . . . the Scandinavians are at the forefront of the movement against racial discrimination." What surprised Baker was that the Brazilian press dedicated many pages to a black athlete. *Última Hora* stressed that the singer praised the consolidation of Brazilian democracy.

Da Silva ended up being elected the representative of something that, in fact, did not exist and never existed in Brazil—the myth of the harmony of races. The valorization of his achievements could not mask the injustices of various orders that surrounded the Brazilian population, including those of a racial nature.

However, we must pay attention to the nuances that permeated Brazilian social life at that time, something that had begun to take shape in the 1930s but that came to life in the 1950s. Culturally, da Silva and other black or brown celebrities were not associated with terms such as "negro," "nigger," or "colored." In the press and the media in general, these connotations were used pejoratively, demonstrating tacit racism, sometimes more, sometimes less. Da Silva and other black or brown personalities were treated as "illustrious Brazilians," and their respective "negritude," so to speak, was "visible" only to foreign eyes.[28]

Nonetheless, the prestige of the country on the international scene, according to the newspapers, was not at all trivial. The day after his victory, *Correio da Manhã*, a Rio de Janeiro newspaper, insisted that da Silva had been hailed as a hero not only for winning the gold medal but also for having performed an "unprecedented event in the Olympic annals," beating the world record four times in a row in the same contest.[29] For the chronicler, this performance helped make the value of Brazil clear to the world.

The applause of the public and other delegations was viewed as a supposed recognition of national qualities—cordiality, empathy, and modesty. For instance, a *Correio da Manhã* article claimed that

> the Brazilian Anthem was sung in chorus by all the fans of Adhemar Ferreira da Silva. Then, the holder of second place in the event, the Russian Scherbakov, made a point of demonstrating to the Brazilian his unspeakable admiration....And when the Brazilian,...launched himself onto the track, on which he made a complete lap, under the ovation of the spectators who cheered him and rose up at his passage, it was felt that even Zátopek had not achieved such a great triumph in his victory in the 10,000-meter race. The public will, for a long time, hold the image of the victor stopping in the midst of the rush to embrace a blond admirer whose enthusiasm brought her to the front row.[30]

José Brígido, from *Diário de Notícias*, another Rio de Janeiro newspaper, called on readers to celebrate the gold medal with "the greatest enthusiasm possible because it made the name of our country in the most important event in the world and in a truly sensational manner."[31] The expectations of the international diffusion of Brazil's positive image were far from modest and, moreover, included all Brazilians as participants in the victory:

> There is no doubt that Adhemar's achievement was worth all the sacrifices Brazilians made to participate in this great event; it will be even more worthy because today, on every page of every newspaper in the world, his name will be stamped next to Brazil. All the voices of the world will speak of his prowess, and the cinema and the television will reproduce the main scenes of his triple jump, and all this will be like great publicity for our land and our people.[32]

Gonçalves, the delegation's coach, went so far as to declare that, given the importance of the event for Brazil, there was no boy who did not want to become "an Adhemar."[33] Regardless of the typical exaggerations of a patriotic coverage, it can be said that Brazil largely came together around da Silva's victory:

> The applause and cheers come from all sides, not only from the sportsmen but also from all the staff of the airlines and the airport, from the most modest to the executives. It was the expression of gratitude of millions of Brazilians, through about seventy people, to the greatest Brazilian champion of all time, the author of a feat that, if not impossible, is difficult to equal by any athlete in the world.[34]

The newspapers sought to synthesize the pride of the country by building symbolic ties between the individual and the nation. Da Silva, the "Olympic champion who haunted the world," declared that "I won because I'm Brazilian."[35] The hero placed himself at the service of the nation, assuming what was attributed to him.

1956:
The Hero as an Expression of the Country's Desires

Adhemar Ferreira da Silva's return to Brazil after winning the gold medal at the 1956 Melbourne Olympics was surrounded by a mixture of expectation and exaltation. The newspapers simultaneously reflected and fostered a certain concern around the "hero" who "once again managed to shake the flag of Brazil on the larger Olympic flagpole."[36]

From the time of his victory and, in particular, in the days leading up to his arrival in Brazil, the newspapers announced his return with increasing excitement. The *Diário Carioca*, from Rio de Janeiro, even reported the full schedule of the ceremonial reception in Rio de Janeiro on the front page of the December 13 edition. The feat of da Silva was considered so memorable that Tupi TV conducted a live broadcast of the whole affair, something that was very unusual at the time.[37]

The ceremony began at the airport, with the delivery of a gold embroidered pennant by the president of the Sport Press Department of the Brazilian Press Association. The country's top official authorities were present, among them the minister of education and culture, Clóvis Salgado, and the mayor of the Federal District, Negrão de Lima.[38] An automobile procession, which passed through Avenue Rio Branco, one of the main avenues of Rio de Janeiro, led the athlete to be received by the president of the republic, Juscelino Kubitschek.

The newspapers published pictures of the presidential reception on their front pages, in which da Silva appeared alongside Kubitschek at the Palácio do Catete (the headquarters of the executive power). The legends that accompanied the pictures are emblematic of the representations that were built around the athlete, in which ideas of the people, the state, and the nation were all mixed. The reader was informed that da Silva received a "consecrating reception . . . from the people of Rio de Janeiro" and heard from the highest authority of the nation "words of encouragement and thanks for the extraordinary exposure he gave to Brazil through his magnificent victory."[39]

This exaltation notwithstanding, Brazil was living in a not-so-bright era. The Getúlio Vargas government, immersed in denunciations and scandals, ended tragically with the suicide of the historic leader in August 1954. The transitional government was marked by great tension, as was the election of Juscelino Kubitschek, who took over and governed the country under many criticisms and conflicts. His administration (1956–61) would be marked not only by the acceleration of the process of industrialization and economic growth, but also by the increase of the public debt and inflation. Brazil received major exposure in the international scene, particularly in cultural aspects, such as in music through bossa nova, modern architecture, and sports achievements, including the 1958 FIFA World Cup title.[40]

While da Silva's victory in Melbourne was unanimously celebrated, there were criticisms of the Brazilian delegation's performance. Although the criticisms did not affect da Silva's image, the absence of other good results in the Olympic Games caught the attention of the public and was a subject of debate. The overall Brazilian performance in Melbourne was considered a sign of the fragility of the Brazilian state. These criticisms were directed toward the performance of the new president of the Republic. Wilson Brasil, writing for *Mundo Esportivo*, a Rio de Janeiro sport magazine, was very explicit about this:

> FAILURE! Disaster! Brazil again fails in the Olympic Games. And what a failure! We achieved nothing but the title of Adhemar Ferreira da Silva. Fortunately, we still have this exception. In fact, sports in our country are this: Adhemar and soccer. Other than that, there is nothing.[41]

If da Silva's victory was previously considered the great triumph of the nation, a fact that would project a good image of Brazil abroad, his second gold medal was regarded by some as an insufficient balm to hide the country's problems. As one chronicler suggested,

> We are always below insignificant countries, which have no importance on the world stage. If it were not for Adhemar Ferreira da Silva, we would have been left behind by the little ones that hardly appear on the map.... It is a fact that we are still very far from maturity. We need to see reality as it is and convince ourselves of our insignificance ... in order to achieve something in the future.[42]

This idea had been outlined after the 1955 Mexico City Pan-American Games, where the Brazilian delegation did not perform well, which for some demonstrated "our sports inferiority."[43] Nonetheless, da Silva's second gold medal and world record–breaking achievement had broad effects.[44] *O Globo*, a Rio de Janeiro newspaper, not only published a special page dedicated to the athlete, but also organized an homage at Maracanã Stadium, the great stage of national sport.[45]

It is worth noticing that, in the political and cultural spheres, the idea of a Latin American identity at that time (something whose roots go back to the nineteenth century) was historically strange to Brazilians. It was equally rare and uncommon to include Brazil in representation of Latin America, at least from the perspective of the countries that viewed themselves as part of Latin America. This would begin to take on different forms, even if tentatively, from the 1960s on, when there was a greater dialogue between Brazilian and Spanish American intellectuals, particularly regarding the place that their respective countries occupied in the center-periphery of international capitalism.[46]

In this sense, some observers believed that Brazil should be ahead of continental neighbors and other countries, which they considered to have smaller international importance. Therefore, they argued that Brazil should be among the highest countries ranked in the medal standings at the Olympic Games, along with, preferably, the United States and other European powers. To that end, they further argued, it would be necessary to win not only a single gold medal, despite its celebrated value, but also to achieve a number of good performances in various events.[47]

In other words, after the 1956 Melbourne Olympics international sport competitions continued to be valued as a form of national projection, but with less patriotism around them. In fact, a few days after the news of da Silva's second gold medal, attention was drawn to the political appropriation of his achievement to exaggerate nationalism. In a *Mundo Esportivo* column presenting the worst and best events of the week, the "worst thing" chosen was the position of "buzzards and demagogues," "vultures" who treated the athlete's achievement with "hollow, adorned, and demagogic speeches, talking about flags, patriotism, etc."[48]

Despite these negative views, a festive and celebratory tone still prevailed regarding da Silva's performance. After all, the victory in Melbourne matched the expectation built in the months before the Olympic Games, even though the athlete faced some difficulties in achieving the qualification standard. A long article on the chances of the Brazilian athletes in Melbourne highlighted—albeit pondering the training difficulties that da Silva had to endure during the year—that he was the national delegation's main hope to obtain a gold medal.[49] The expectation also gained continental coverage. *Jornal do Brasil*, another Rio de Janeiro newspaper, called attention to the fact that he was the only Latin American with the possibility of victory in the athletic events and noted that European journalists considered him the "most outstanding" athlete.[50] Jesse Owens, the "Man of the Four Gold Medals in Berlin," had stated a few days before the Olympic Games that da Silva was "undoubtedly one of the greatest athletes in the world at the time."[51]

On the very day of the triple jump event, the Rio de Janeiro *Diário Carioca* reported on the cover, increasing the reader's expectation, that "reserving energy" da Silva qualified for the final that would occur in the afternoon.[52] *Globo* and *Última Hora* positioned themselves as privileged witnesses and, indirectly, as participants in and followers of his accomplishment.[53]

The popularity and prestige of da Silva became evident in the period between the two Olympic Games in which he won his two gold medals. His name was often cited as that of the greatest sportsman in Brazil, including athletes of other sports, such as soccer.[54] Articles and columns dedicated to the life of "celebrities"[55] and "personalities," included him in such categories.[56] The track and field stadium of Belo Horizonte (capital of the state of Minas Gerais) was christened with his name.[57]

Surprisingly, *Última Hora*'s headline announced his victory in Melbourne—"Adhemar jumped 16.35 meters, defeated the Russian, and became the Olympic champion!"[58] The newspaper offered a glimpse, albeit indirectly, of a nationalist reading in the context of the Cold War. Perhaps the emphasis would have gone unnoticed had it not been in the midst of other news such as "Lott in the name of the army: against communist tyranny in defense of nationalism."[59]

This nationalist approach, however, was an exception. The nationalistic feeling, dear to the participation of Brazilian athletes in international competitions since the beginning of the twentieth century, gained new contours in da Silva's second Olympic victory.[60] The exaltation of the athlete as a symbol of the success of the nation was reconciled with the emphasis on certain individual qualities possessed by the Olympic champion, something that figured less intensely in his first Olympic victory of 1952.

Black, cultured, and bearing athletic, psychological, intellectual, and moral virtues, the representations of da Silva incorporated the self-image of a nation that continued to seek to consolidate, internally and externally, a narrative in terms of racial identity, understood as a positive sign of the Brazilian social formation. These representations reinforced the interpretation of a social configuration that, in Freyre's terms, was "original"— multiracial, hybrid, cohabited by opposites, and culturally plastic, not a backwardness or a mere characteristic but, rather, an advantage for the country's future. Da Silva, from this perspective, would be the proof par excellence of the grand destiny of the nation.

There were many features that were appreciated, sometimes diffusely, in the newspaper coverage of da Silva. They ranged from issues such as da Silva's readiness to express himself publicly (including in other languages, such as English, French, and Spanish) to his broad training and educational trajectory, his personality, his family relations, his professional vocation, and his position in the world of sport.

One day after winning the medal in Melbourne, *Última Hora* sought to synthesize all of these qualities in a column honoring da Silva. He was—as the newspaper noted in bold letters—an "ambassador" who "honors all of Brazil:"

> The reader will perfectly understand that these columns give a particularly vibrant and moving homage to the exceptional athlete who made the whole world, yesterday, pronounce the name of Brazil with admiration. For the qualities of Adhemar's heart and spirit match the exceptional value of his muscles. And wherever the great champion of the triple jump goes, he becomes, in fact, a magnificent sport ambassador. [61]

Part of da Silva's recognition was related to the idea of Brazil's positive representation in foreign lands due to his ability to be a symbol of the nation. In these terms, da Silva would be heralded as an exemplar of a certain laudatory "Brazilianness":

> Good son, good husband, good father, Adhemar is an intelligent, studious, more cultured man than the average athlete, who always thinks of making the best impression in every country he goes to visit and in making the most beneficial publicity for the things and the people of Brazil.[62]

Da Silva's cultural background and "diplomatic" character were recurrently highlighted in the newspapers. On tour in 1955 in the United States and sponsored by the US State Department student program to "take part in athletic events and get to know the country," he appeared with the book *Abraham Lincoln* by the biographer Emil Ludwing under his arm, written in "English, a language that he speaks fluently."[63] In the same language, he greeted those who waited for him and gave a speech in Spanish to the United Press correspondent, demonstrating his joy at being in the United States and noting, in particular, that the trip had less to do with victories and records: "I will participate . . . joyfully with a fraternal sporting spirit. Of course, I will try to win . . ., but the main thing will be to compete and interact with the North American athletes." [64]

In 1956, already having pursued a degree in art, da Silva was a student at the School of Physical Education of São Paulo, a sculptor, a journalist, a broadcaster, and an amateur athlete.[65] When asked about what he liked to read, he was categorical: Érico Veríssimo, one of the leading Brazilian writers of the twentieth century. Humbly and generously, he said that, in his opinion, the most complete Brazilian athletes were his fellow track and field competitors José Telles da Conceição (triple jump, high jump, and sprints) and Ary Façanha de Sá (long jump).[66]

The athlete was aware of his good public image. Upon returning from Melbourne, "he made a point of writing" a letter in his own hand to thank the "Brazilian people," which was published in its entirety in *Última Hora*, along with his photograph.[67] For all of these reasons, his social networks kept expanding. In 1956, he was invited to perform in a play that subsequently became famous, *Orfeu da Conceição*, written by Vinícius de Moraes, with a score composed by Tom Jobim and a scenario by Oscar Niemeyer.[68] Although he played a secondary role, he was remembered as having completed what was then considered the "greatest black cast" of Brazilian theater.[69]

Public admiration for da Silva even reached the uppermost strata of society. A few days before the trip to Melbourne, at a dinner hosted by the Society of Theater and Art—a group of members of the exclusive Rio de Janeiro Country Club, an association of the social elite of the city— honored him with a shield and pennant.[70]

The celebrated journalist and playwright Nelson Rodrigues dedicated a column to creating a "portrait" of da Silva in which he emphasized that the athlete, despite all adversities, had, first of all, a "state of mind."[71] In a special report from Melbourne, the journalist Marc Gauldichau suggested that the "sculptural black athlete" was a true God in a "recital."[72]

For the newspapers, the qualities of da Silva seemed to be endless, as *Última Hora* in his column-tribute highlighted:

> But the list would be very long if we wanted to tell you all these small facts that would lead us to the same conclusion anyway: Adhemar always knows how to act at any moment, like a real "sportsman", a "gentleman" who respects the sporting spirit of "fair play," earning unanimous sympathies in favor of Brazil. That is why all of us from *ÚLTIMA HORA*, from Samuel Wainer to the humblest of the collaborators of this newspaper, who are in daily contact with this real man, simple and smiling, hardworking and talented in his activities as a sports journalist, as responsible for our athletics and amateur sports section as he is in the competition tracks, are today proud of the magnificent triumph of our friend, Olympic double champion, Olympic record holder, and world record holder, who once again

made the Brazilian flag flutter on the largest mast of the Olympic Stadium in Melbourne. Well done, dear Adhemar, thank you very much from ALL OF US.[73]

Da Silva's "sporting spirit" extended beyond the sandpits. His concern for the condition of the state of sport, in addition to his solidarity with the athletes and coaches, can be observed in several articles written both by the sportsman himself and by other journalists. He repeatedly denounced the precariousness of the structure of athletics and the institutions responsible for its organization.[74]

In fact, this sense of "class" or "fellowship" was present at various points of his career. In the first interviews published after the victory in Melbourne, *Última Hora* called attention to the phrase "I dedicate my victory to all sportsmen of Brazil." In addition, da Silva stated: "I have to confess that I owe my victory to my coaches."[75] Da Silva's humble personality caught the attention of the journalist Marques Rebelo:

> Adhemar has arrived! Tall, modest, delicate, bi-Olympic, the best of comrades, and decent, so decent that after his spectacular speeches, he never forgets to speak of his old coach and share credit with him for his achievements. Adhemar, the man of the year! He did not land with the gold medals on his chest; what he brought in the chest was the heart of the noblest gold.[76]

When he was received at the Catete Palace upon his return to the country, he departed from the protocol of only listening to the president's expressions of gratitude and appealed to him to continue "looking and supporting children and sports."[77] He thus showed his concern for the future of the country, for a better life for the common people, the social stratum from which he emerged and which he never denied. Undoubtedly, his diplomatic personality traits, in addition to his successes on the sport field, played a fundamental role in his post-athletic trajectory. In the 1960s, da Silva served as a cultural attaché at the Brazilian embassy in Nigeria, graduated in law from the University of Brazil (1968) and public relations at the Cásper Libero Social Communication School (1990), and served as advisor to the São Paulo Government Council, which was fighting against racism and racial discrimination.

In short, da Silva was represented as an image of what Brazil would like to do internally but, above all, for the world as a form of self-assertion. Da Silva would be "undoubtedly . . . one of the very rare institutions in Brazil, which does not disappoint or content itself with vices."[78] Moreover, da Silva would be the bearer of an original and virtuous element of Brazilian cultural identity:

> Such is the Brazilian. When the feeling is applied, no one contains it, no one holds it, no one binds it. My friends, allow me to sneer with patriotism, in the manner of Olavo Bilac of the reservists:—With his Olympic victory, Adhemar Ferreira da Silva rubbed in the face of the world the soul of each one of us, which is equivalent to say:—the soul of Brazil.[79]

For the press, da Silva was the materialization of a great national project. Da Silva was the imprecise hope for Brazil to be something that, unfortunately, the country had not really become. Brazil's real problems were more comprehensive and elaborate than those presented by the press. In other words, history shows how the construction of the sense of the "imagined community" in Brazil has taken other paths, which have spread in heterogeneous and uneven ways—and not just through soccer.

CHAPTER 6

Solving "the Problem of Argentine Sport"

The Post-Peronist Olympic Movement in Argentina

CESAR R. TORRES

Alberto P. Petrolini was an Argentine sport official with a long record of service. In his younger years, Petrolini played basketball for Buenos Aires's Hindú Club, taking part in the European tour that its thriving basketball team undertook in 1927, the first of its kind for an Argentine team in said sport.[1] Despite his initial venture in basketball, Petrolini's career as a sport official grew out of his involvement with swimming. He would eventually serve as president of the Federación Argentina de Natación (Argentine Swimming Federation) and as secretary of the Comité Olímpico Argentino (Argentine Olympic Committee). While in 1936 he was appointed as attaché of the Argentine delegation to the Berlin Olympics, twenty years later he became the country's *chef de mission* at the Melbourne Olympics. Petrolini wrote a thorough report of Argentina's 1956 Olympic excursion. Tucked in between details of the delegation's wearing journey from Buenos Aires to Melbourne, descriptions of the Olympic Village and the Argentine athletes' training and competitive schedule, accounts of the opening and closing ceremonies, and words of praise to the delegation's technical director, medical staff, and administrative personnel, Petrolini inserted a section entitled "Gestiones Realizadas" (Negotiations Undertaken). In this section, Petrolini specified a number of interrelated negotiations he undertook in Australia along with Enrique Alberdi, an Argentine polo official who in addition to having won the

DOI: https://doi.org/10.34053/scs2019.0.6

gold medal in that sport at the 1936 Berlin Olympics was also a member of the International Olympic Committee (IOC), that were meant to solve "the problem of Argentine sport."[2]

Petrolini's report did not explicitly mention Juan Domingo Perón, who governed Argentina from 1946 until 1955, when his government was ousted by the so-called Revolución Libertadora (Liberating Revolution) through a coup d'état, nor did he elaborate on the specifics of the problem of Argentine sport that Petrolini and Alberdi addressed during the Olympic Games in Melbourne. However, the predicament had originated during Perón's decade in power. Petrolini related that Alberdi had had to explain to his IOC colleagues Argentina's adverse experience during that decade, the undue influence that Perón had exerted over the Comité Olímpico Argentino, and the chaotic condition of sport in the country that resulted from the Peronist regime's policies. According to Petrolini, the negotiations were productive. The IOC left the problem of Argentine sport to the Comité trusting that the Argentines would follow Olympic principles when solving the sport predicament inherited from the ousted government.[3] Peronism was a populist and nationalist movement that assigned the state a prominent role in economic, social, and cultural affairs. Led by Perón, this movement transformed all areas of Argentine life, both public and private. This transformation included sport, through which Peronism sought to express and reaffirm its populist and nationalist character, and also politically profit from its unprecedented support and control of sport. The Revolución Libertadora detested the Peronization of Argentina and undertook a process to excise Peronism from the country, including sport. Petrolini and Alberdi's efforts in Melbourne on behalf of the Comité were part of an ongoing process to remove any vestige of Peronism from sport.

It is hardly surprising, then, that the size of the Argentine delegation to the Olympic Games in Melbourne paled by comparison to the one sent to the Olympic Games in London eight years earlier, one of the two Olympic forays organized under Peronism. There were over two hundred Argentine athletes in London but fewer than 30 thirty in Melbourne.[4] It is also unsurprising that Petrolini, an ascending figure in post-Peronist sport, had no official role in his country's delegations to either the 1948 or the 1952 Olympics. Revolutionary sport official believed that these sorts of changes, along with other corrective measures, were needed to restore Argentine sport to "normalcy," even if they proved distressing to the sport community. The central problem for the revolutionary government was the noticeable political use—and abuse—that Perón made of sport, thereby corrupting its practice and administration. This chapter examines the de-Peronization of Argentine sport and, more specifically, of the local Olympic bureaucracy and its relation to the international Olympic Movement. It covers the period from the coup d'état to 1960, when those who led the de-Peronization of Argentine sport believed that it had been freed from the vices that Peronism supposedly brought to the life of the country.

The Peronization of the Argentine Olympic Movement[5]

Up to the advent of Peronism in the mid-1940s, Argentina's sport and Olympic Movement were primarily organized, controlled, and funded by civil society. The main actors were sport clubs, national sport federations, and, as of the 1920s—the decade during which these institutions were created and officially recognized—first the Confederación Argentina de Deportes (Argentine Confederation of Sports) and the Comité Olímpico Argentino, and then the Confederación Argentina de Deportes-Comité Olímpico Argentino (CADCOA).[6] Governments did not overtly, directly, or consistently attempt to control sport and Olympic affairs, nor did they expect related political dividends. Before Peronism, Olympic and sport officials were mainly Argentine elites who saw Argentina as a Latin American preserve of Western civilization. In that context, they sought to demonstrate their commitment to the international Olympic Movement and, as Ricardo C. Aldao, an Argentine jurist with a distinguished career in sport and Olympic circles, put it, to Argentina's "prominent place in sports throughout Latin America."[7] They did so by sending robust delegations to the Olympic Games and by attempting to bring the event, as well as other multisport festivals such as the Pan-American Games, to Buenos Aires.

Peronism's influence on and significance for every aspect of Argentine life have been as dramatic as they have been durable. As Matthew B. Karush and Oscar Chamosa underscore, "Virtually all accounts of Argentina's modern history have identified the first Juan Domingo Perón regime, from 1946 to 1955, as the critical turning point."[8] Perón's populist and nationalist vision was for "a New Argentina based on social justice, political sovereignty, and economic independence."[9] Peronism's departure from the past drew on the empowerment, legitimization, and inclusion of the working class in the political process. Unlike previous governments, Perón's administration attended to the masses' demands through innovative social, labor, and political legislation along with social policies that translated into a myriad of social services and programs. Besides improving workers' standard of living, these benefits "offered them both an identity and a convincing interpretation of the society in which they lived."[10] Sport, and the local Olympic Movement, became preferred forums in which to articulate and convey the Peronist identity and interpretation of Argentine society, both domestically and internationally.

For Perón, sport represented a formidable social technology—an organization of human energy designed to arrange and rearrange social patterns—that could be effectively used to build, cement, and advertise his New Argentina. The Peronist belief that sport had a tremendous capacity to sway the "soul" of a people and presumably to unite its members set in motion an unprecedented emphasis on its practice, promotion, and support. As Raanan Rein remarks, "No Argentine government prior to Perón had invested as much energy and as many resources in developing and encouraging athletic activities and in the effort to earn political dividends from this policy."[11] His regime implemented policies aimed to greatly expand the opportunities for the masses to practice sport. Numerous sport organizations were aided, and sport facilities were built throughout the country. The regime established an organization for high school students, with two sections divided by sex, at the center of which was the practice of sport. Beginning in 1948, the Fundación Eva Perón (Eva Perón Foundation), led by the president's wife, organized national sports championships for children and youth, with ample financial backing from the government. In 1954, more than 215,000 children and youth participated. While expanding access to the practice of sport, these policies showcased the regime's effort to politically socialize citizens into the mores of the New Argentina. Such efforts overtly sought to link the newly created opportunities to practice sport to the values and beliefs that constituted the Peronist culture.[12]

Elite sport, which, in contrast to mass participation, focused on high-level athletic performance, also benefited during the Peronist decade and represented the regime's effort to politically socialize citizens. This was mainly due to Perón's vision of sport as a tool for cultural diplomacy and of athletes as ambassadors of the New Argentina. The participation of the country's athletes in elite sport, especially in international sport competitions, allowed his regime to advertise globally the goals, achievements, and progress of the New Argentine citizen in the New Argentina. These were related not only to the integration of the masses to the political process but also to their increasing access to social services and cultural goods as well as the increase of their income and level of consumption. The Peronist regime sponsored the careers of many athletes who competed both in Argentina and abroad. They include the race car driver Juan Manuel Fangio and the boxer Pascual Pérez, both of whom became world champions under sustained Peronist patronage. Likewise, the Peronist regime underwrote numerous international sport championships, including the 1949 Men's World Shooting Championship, the Formula One Grand Prix from 1953 to 1955, and, most notably, the 1950 Men's World Basketball Championship and the 1951 Pan-American Games, both of which were inaugural editions of the events. The regime bid to host the 1956 Olympics in Buenos Aires, losing by one vote to Melbourne, and also underwrote the country's delegations to the 1948 London and 1952 Helsinki Olympics. In each of these Olympic Games, the Argentine delegation was the largest in Latin America. These athletes, whether successful or not, were celebrated as ambassadors of the New Argentina, showcasing it to the world. In turn, hosting a large international sport event was also conceived as an avenue to accomplish the same goal, in this case by reversing the strategy and welcoming the world to the New Argentina; in other words, bringing this kind of event to the country also became a means to structure and disseminate the Peronist narrative, simultaneously solidifying it at home while projecting it internationally.

To implement and advance its sport policies as well as the goals they were meant to achieve, the Peronist regime sought to centralize the supervision of sport. Perón rationalized his scheme by claiming that, prior to him taking office, sport clubs received negligible support from the state, and that sport occupied a prominent role in the New Argentina.[13] In order to do what its leader thought necessary for Argentine sport, the Peronist state attempted to control sport institutions, particularly the national sport federations and CADCOA. Such control secured not only domestic influence but also access to the international sport system. Thus, for instance, Perón attempted to appoint, or have elected, associates or sympathizers to lead national sport federations. A case in point was the Asociación del Fútbol Argentino (Argentine Football Association), which oversaw the most popular sport in the country. From 1947 to 1955, it had several presidents, all of whom strongly identified with Peronism and advanced its narrative through their posts to generate consensus for the regime; in other words, they committed to Peronize the sport. These presidents included Oscar L. Nicolini, minister of communication from 1949 to 1955 and a friend of Perón's wife; Valentín Suárez, a close aide of the Fundación Eva Perón; Domingo Peluffo, a Peronist delegate to the 1949 constitutional convention; and Cecilio Conditti, an influential labor union leader loyal to Perón. Similarly, the Confederación Argentina de Basket-Ball (Argentine Basketball Confederation), which oversaw another popular sport in the country, was presided over by Carlos A. Juárez, a Peronist who served as governor of the province of Santiago del Estero from 1948 to 1952, when he was elected as a senator. Lower levels of sport administration were also of Peronist concern. For example, vice president Alberto Teisaire, along with other Peronist politicians, tried to replace the president of the basketball federation of the province of Corrientes because it opposed the regime.[14] Individual clubs were also the targets of Peronization efforts.[15]

If the Peronization of national sport federations, as well as lower levels of sport administration and clubs, was of central concern for the regime, even more so was the control of CADCOA, an institution in which all national sport federations were represented that supervised the organization of sport in the country and served as a nexus to the international sport system. When Perón took office in 1946, Juan Carlos Palacios had been the president of CADCOA since 1938. He had also presided over the institution in 1927–28 and 1932–33. Perón promised Palacios that he would bankroll the national delegation that CADCOA would send to the 1948 London Olympics. This promise notwithstanding, Palacios resigned from CADCOA in September 1947. It is unclear whether he was pressured by the regime to resign his longstanding post in CADCOA. Three months earlier, Ricardo C. Aldao, one of two Argentine IOC members, had written to Sigfrid Edström, then presiding over the committee, arguing that Argentina deserved to be represented by a third member in the committee, nominating Palacios as the "best candidate" to become that third member, and informing Edström that Horacio Bustos Morón, the other Argentine IOC member, agreed with his nomination.[16] Had Aldao, a member of a political party that opposed Perón, suspected that Palacios's future in CADCOA was uncertain and tried to protect his standing in the international Olympic Movement by having him elected to the IOC? Rumors were circulating that Perón favored some officials over others to lead CADCOA. Whatever the reason for Aldao's move, shortly after Palacios's resignation Carlos Aloé, a representative of Perón who would later serve as governor of the province of Buenos Aires, clarified in a CADCOA meeting that those rumors were baseless, adding that the president believed that it was sportspeople who should elect their leaders. Palacios's term as president of CADCOA was completed by Ricardo Sánchez de Bustamante, who had served as vice president until his resignation.

Sánchez de Bustamante was replaced by Rodolfo G. Valenzuela, an Olympic fencer in 1932 and 1936, the chief justice of the Supreme Court, and a devoted Peronist, who served as president of CADCOA until the coup d'état that ousted Perón in 1955 (Image 6.1). Football official Peluffo was appointed as the institution's first vice president, also serving in that capacity until the end of the regime. No member of the previous CADCOA leadership remained during the Peronist decade. Leaving nothing to chance, in 1951 CADCOA modified its bylaws, which now allowed the president of the country to appoint the institution's president. Perón and his wife were appointed CADCOA's honorary presidents. This was hardly surprising in a regime that glorified their images through a political culture characterized by symbols and rituals that presented them as charismatic and benevolent leaders.[17] In CADCOA, the regime had an enormous platform to exercise considerable control of sport, both elite and mass, and the national Olympic Movement. It was through CADCOA that the Peronist regime sponsored the careers of many athletes, underwrote numerous national and international sport championships as well as the country's Olympic delegations, and bid to host the 1956 Olympics and the 1950 IOC session in Buenos Aires. CADCOA worked with other state agencies such as the Consejo Nacional de Educación Física (National Council of Physical Education), created by Perón in 1947, to carry on its mission.[18] Perhaps one of CADCOA's finest hours was at the conclusion of the inaugural Pan-American Games hosted in 1951 in Buenos Aires. The regime saw the 1951 event, whose organizing committee was chaired by Valenzuela, as a great success. Argentina won the most medals, and an exultant Perón declared that such an honor was "a new victory that the Peronist movement offers at the altar of the Nation."[19] Controlling sport and the national Olympic Movement facilitated scoring these material and symbolic victories.

While it seems that Peronism's centralized supervision of sport and the national Olympic Movement enjoyed ample support, it also had critics. As Rein asserts, critics "claimed that Peronism distorted the spirit of sports, violated the sporting ethic, encouraged the routine use of bribery,

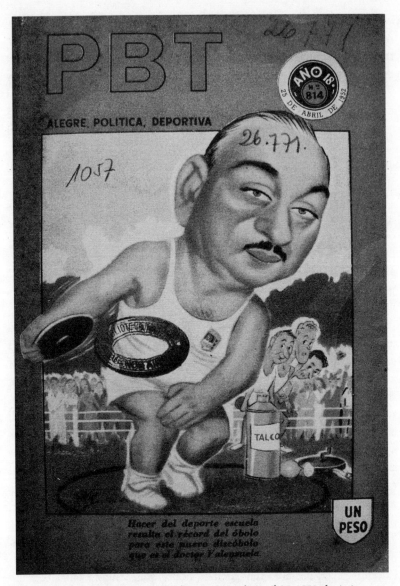

Image 6.1. Cover, *Revista PBT* (Buenos Aires), April 25, 1952, depicting
Rodolfo G. Valenzuela, president of the *Confederación Argentina
de Deportes-Comité Olímpico Argentino* (1948–1955).

corruption and special favours."[20] In addition, they contended that the regime "sometimes even sanctioned the employment of dubious means to guarantee Argentine victory in international competitions held in Buenos Aires."[21] Peronists rebuffed the criticisms and pointed to what the regime had accomplished through its unprecedented support and encouragement of sport. In 1954, CADCOA launched *Olimpia: Revista de Capacitación Deportiva*, a magazine that published articles on different issues related to the practice and management of sport that also doubled as a venue to promote the regime's sport accomplishments. In its first issue, it featured a list of the world championships and Olympic victories achieved by Argentine athletes before and after the rise of Peronism. The list was accompanied by a picture of the CADCOA headquarters in Buenos Aires. At the end of the list was a brief vignette entitled "State Support" that invited readers to analyze the achievements.[22] The list, the magazine's editors presumed, spoke for itself and was proof of the success of the regime's sport policies. Some sport officials were more explicit than the magazine's editors about the state of sport under Peronism. Writing to Armand Massard, a French IOC member, Roberto J. Monteverde, president of the Federación Argentina de Natación, boasted in 1952, "As you know our country occupies one of the principal sporting places in the world."[23] When Perón was ousted from power three years later, CADCOA was already planning the delegation for the following year's Olympic Games and hoping that it would add more achievements to the Peronist sport's roll of honor. Instead of Olympic success, what followed was a concerted campaign not only to question the means by which the accolades of Peronist sport had been achieved but also to remove any vestige of Peronism from sport. That cleansing would significantly impact the Argentine Olympic Movement.

De-Peronizing the Argentine Olympic Movement[24]

Juan Domingo Perón's regime was overthrown in late September 1955. Immediately after proclaiming himself president, Eduardo Lonardi, an army general, also proclaimed his intention to restore democracy. Lonardi did not have any sympathy for Perón, yet he opposed dismantling the Peronist system altogether and sought to negotiate with some of the groups that had supported the ousted president. Despite Lonardi's intentions, a short two weeks after the coup d'état, the revolutionary authorities created by decree the Comisión Nacional de Investigaciones

(National Investigating Commission), charged with investigating the irregularities during Perón's decade in power. This Comisión covered a wide range of the Peronist regime's undertakings, including sport. Indeed, a special investigating commission (number 49) was set up to inspect the structure and operations of sport under Peronism. For those who clamored for the suppression of Peronism, Lonardi's policies were too bland. The wrangles between Lonardi and his detractors escalated to a point where in mid-November, less than two months after his proclamation as president, Lonardi was replaced by Pedro E. Aramburu, another army general. As David Rock explains, under Aramburu's authority "the assault on Peronism began forthwith."[25] Peronism was proscribed, and its leaders, as well as numerous supporters, were investigated, persecuted, and in some cases arrested. Public administration was purged of Perón's loyalists, and the constitution sanctioned in 1949 was abolished. In his attempt to de-Peronize Argentina, early in 1956, Aramburu went as far as prohibiting, through another decree, the use of Peronist symbols and mentioning Perón by name.

Aramburu's assault on Peronism led to a forceful resolve to dismantle Peronist sport. Soon after the coup d'état, Fernando I. Huergo, an army general who had fenced at the 1948 London Olympics, was appointed intervenor of CADCOA (Image 6.2). In turn, Huergo appointed intervenors to the national sport federations. In the meantime, Rodolfo G. Valenzuela was arrested and reportedly tortured by the revolutionary government.[26] The systematic character of Aramburu's takeover of sport and his determination to place its structure under non-Peronist control is evident in the fact that Investigating Commission 49 of the Comisión Nacional de Investigaciones established its offices at the CADCOA headquarters. Investigating Commission 49 was presided over by Alejandro C. Ojeda, an army colonel, and it promptly established subcommissions to investigate the national sport federations. The underlying assumption of Investigating Commission 49 and its subcommissions, widely shared by anti-Peronist groups, was that under Peronism sport had been corrupted. Juan K. Lang, an anti-Peronist businessman and sportsperson, wrote to Otto Mayer, then IOC chancellor, lamenting that "the dictatorship of Perón used these [sport] organizations just for political propaganda" and was convinced that "it is exactly to eliminate the influence of politics, that the Argentine Government had to intervene these organizations."[27] The procedures of Investigating Commission 49 and its subcommissions, combined with the character of Huergo's intervention of CADCOA and

Image 6.2. Ricardo C. Aldao (center) visits General Fernando I. Huergo (second from the left), intervenor of the of the *Confederación Argentina de Deportes-Comité Olímpico Argentino* (1955–1956) and president of the *Comité Olímpico Argentino* (1956–1957), on November 4, 1955. *Courtesy of the Archivo General de la Nación, Buenos Aires.*

the national sport federations, illuminate the revolutionary authorities' zeal to de-Peronize sport. One strategy the anti-Peronists utilized to carry out their agenda was to establish that athletes, officials, and institutions had illegitimately benefited, primarily in material terms, from their association with the deposed regime. Whether from ignorance or blatant disregard, they failed to see that many Argentines considered these benefits an important aspect of the novel Peronist policies that aimed to dignify life for the masses.[28]

Basketball seemed to have been specially targeted by the post-Peronist authorities. This was likely because of the successes and support that the sport had enjoyed during the Peronist decade. Argentina had won the 1950 Men's World Basketball Championship, organized in Buenos Aires under the aegis of Peronism; had been runner-up in the men's basketball tournament of the 1951 Pan-American Games; had placed fourth in men's basketball at the 1952 Helsinki Olympics; had won the men's basketball tournament at the 1953 Summer International University Sports Week in Dortmund; and had been runner-up in men's basketball at the 1955 Pan-American Games. In late November 1955, the Confederación Argentina de Basket-Ball received a letter from the Comisión Nacional de

Investigaciones introducing Investigating Commission 49 and requesting a report on irregularities from the Peronist decade. Early in 1956, several members of the national team were requested to appear before the Comisión for questioning. In the meantime, the subcommission set up to investigate the sport went over the Confederación's minutes, balances, and other documents from the Peronist decade. In February, the subcommission alleged that, on their return from the 1952 Helsinki Olympics, members of the national team had smuggled in goods bought abroad and that CADCOA had instructed customs officers to look the other way.

The first post-Peronist sanctions in basketball were directed at Racing Club, based in the municipality of Avellaneda in greater Buenos Aires with strong ties to Perón, a notorious supporter of Racing Club's soccer team. In 1953, the Racing Club's basketball team undertook a lengthy tour of South America. The following year, the Confederación Argentina de Basket-Ball alleged that the basketballers had violated the rules of amateurism by illegally importing goods and suspended them for life. However, CADCOA pardoned the basketballers prior to the 1955 Pan-American Games, which prompted an investigation by the Confederación and a lifetime ban on competition for the players, the coach, the officials, and the referees that accompanied the team, as well as on the club itself.

A few days after the sanctions against Racing Club, Aramburu signed a decree terminating the investigations of the Comisión Nacional de Investigaciones. Even so, the investigation of Peronist sport continued through the interventors that Huergo's CADCOA had appointed in each of the national sport federations. CADCOA had made clear to the interventors that it was particularly interested in uncovering both violations of the amateur code and cases of fake amateurism that had occurred under Peronism. CADCOA had also made clear that the interventors were to modify the national sport federations' bylaws in order to prevent future violations to the amateur code. Basketball was again strictly scrutinized. In a confidential report dated May 7, the Investigating Commission 49's subcommission on basketball established that, with few exceptions, basketball team representatives to the 1951 Pan-American Games and the 1953 Summer International University Sports Week had economically benefited from participating in said events. The benefits included receiving permits to import cars, illegally importing goods bought abroad, and selling passports. The subcommission suggested that they be declared professionals and sanctioned accordingly. On June 5, the subcommission issued its final report. Almost three months later, *La Nación*, a mainstream newspaper, speculated that a sanction was imminent.[29] This, however, was only made official in early 1957. The sanctions, which included a lifetime suspension due to violations to the amateur code, would extend to several other sports that were still under investigation.

The International Impact of the De-Peronization of the Argentine Olympic Movement

The nature and intensity of the changes imposed on Argentine sport by the leaders of the Revolución Libertadora preoccupied international Olympic officials and jeopardized Argentine participation in the upcoming Olympic Games in Melbourne. As early as October 1955, IOC president Avery Brundage anticipated "a reorganization of the Argentine Olympic Company [sic] and the amateur sport federations," hoped that IOC rules would be followed, and urged "that all these organizations will be kept under the control of amateur sportsmen and not politicians."[30] The following month, Fernando I. Huergo informed Brundage that he had been appointed interventor of CADCOA.[31] For the IOC, which deplored political interference in the organization and work of national Olympic committees, the appointment rendered CADCOA illegitimate. Huergo, who appeared unconcerned, had no intention of complying with the IOC's regulations. In March 1956, Enrique Alberdi reported to Brundage that Huergo "does not intend for the moment, to modify the statutes of the A.O.C. [Argentine Olympic Committee] to bring it in line with rule N. 25 of our regulations, nor to call for elections to form a new Committee in accordance with said regulations."[32] Rule 25 of the IOC's charter, which was put into effect in 1956, stipulated that "National Olympic Committees must be completely independent and autonomous and entirely removed from all political, religious or commercial influence."[33] Moreover, in contravention of rule 24 of the charter, also put into effect in 1956, which established that only recognized national Olympic committees could enter athletes in the Olympic Games, Huergo claimed that he would personally take care of the entry of his country's athletes to that year's Olympic Games and threatened that, if this was unacceptable, "not a single Argentine athlete will take part in these Olympic Games."[34] Alberdi, faithful to the IOC, admitted that "the Argentine Olympic Committee, to all intents and purposes does not exist." He also admitted that his attempts to have the national sport federations freely elect their officials had gone nowhere and that "this situation is in every way contrary to our regulations."[35] In short, the de-Peronization of sport risked Argentina's membership in the international Olympic Movement.

Late in April 1956, Brundage left no doubt about the IOC stance regarding the situation in Argentine sport and pressed for a resolution that complied with its regulations. To Raúl Aguirre Molina, the Argentine ambassador to Switzerland who had officially informed the IOC of Huergo's appointment, Brundage repeated his presumption that Huergo was "reorganizing Argentine amateur sport in conformity with international regulations," stressing that "political influence must not be permitted" in sport.[36] To Alberdi, Brundage underscored that "as the matter stands it seems that no team from the Argentine can be entered in the Melbourne Games because there is no NOC," albeit he mentioned that a special request could be petitioned.[37] In May, Alberdi reiterated to Huergo, whom he had personally met in February, the IOC expectations, to no avail.[38] Oblivious to the increasing IOC disapproval of the situation in Argentine sport, or perhaps defying such disapproval, Huergo informed international Olympic officials of the sanctions that the interventors of the national sport federations imposed on athletes or officials.[39] Several months went by without news of a reorganization that respected IOC's regulations, during which CADCOA was busy with its campaign to de-Peronize sport. Brundage grew impatient, for he thought that Huergo had had plenty of time to reorganize the Argentine Olympic Movement in accordance with Olympic principles, and concocted a strategy to twist Huergo's arm. He requested that the organizing committee of the 1956 Olympics send a letter to Huergo informing him that "since the Argentine Olympic Committee is not recognized by the IOC it is not possible for it to participate in the 1956 Games."[40] The letter was dated July 30, and by the end of the following month Brundage wrote Lewis Luxton, an Australian IOC member and vice president of the organizing committee, that "the letter to the Argentine Olympic Committee produced results in a hurry."[41]

Brundage's strategy certainly caused a stir. By mid-August, the press, both in Argentina and abroad, announced that the country had been prevented from participating in the 1956 Olympics because the revolutionary government had interfered with its national Olympic affairs. However, as the *New York Times* reported, quoting Otto Mayer, "If the Argentine sports federations can organize proper elections of a new committee before the closing date for entries, Oct. 10, the readmission of Argentina might be considered."[42] Huergo was displeased, but he was hardly the only one. Juan K. Lang wrote to Mayer, chastising him for the IOC decision, which he thought was taken without knowledge and consideration of the state of Argentine sport. Lang lamented that the IOC had not objected to political influence on the Argentine Olympic Movement during Peronism.[43] Similarly, reporter Milton Bracker, writing for the *New York Times*, postulated that banning Argentina from the 1956 Olympics was "one of the most ironic decisions in the recent history of international athletics" and argued that CADCOA "had for nearly a decade made all Argentine sports an adjunct to the Peronista state."[44] Despite the protests, the IOC proceeded to "intervene energetically" in Argentina, as it had decided to do in its January executive board meeting.[45] Alberdi insisted to Huergo that, once intervened, CADCOA had effectively been dissolved, and thus Argentina had no national Olympic committee authorized to enter athletes in the Olympic Games.[46]

Yielding to international pressure, on August 20 Pedro E. Aramburu signed a decree ending the intervention of CADCOA. Aguirre Molina wrote to and visited the IOC headquarters in Lausanne shortly thereafter to inform its officials of the decree and that the national sport federations would freely elect a new Comité Olímpico Argentino early in September. Brundage was kept abreast of developments.[47] As promised, on September 3, CADCOA called the national sport federations to an extraordinary constitutive assembly that would take place on September 14. The call explicitly underlined that this was in accordance with rules 24 and 25 of the IOC's charter.[48] The next day, Brudange disingenuously told Mario L. Negri, the Argentine president of the International Amateur Swimming Federation, that he had known "that all was going well" in Buenos Aires, adding that his only intention all along had been "to expedite the proceeding, so that everything would be in order before the Melbourne Games."[49] The expedited proceeding continued, and the extraordinary constitutive assembly took place on September 14. Alberdi was invited to the meeting, which was presided over by Raúl Almeida, a CADCOA adviser, and enlisted representatives of ten national sport federations. Conspicuously, seven other federations did not send representatives because they were still intervened. Huergo was nominated as president and Alberto P. Petrolini as secretary. Ireneo V. Zocca, the representative of the rowing federation, was nominated as treasurer while the rest of the representatives would become members at large. Following a lengthy discussion, it was agreed that the IOC could not object to the meeting because it was taking place in "the most absolute freedom" and without any political, religious, or commercial intrusion. The nominees were then elected unanimously, and the new Comité was finally established. Huergo, who had been in the building in which the meeting took place but had not been at the meeting, was invited in. He thanked the gathering for his election and accepted the post, proclaiming that it amounted to a recognition of his labor at CADCOA, "totally eliminating politics from sport and to the purity of his intentions."[50] Despite formally complying with the IOC regulations, it was all rigged. After almost thirty years the two institutions that made up CADCOA had become once again independent.

Alberdi informed Brundage and Mayer at once of the creation of the new Comité Olímpico Argentino.[51] Huergo took a week.[52] Brundage might have harbored some doubts about the election but told Alberdi that "you can grant professional recognition to the new Argentine Olympic Committee, so that the Argentine team may participate in Melbourne."[53] If the election of Huergo raised any eyebrows in international Olympic circles, Alberdi promptly dispelled them. On September 24, Alberdi reported that Huergo had urged the intervened national sport federations to freely elect new officials and that he was of the opinion that since Huergo "is solving the problems of the sports for the Olympic Committee of Argentina his election as president should be amply accepted."[54] Alberdi revealed something else: the new Comité "will take the necessary steps with those directors or players who have not maintained themselves in the amateur field."[55] In other words, Huergo would continue his campaign to de-Peronize sport. Despite this fateful continuity, the new Comité was provisionally recognized by the IOC two days after Alberdi reassured Brundage that Huergo was a positive influence on Argentine sport.[56] The new Comité was authorized to participate in the 1956 Olympics.[57]

Mayer's notification meant that the new Comité Olímpico Argentino had less than a month to determine the composition of its delegation to the 1956 Olympics. The intervened CADCOA had started preliminary work in this regard in December of the previous year and had decided that only athletes or teams that could potentially finish among the top six in their competitions would be included in the delegation. Following this standard, the delegation would be much smaller than those sent to the two previous Olympic Games by the Peronist CADCOA. Austerity was mentioned as a main reason to justify a small delegation, which also served as an attempt to distance the intervened CADCOA from the funding model bestowed on CADCOA by Perón. By late January 1956, CADCOA estimated that the delegation would include sixty-one athletes but clarified that basketball and boxing, the largest contingents, would make the trip to Melbourne if the respective national sport federations could finance them. By October 5, five days before the deadline to submit the entries, the delegation had been reduced to forty-eight athletes. Basketball, above which hung the accusation of professionalism and whose interventor did not try to raise any funds, and rowing, which had been disqualified by the sport's international federation for violations to the amateur code, were absent from the list. On the other hand, fencing was added, and there were some minor changes in the number of athletes in other sports. In the end, the final delegation included only twenty-eight athletes from eight sports. This further reduction, the Comité conveyed in the official report of Argentina's 1956 Olympic excursion, was due to the accusation of professionalism that loomed over several athletes.[58] The evidence came from the Investigating Commission 49 and its subcommissions as well as the interventors of the national sport federations. This was a covert way to communicate that the athletes removed from the delegation at the eleventh hour had also been, or were believed to have been, associated with Perón and/or benefited materially from their sport participation during the Peronist decade.

The cycling and swimming teams, with six athletes each, three shooters, two fencers, one wrestler, and two track and field representatives, were the last to be barred from the delegation.[59] An emblematic case was long-distance runner Osvaldo Suárez, a candidate to win the marathon, who was informed that he would not travel to Melbourne a few days before the delegation's scheduled departure. Like the other barred athletes, he was accused of supporting Perón and materially benefiting from his athletic ascent during Peronism. For that he was banned from competition for fourteen months.[60] The absence of talented athletes such as Suárez from the delegation because of the de-Peronization of sport undertaken by the revolutionary authorities severely weakened its prospects in Melbourne. For the first time since Argentina began its official participation at the Olympic Games in 1924, the country did not win any gold medals, a drought that would last until the 2004 Athens Olympics. Argentina brought home two medals from Melbourne, compared to the seven and five that the Peronist Olympic delegations did won in 1948 and 1952, respectively. This did not much concern the Comité Olímpico Argentino, for which the most important achievement in Melbourne was that the country had been formally welcomed back to the Olympic fold.

In this sense, Petrolini rejoiced that the negotiations he and Alberdi had undertaken in Australia had been a resounding success.[61]

Once the delegation returned home from Melbourne with the full recognition of the IOC, which ignored the nature, extension, and outcomes of the ongoing de-Peronizing campaign, the Comité Olímpico Argentino pursued the final stages of the "institutional recovery"[62] of national sport. Before the end of the year, representatives of the national sport federations that had not taken part in the September 14 extraordinary constitutive assembly were incorporated into the Comité. Likewise, a commission was formed to write the bylaws of the new institution. The investigation of athletes and officials associated with Peronism continued. Early in 1957, it was announced that more basketballers and track and field athletes had been declared professionals and that track and field officials had been prohibited from engaging in any activity related to their sport for two years.[63] Perhaps sensing that his work had been accomplished, on May 30 Huergo resigned from the Comité. After all, two weeks before tendering his resignation, Brundage had clarified that, in Melbourne, "recognition was granted to the reorganized Argentine Olympic Committee" and emphasized that "we [the IOC] understand that amateur sport in the Argentine is now conducted in full conformity with the Olympic spirit."[64] The Comité offered Huergo a medal for his services. In June, José Oriani, a boxing official, was unanimously voted in as Huergo's replacement as president. By July, the new bylaws were approved, an important step in the consolidation of the Comité. That month the rest of its authorities were named in accordance to the new bylaws.[65] Oriani and Petrolini would retain their grip on the Comité until 1964.

The same month of Huergo's resignation, Alberdi told Brundage that the Comité Olímpico Argentino wished "to solve the situation created to more than an athlete for having accepted facilities or prizes, while in their category of amateurs, from persons belonging to a former regime in this country." This, Alberdi thought, would bring "reassurance to national sport in our country."[66] The investigation and sanction of athletes and officials were the ways the revolutionary government's sport authorities found to solve the issue of amateurism. Gradually, though, the sanctions expired or were lifted. For example, Suárez would compete in the 1960 Rome Olympics, placing ninth in the marathon. However, he remained upset until his passing early in 2018 with how the revolutionary government treated him, asserting that it ruined his athletic career.[67] Other sanctioned athletes never competed again at the elite level. The sanction against the basketballers, for instance, was only lifted in 1967. The strategy that Huergo and his acolytes implemented to de-Peronize sport was far from reassuring, and it hardly achieved, as Alberdi had hoped, "the complete normalization of our sports."[68] Predictably, the Comité was convinced of what it had done, and in late 1960 it named Huergo and Juan Carlos Palacios, who had resigned as president of CADCOA after Perón took office, as honorary members. In a sense, the bestowing of such honors at the conclusion of the 1960 Olympics and the temporary return of democracy, however defective, to Argentina represented the conclusion of the de-Peronization of sport. Over two years earlier, Aramburu's failure to rescind, and opposed by, Peronism called elections. Nonetheless, Peronism remained proscribed. Much like in Argentine society at large, the campaign to de-Peronize and normalize sport, whatever its promoters claimed, only added more grievances against Aramburu's government by both Peronists and not a few anti-Peronists.

Conclusion

In 1961, when he thought that the latest developments in Argentine sport did not even amount to history, journalist Félix D. Frascara reflected on the impact that the Revolución Libertadora had had on this most important area of national life. A critic of Juan Domingo Perón's sport policies, Frascara believed that the revolutionary authorities had "found sport weakened as a partier after an orgy," yet he admitted that they had not only failed to solve its problems but rather had managed to deepen them. For Frascara, the campaign to de-Peronize sport "did nothing but increase confusion and discouragement." What was left was "a pile of files and another pile of resentments."[69] This is a candid assessment of the state of Argentine sport when Pedro E. Aramburu left office in 1958. His promise to put Argentina back on the path of decency and democracy had amounted to the prosecution of Peronist officials and sympathizers. The purported depoliticization of sport, if accomplished at all, came through political interference of the kind that the revolutionary authorities criticized. Despite the IOC's recognition of the new Comité Olímpico Argentino, which in part reflected Avery Brundage's and his IOC colleagues' own ambivalence regarding Argentine sport, and the ending of the intervention of the national sport federations, the status of the country's sport institutions was anything but normal. Scores of athletes had been sanctioned for their sympathy for Perón and/or their supposed material gains during his regime, and Peronist leaders remained excluded from the country's sport institutions. What was left was only a charade, a blurry patina, of "normalcy."

The revolutionary authorities' failed campaign to solve the problem of Argentine sport would linger for a long time. Demonizing Peronist sport meant curtailing state support and encouragement for athletes and sport institutions, which in turn translated not only into the loss of international accomplishments but also the loss of opportunities for the masses to practice sport. The deteriorated image of Argentina as well as its Olympic and sport institutions was evident in 1963, when the bid to host the 1968 Olympics in Buenos Aires put forward by the new Comité Olímpico Argentino's officials that emerged from the intervention of CADCOA garnered a mere two votes in the IOC session that chose Mexico City for that honor. By then, Argentina, suffering from the instability inherited from the Revolución Libertadora and the proscription of Peronism, was in its second experiment with democracy in six years. Alberto P. Petrolini and José Oriani's promise on behalf of the Comité that an Olympic Buenos Aires in 1968 would promote national unity was futile and only convinced one IOC member, the other vote coming presumably from the then-lone Argentine in the committee.[70] The situation in Argentina, including its sport structures, was so precarious that the bid for a 1968 Buenos Aires Olympics was neither favored internationally nor at home. Brundage opposed the Comité's bid and Jorge N. Parsons, one of the institution's vice presidents, expressed his qualms about it, claiming that "one hesitates to decide . . . right now things are so unsettled here."[71] Both men's reaction to the possibility of an Olympic Buenos Aires in 1968 condensed the legacy of the campaign to de-Peronize sport and its current state. As Frascara said, Argentine sport could not be fixed: "We have to do it all over again."[72] As with everything else, whatever its initial intentions and whatever the flaws of Peronism, the Revolución Libertadora ended up doing more harm to sport and its structures than good.

Acknowledgements

The author would like to thank David M. K. Sheinin for his helpful comments and criticisms on an earlier version of this chapter, Richard V. McGehee for his suggestions and corrections of several translations, and Marcelo Massarino for his assistance in facilitating access to important material for this chapter.

CHAPTER 7

Un compromiso de tod@s

Women, Olympism, and the Dominican Third Way

APRIL YODER

From a podium erected on the field of the Juan Pablo Duarte Olympic Center, organizing committee president Bienvenido Martínez Brea made the commencement address for the XII Central American and Caribbean Games in 1974. Looking at the crowd of thirty thousand men and women, some who had waited hours in the sun, Martínez Brea declared the Games *un compromiso cumplido,* a promise fulfilled.[1] With reference to this promise, Martínez Brea invoked the motto of the Games—*Un compromiso de todos,* a duty of everyone—used since 1970 to rally Dominicans to a national project to prepare and host the event. The largest international sporting event hosted in the country to that date, the Games mobilized Dominicans to build the physical infrastructure and human capacity necessary to fulfill the "extraordinary national responsibility" of overseeing nearly two thousand athletes competing in eighteen sports.[2] Work to expand amateur sport and build sport installations began even before the Central American and Caribbean Sports Organization (CACSO) confirmed the bid. Once the bid was confirmed, national sport and government leaders intensified their efforts to construct the Olympic Center and renovate existing facilities, to establish new federations for sports played for the first time in the country and strengthen existing organizations, and to recruit new athletes and prepare the delegation to achieve success on the field.[3] Fulfilling the promise to host twenty-two neighboring countries in a two-week celebration of sporting fraternity spread the Olympic spirit through Dominican society.

The motto *Un compromiso de todos* was intended to unite Dominicans

DOI: https://doi.org/10.34053/scs2019.o.7

long divided over the shape of democracy in their country in a national project led by President Joaquín Balaguer, who was officially designated Patron of the Games in 1971.[4] The Games were the culmination of Balaguer's incorporation of sport into his "Third Way" model of government, a means of aligning Dominican expectations for democracy with his national program centered on capitalist development. The Third Way describes Balaguer's use of social programs and public investment in infrastructure, housing, and sport that aligned with the Cuban and Soviet models of social justice to bolster his claims of democratic governance while engaging in authoritarian repression to maintain stability and order. Dominican historian Roberto Cassá identified "despotic and democratic elements" in the Balaguer government, with patronage—a system of favors or investment directed to popular and powerful actors—operating to legitimate claims of democracy.[5] The Third Way as Balaguer practiced it relied on clientelistic relationships similar to those that sustained the authoritarian regime of Rafael Trujillo (1930–61),[6] but Balaguer's distance from the military and Dominican demands for democracy required him to popularize this patronage, creating what Elizabeth Manley calls a "new kind of paternalism."[7] The project to build the 1974 Games and the centralization of sport in the Secretary of Sport, Physical Education, and Recreation (SEDEFIR) after the Games helped to institutionalize this paternalism as a democratic Third Way.

The Third Way emerged as a means for Balaguer to serve the interests of domestic and international business leaders through his development program while upholding an illusion of political and economic democracy. Policies that limited the right to strike, froze wages, and provided incentives for wealthy industrialists helped to increase national production, but Dominicans saw them as violations of the democratic freedoms that they had earned when they brought dictator Rafael Trujillo to justice in 1961.[8] When they participated in the first free elections in 1962, Dominicans dreamed of a new society where everyone would have economic opportunity and a political voice.[9] A military coup against President Juan Bosch only seven months after he took office stifled their optimism. Tired of waiting for the return of constitutional government, given the Triumvirate's continual delay of elections, Dominicans formed a popular insurrection in April 1965. Although the insurrection forced the Triumvirate from power, a US-led intervention and occupation by forces from the Organization of American States (OAS) prevented them from restoring Bosch to his elected position. The election of Balaguer in 1966, with OAS forces still in the country, was a compromise: the United States and Dominican business elites implanted a pro-business, anticommunist candidate while Dominicans elected a constitutional government headed by a civilian.[10] To uphold his legitimacy and earn reelection, Balaguer relied on the paternalist Third Way. He fulfilled Dominican requests to develop themselves through sport to bolster the image of a government attuned to the needs of its people.

Even in sport, the paternalism of the Balaguer government required maternalism, the inclusion of women in the nation in roles prescribed by gender norms around caretaking.[11] As Manley has explained, Balaguer appointed women as civil governors in all the provinces to give the national government a face of peace and reconciliation in the position closest to the people.[12] This association of the women governors with peace continued Trujillo's use of women as foils to his militaristic masculinity and bolstered Balaguer's image as the father of the country.[13] The women governors supported Balaguer's Third Way as symbols of democracy and reconciliation. They actively created that peace as liaisons between the Balaguer government and their communities, often serving as "deliverers" of government patronage.[14] The governors lent their moral and economic support to sporting events in addition to delivering and requesting the sport equipment, baseball stadiums, and volleyball-basketball courts their communities need to participate in the national project of preparing for the Games. Beyond official channels, women also incorporated themselves into the Games as athletes, marking a new era of increased women's participation in international events.[15] Their efforts joined those of women across the globe who asserted themselves as national representatives in international events and, decades later, forced the International Olympic Committee (IOC) to advocate for women's access to sport.

The Games in the Dominican Republic offer a case study of what Greg Grandin describes as the "politicalization and internationalization of everyday life" during the Cold War.[16] Acts as mundane as signing up for Little League or attending a volleyball match became political as citizens read even habitual actions in the context of ongoing ideological debates divided along Soviet-US or Cuba-US axes.[17] In the Dominican Republic, these ideological debates manifested as demands that the government invest in amateur over professional sport. Amid growing inequality and stagnating wages under the pro-business Triumvirate government, Dominicans demanded more government investment in amateur sport as a means for building the nation. They criticized government welfare for businesses, including the professional baseball league, which received tens of thousands of dollars of support each year while amateur sport languished. After winning reelection in 1970, Balaguer initiated the project around the 1974 Games to respond to these criticisms. The Games would be the culmination of Balaguer's commitment to developing the hearts and minds of the Dominican people—and just in time for the 1974 presidential elections.

Looking at the Balaguer government through the Games reveals the ways that Dominican citizens applied both the US Cold War rhetoric of rights and freedom and the Soviet and Cuban rhetoric of justice as they worked to create a democratic society. In contrast to the superpowers' polarization, Dominicans imagined democratic society as one that incorporated both the freedom touted by the United States and the equal opportunity, or justice, promised by the Soviets and Cubans. This middle path had international implications. The outcomes of Dominican interactions with the Third Way, both that promoted by Balaguer and their own understandings, fed back to reshape the international discourse—specifically in acknowledging a place for women. Sport offers a glimpse of how these domestic and international influences came together. After describing how Dominicans negotiated global forces and Balaguer's Third Way in the project for the Games, this chapter will look at how women contributed to this "extraordinary national responsibility" and expanded Olympism in the process.[18] Women's participation in national sport projects such as the *compromiso de todos* under Balaguer ultimately led to one of the greatest points of convergence in the Cold War: women's increased access to sport.

Balaguer's Third Way and the XII Central American and Caribbean Games

The 1974 Games were the culmination of many smaller projects that the Balaguer government had undertaken to incorporate sport into the Third Way. Rhetoric about the moral and physical benefits of sport and the apparent commitment to make sport accessible to all Dominicans, especially those in the rural interior, mirrored populist sport programs fostered by Luis Muñoz Marín's Popular Democratic Party (Partido Popular Democrático, PPD) in Puerto Rico in the 1940s,[19] Juan Domingo Perón in Argentina in the 1940s and 1950s,[20] and even Trujillo in the first two decades of his regime.[21] But the sport program in Cuba was the proximate influence for Dominican sport in the Third Way and the most important for the related project of promoting the Dominican Republic as a leader in hemispheric unity and solidarity.[22] Cuba's domination of the Central American and Caribbean Games after 1970 grasped the attention of Dominican sport officials, who joined sportswriters to advocate for investment in amateur sport.[23] Hosting the Games would not only prove the capacity of the Dominican Republic to uphold Olympic fraternity and the spirit of regional solidarity,[24] but also instill a "sporting mystique" as the basis for unity and progress throughout the nation.[25] Midway through Balaguer's first term (1966–70), Dominican sport officials began to implement projects similar to those in Cuba, even writing legislation that defined sport as a government obligation in 1968. The next year, and through the rest of the Balaguer government, they coordinated a project to construct sport installations across the country, targeting rural communities that had previously received little governmental attention and that lacked infrastructure. When Balaguer sought reelection again in 1974, the Dominican Republic had a growing amateur sport program and had fulfilled the promise of Olympic fraternity to its regional neighbors.

Dominican citizens pulled Balaguer toward the Cuban sport model rather than being lured by him into it. During the first half of the period known as the twelve years (*doce años*), Balaguer attempted to win Dominican hearts and minds through professional baseball. He supported a charity event that brought the Pittsburgh Pirates to play a five-game exhibition series against a team of Dominican All-Stars. Though successful in easing popular resentment toward the United States and well-intentioned in donating profits to local farmers, the exhibition series exposed the limitations of professional baseball and Balaguer's emphasis on capitalist development as the means to build the nation and its future.[26] Seeing national baseball heroes including Matty Alou play for the Pittsburgh Pirates rather than the local All-Stars showed Dominicans how capitalist development robbed the nation of some of its best resources. The All-Stars's 1–4 record against the Pirates exposed the inequities in their relationship with the United States. The limitations of professional baseball moved Dominicans to join sportswriters' calls for the government to protect amateur sport, using baseball as what scholar Thomas Carter describes as a "language of contention" in negotiating the meanings and forms of sport with the state.[27] The lure of individual profit in professional baseball had caused amateur players to professionalize prematurely, leaving them stranded outside of baseball and depleting national rosters in the process. Legislative and financial support for amateur sport would, in the words of one sportswriter, help restore these rosters and make sport a sight of national prestige and progress.[28]

After the failure of the Pirates exhibition to co-opt Dominicans into his development program, Balaguer adapted to popular sentiments and shifted the emphasis to amateur sport. By 1968, Director of Sport Horacio Veras and Dominican Olympic Committee chair Juan Ulises García Saleta had drafted legislation that defined sport as a right of the people and acknowledged the government obligation to provide for "the betterment and moral, intellectual, and physical improvement of Dominican youth"[29] through sport. To fulfill this obligation, Veras and García Saleta coordinated efforts to construct sports installations across the country. They received hundreds of letters and telegrams from promoters, local officials, private citizens, and the executives of sport clubs asking the government to build or renovate sport facilities. Though they lacked the resources to fulfill all of these requests, their initiatives laid the groundwork for the larger national project to prepare the Games and Balaguer's alignment with amateur sport.[30] Many Dominicans embraced these projects as a sign of partnership between the president and the population. For example, Governor Peggy B. de Bautista of La Vega projected popular desires for amateur sport onto Balaguer in a letter requesting a new roof for a local boxing gym. She told officials that the president had ordered the secretary of public works to construct the gym "with the hope of increasing Sport in all the Country."[31] Assisting with the roof would show Dominicans that Balaguer shared their desires and would follow through to achieve them.

The national project to prepare the 1974 Games created a paternalistic relationship between the president and the people as they shared the *compromiso de todos*. Dominican youth demonstrated their willingness to fulfill their side of this partnership by incorporating Balaguer's rhetoric of the unity and educational potential of sport into their requests for patronage. A group calling themselves the "legitimate representatives of the entire Azua community"—likely to distance themselves from groups associated with the opposition—shared their desires to "develop ourselves morally, culturally, and physically through sport" in their request for a new sport center.[32] Training athletes and hosting competitions to select athletes for the Games, the *azuanos* noted, would create "a very necessary permanent closeness among all in the southern community" and instill in them the Olympic spirit. Balaguer hoped that the Games could do the same on a national level, taking the *azuanos* at their word "that only sport and culture can unite peoples permanently without political, racial, or religious problems."[33]

While the earlier attempts by Veras and García Saleta to unite Dominicans through amateur sport faltered for lack of financial support, the project to host the Games mobilized resources to fulfill citizens' requests. In addition to symbolic gestures such as designating 1971 as the "Year of Sport," the government created a special fund for the promotion of sport. Though the initial appropriation of just over $15,000 in 1971 was relatively modest, the budget more than tripled the next year and rose to almost $54,000 by 1974.[34] The government increased funding for the development not only of amateur sport but also physical education. The overall budget for the development of sport, including school programs for physical education, increased by more than $100,000 between 1970 and 1971. Before the "Year of Sport," the government had allocated more funds to physical education than to more general programs for the development of sport. That, too, changed by 1972, when the budget for sport development increased by nearly $200,000 to $521,716. In 1974, the year of the Games, the government directed almost $900,000 to sport. These budgets and "the interest that the Honorable Mr. President of the Republic has shown in offering all his cooperation for the increase and development of national sport" attested to Balaguer's willingness to invest in Dominican citizens.[35] And Dominicans responded: they sent so many requests for installations and equipment that Balaguer's office had to assign a special military assistant to administer what officials called the Plan for the Promotion of Sport (*Plan Promocional Deportivo*).[36]

Just as Dominicans had pulled Balaguer to amateur sport, the Balaguer regime employed the educational benefits of sport both to raise youth in the norms of democratic participation and to promote order in the country. Sport served as a means for social control, an antidote to vices like alcohol, drugs, and politics, which editors and officials in the Dominican Republic worried would undermine the social order.[37] Press reports about the construction of new installations and requests by sport promoters emphasized the benefits of sport, declaring them the best means to eradicate drugs in the country. One sportswriter hailed basketball and volleyball courts as "determinate in stopping the use or the trafficking of narcotics among Dominican youth."[38] Similarly, sportsmen suggested that the government might prevent youth from joining seditious political groups by delivering a "message of true interest" through its support for events such as national baseball tournaments.[39] Those who missed this message or who criticized the paternalist model could be dismissed as bored teenagers or branded as communists.[40] Sport could bring the nation together in a common project and end political violence by offering Dominican youth the opportunity to be "better men for the Fatherland."[41]

After winning reelection in 1974, Balaguer rewarded Dominican citizens for fulfilling their *compromiso* by making good on a campaign promise to institutionalize the national sporting project in the Secretary of Sports, Physical Education, and Recreation (SEDEFIR). The new SEDEFIR elevated sport from a directorate under the secretary of education to its own cabinet-level position, establishing a centralized system similar to Cuba's National Institute of Sports, Physical Education, and Recreation (Instituto Nacional de Deportes, Educación Física y Recreación, INDER) and promoting Balaguer as the patron of national sport. As the patron, Balaguer led Dominicans to progress much as a parent or teacher might guide a child. A cartoon published in April 1976 depicted this paternalism. A boy in short pants representing "Dominican children" grasped the fingers of a man in a suit labeled "Sports Plans of the Secretary of Sports." The boy gazed up at the man, whose head extended beyond the frame to stress his stature. His eyes shining with gratitude, the boy commented, "It is good to know that one is not so alone." The creation of the SEDEFIR to lead Dominican youth on the path to progress completed the message of Balaguer's concern for the Dominican people and reinforced the trust in his leadership on their Third Way "to peace, harmony, and development."[42] The Games normalized the Balaguer government's conflation of requests for patronage with political participation. The Third Way helped to build sport, and sport sustained the Third Way.

Dominican Women, Sport, and the Third Way

The 1974 Games were a turning point in Dominican sport.[43] The mobilization of resources, especially in preparing athletes, created the opportunity for Dominicans to represent the nation in events that they had previously left uncontested. In some sports, such as basketball, the Dominican delegation sent a women's team for the first time; in others, such as gymnastics and judo, the country sent its first representatives of either sex. Dominican women of various class and social backgrounds participated in the *compromiso de todos*, using many of the same channels as their male compatriots: training in sport and sending letters and telegrams to request patronage in their communities. Because of their positions between the national government and communities, women governors were particularly important in facilitating these exchanges. They backed local requests and followed up on promises that Balaguer had made to the communities they represented. The governors, like their compatriots, employed democratic rhetoric in their requests, echoing official statements about the educational and social benefits of sport. Though legislation and state policies failed to recruit them explicitly in the national sporting project, Dominican women seized the opportunities they found through the Third Way to assert themselves as part of the nation and to contribute to the struggle for democracy. Women governors, athletes, and administrators—not to mention those who supported male athletes—made the Games a success. They also built one of the greatest legacies of the Games: Dominican women's increased participation in sport.

Balaguer's use of sport for political ends coincided with the politicization of sport on a global scale and with a corresponding rise in women's representation on national delegations. This representation was motivated in part by the same feminist discourse that pushed Balaguer to appoint women as civil governors. Despite the IOC's claims to separate sport from politics, the Soviet Union's entry into the 1952 Olympics in Helsinki made the Olympic Games a proxy ideological battlefield. Medals won in women's events counted the same as those won in men's events, leading some countries to pressure local organizing committees and the international federations of various sports to include more women's events in the program.[44] The Soviet Union was especially outspoken about expanding the program to include women, pointing to this advocacy as evidence of Soviet egalitarianism. The expansion of competitive opportunities for women at the Olympic Games rose notably from 25 women's or mixed events of 149 total events (16.8 percent) in 1952 to 86 of 257 total events (33.5 percent) in 1992. Women and National Olympic Committees seized these opportunities: women's participation increased from 10.5 percent of total athletes in 1952 to 28.8 percent in 1992.[45] This expansion for women and men granted countries in the Third World more opportunities to participate on the global stage. The Dominican Republic, which participated in the Olympic Games for the first time in 1964, benefited from these opportunities. The country sent its first woman to the 1976 Montreal Olympics and at least one woman has qualified for each Olympic Games since, representing the country in track and field, tennis, synchronized swimming, weightlifting, judo, taekwondo, table tennis, gymnastics, and volleyball.[46]

Dominican women participated in the Central American and Caribbean Games at higher rates than in the Olympic Games, although the Dominican delegations before 1974 had left even all-male events uncontested.[47] Before the Games in Santo Domingo in 1974, Dominican delegations to the Central American and Caribbean Games comprised mostly men. While women made up over 17 percent of all participants in 1966 and 15.75 percent in 1970, the Dominican delegations included only 13.8 percent and 11.6 percent women, respectively. These delegations were relatively small overall, but the opportunities for Dominican women were limited further by the sports available to them: they participated only in volleyball, track and field, and tennis.[48] Hosting the 1974 Games changed that. New sport federations and increased funding brought more women to gyms, stadiums, courts, pools, and fields. Sixty-one of the 203 Dominican athletes were women in 1974. They participated in seven disciplines: basketball, gymnastics, swimming, tennis, track and field, softball, and volleyball. After sending only thirteen women—the volleyball team and a javelin thrower—to the XI Games in Panama City in 1970, women represented 30 percent of the Dominican delegation in 1974 and 34 percent of that in 1978.[49] While all the coaches and most officials were men, one woman served as a voting member of the organizing committee, and another, Dra. Beatriz Martínez, as a director of protocol.[50] Though still far shy of parity or equality, these advances were significant.

The politicization of sport during the Cold War increased opportunities for women to participate, but these opportunities did not represent a movement toward gender equality in sport or in society at large. Gains for women athletes were secondary to winning medals and the national progress and modernization those medals symbolized, especially for countries in the Third World. As Brenda Elsey demonstrates in her study of the Pan-American Games of the 1950s, the failure of most countries to explicitly include women in sport reflected and deepened women's exclusion from national politics more generally.[51] Women were *allowed* to participate rather than recruited to represent the nation.[52] Despite fielding a nearly complete roster in women's events for the first time, the Dominican press was silent on the increased participation of women at the 1974 Games. Exchanges among Dominican officials mentioned no specific efforts to recruit women athletes or to provide additional accommodations for their training. One Dominican runner revealed that she felt underprepared: she had trained for only seven months.[53] She may have been an exception, or shared these complaints with male athletes, but her experience suggests a relative lack of attention to women athletes. By contrast, a sport supplement published the day before the opening ceremonies cited two Puerto Rican Olympic Committee executives who proudly declared that their delegation included a complete women's team of sixty-four athletes as part of their goal to promote women's active participation in sport. Though they noted that women in sports other than tennis, basketball, and swimming were there to "acquire experience and knowledge" rather than earn medals, the officials acknowledged women as part of the national sport community and for their potential to improve the nation's standing on the medal table.[54]

Dominican women's basketball was one of the beneficiaries of the expansion of the national sport program. Though Dominican men and women had played basketball recreationally for decades, the women's national team formed only in 1971, after the Central American and Caribbean Basketball Confederation organized its first women's tournament, the Centrobasket. The 1974 Games were the first time Dominican women competed in basketball at an Olympic-sponsored event. Expectations were low, and the disparities in experience among the teams manifested in the scores. In their first game, the Dominican women fell to Cuba by a score of 99–33—a discouraging loss, but a marked improvement from their losses by over a hundred points to Cuba and Mexico in the first Centrobasket. During the three years between the events, the Dominican women had trained hard and even traveled for scrimmages and camps with the Cuban national team. Their efforts paid off. They defeated El Salvador twice and took the bronze medal from Puerto Rico because of point differentials, even after losing a close final game.[55] The next year, the team qualified for the Pan-American Games in Mexico City, joining the largest Dominican delegation (seventy-seven) to the Pan-American Games to that date, along with five women from track and field and one from gymnastics.[56]

The Dominican Republic was ill-prepared for the influx of the hundreds of women athletes who joined the amateur sport program for the Games, but the renewed sporting fraternity with Cuba since 1969 helped alleviate some of the stress on the system. For the first time, Dominican women participated in numbers close to their Cuban sisters in the 1974 Games: the Dominican delegation included sixty-one women, the Cuban delegation sixty-nine.[57] Long plagued by a lack of physical education teachers and sport coaches, the Dominican Republic relied on reinforcements from Cuba and other countries in the region. The Manuel Fajardo Superior Institute of Physical Education, an institute of higher learning that trained Cuban and international students as teachers, trainers, coaches, and experts in the technical and scientific practice of sport, offered technical assistance to the Dominican women's basketball team. Perhaps as a reward for their coach Mayobanex Mueses, who was honored as "Director of the Year" at the Centrobasket tournaments in 1971 and 1973,[58] García Saleta arranged for the women's basketball team to make at least two trips to Cuba for "intense training and scrimmage" the year before the Games.[59] Other women's teams had similar opportunities at exchanges with Cuba, perhaps as a way to compensate for the more regular international exchanges available to men's teams, especially in baseball, and for women's teams with longer histories in the Dominican Republic, such as a volleyball.[60] Cuba's fraternity and practical expertise helped Dominican women claim their place in the nation under Balaguer's Third Way.

In addition to training themselves for athletic competition, Dominican women helped to build the Games, often working through and validating the paternalistic channels of Balaguer's Third Way. Balaguer and his officials actively sought the input of women in his administration, even making their inclusion official by appointing women governors in all the country's provinces. Appointing women in such posts was strategic. First, bringing women into his administration conformed to demands in the feminist movement that women gain a seat at the table and bolstered Balaguer's progressive image.[61] Second, public associations of women as maternal figures, caretakers, and conciliators offered a helpful counter-narrative to accusations that Balaguer was complicit in "old-style killings and political repression" against members of the opposition.[62] The women's social and marital status—they were comfortably middle-class, many of them former principals or teachers, and nearly all married—eased the fears of many that women in official positions might upset the social order by conceding to radical feminist demands. The governors claimed these familial connections and their maternalism as unique qualifications for their jobs that would allow them to unite the country under their leader.[63] The governors promoted Balaguer's Third Way and the Games in their communities, providing a crucial meeting point between the populations they served and the state.[64]

Those charged with organizing the Games made use of the gendered implications of the governors' positions by pairing them with Balaguer at the head of the Dominican national family. By designating San Francisco de Macorís Governor Doña Juanita Castellanos Vargas as Patron and President Balaguer as Honorary Patron of the First Northeast Regional Games, the organizing committee projected an image of familial peace onto the event in the hopes of inspiring the support of local athletes and spectators. Highlighting the patronage of both local and national representatives—Governor Castellanos and President Balaguer—also confirmed the unified moral and material support for the event and secured more financial support through the executive branch.[65] This coordination was essential to the national sport project because, as organizing committee director Francisco Medrano Basilis explained to Balaguer, youth selected at the regional games would help form the rosters for the Games.[66] By lending their support to the regional games, and, by implication, to the 1974 Games, President Balaguer and Governor Castellanos Vargas provided local youth the opportunity to join the rest of the Dominican family in the Olympic project. Their support, Medrano explained, would be reflected back in "the confidence, admiration, and sympathy that the Dominican People have for their President."[67]

The governors' ability to mobilize youth in their regions and to provide feedback about what their communities needed proved essential to Balaguer's paternalism. Early sporting projects such as the National Games scheduled for 1968 offered a test run. García Saleta wrote to all the governors, asking them to "put all their enthusiasm" into recruiting youth for the competition, which would "honor above all our Country, [allowing] us to put it on par with other civilized countries in the world, in the beautiful affairs of amateur sport."[68] The governors offered their moral support to national projects in exchange for government largesse to their communities. Governor Librada Báez de Socias of Dajabón, a province on the border with Haiti, asked that the organizing committee for the Border Games intervene with President Balaguer to speed construction on a $25,000 baseball stadium in her province. She wisely invoked the rhetoric of the educational benefits of sport, asking the committee to "[keep] in mind that our youth need to incorporate themselves into the practice of sport to create healthy minds and bodies, as Dr. Joaquín Balaguer, the First Dominican Sportsman, wishes."[69] The governor's ability to align her demands with Balaguer's stated objectives for sport likely helped her secure the promise for the stadium and the support to see it through completion.

Though often under the radar, this participation in the national project demonstrated how Dominican women negotiated their expectations for democracy with the Balaguer regime. Using the honorable designation of Balaguer as the "First Dominican Sportsman" and invoking his wishes created a sense of unity on the one hand and an obligation for the government on the other. Balaguer claimed to want what Dominicans wanted, so they expected him to follow through. Other communities were less subtle than Báez in holding Balaguer accountable to their shared objectives. Members of a cultural and sport club in Santo Domingo requested a meeting with Balaguer after Director of Sport Veras failed to construct a volleyball-basketball court that Balaguer had promised. They were certain that Balaguer shared their desire to give youth a place to stretch and build their muscles. They had even acquired the land to build the court.[70] Though they intimated that Veras was to blame for the construction delays, club members hoped that discussing Balaguer's "useless promise" might compel him to uphold his part of the paternalist pact.[71] Even when they recognized the limits of democracy in their constitutional government, Dominicans worked to hold Balaguer accountable to the obligations defined by his Third Way.

The mobilization of national resources to increase access to sport across the country provided the hope that women and girls could integrate into the national sport community. But many women and girls faced obstacles to participation even when they had access to fields and training. As Paula Pettavino and Geralyn Pye showed for Cuba, women's participation in organized sport and recreational activities lagged behind that of their male comrades even after the sport infrastructure was firmly established, and despite the rhetoric of inclusion in the socialist sport systems.[72] In Cuba, as in Puerto Rico and the Dominican Republic, the emphasis on measuring national progress through medal counts separated women's sport from the global movement for gender equality. Although the competition for medals that characterized the Cold War expanded sport access to women, the lack of specific attention to their training meant that only women with more leisure time and expendable income could seize the opportunities.[73] Even with access to child care, maternal responsibilities and political action kept many women out of the gym altogether or pulled them from training programs earlier than their male counterparts.[74] The rhetoric of rights and justice from the poles of the Cold War converged to expand the Olympic program and increased opportunities for women athletes to represent their countries.

The cultural biases and maternal obligations that prevented more women from seizing those opportunities went beyond the limited number of events on the Olympic program.

Un compromiso de tod@s

By incorporating the population under the *compromiso de todos*, Balaguer hoped to co-opt the democratic meanings that Dominicans projected onto amateur sport and to direct them to his development plan. The project around the Games helped secure Balaguer's second reelection in 1974 and, in the process, instituted a paternalist pact around sport that legitimated Balaguer's claims to lead the country along a path of democratic peace and progress. Even as tensions surged amid rumors that Balaguer would seek a third term in the May 1974 elections, Dominicans united in the Olympic spirit to fulfill their promise to their Central American and Caribbean neighbors and to create a new sporting era at home.

This new sporting era created new opportunities for Dominican women to represent their nation on international sport fields and to deepen their connections and exchanges with their sporting sisters. Yet Dominican women's participation in the national sporting project was not so much encouraged as tolerated or accepted. The political significance attributed to medal counts as measures of national strength and potential during the Cold War subsumed women and their social position under their identity as Dominicans and their utility to Balaguer's political project. Women athletes could add their medals to the national count, and women governors could strengthen Balaguer's paternal image at the head of the peaceful Dominican family. But their participation in these national projects ultimately served Balaguer's Third Way, boosting his narrative of opportunity while maintaining the authoritarianism and inequality behind the paternalist structure. As Manley has found, maternalism gave women a place in the national dialogue, but defined their participation along gender norms. Only after the Games, and through their participation in events such as the United Nations International Women's Year, did Dominican women and their male allies unite across partisan divides to demand equal rights and justice.[75]

The place of sport in Balaguer's Third Way, and women's participation in it, mirrored the convergence of US and Soviet ideologies in the Cold War more generally, especially in the realm of sport and culture. Internationally, the Cuban system had already confirmed the power of sport to accommodate state-run programs with citizen expectations. It rewarded star athletes with incentives such as cars or the opportunity to earn a salary in foreign currency as a coach or trainer abroad.[76] Capitalist countries adopted pieces of the socialist sport model, or adapted earlier models such as Puerto Rico's 1940s A Park for Every Town program, to join their communist adversaries in defining sport as a (male) human right.[77] The commitment to developing women athletes and helping them overcome obstacles to participation varied by country. But women themselves seized a place as athletes in international competition and as citizens of the nation. Whether as governors supporting programs because they believed that sport developed stronger citizens or as board members of sport clubs calling on Balaguer to build volleyball courts in their communities, women not only participated in the Third Way but molded it to align with their democratic visions. By invoking democracy as they claimed their place on the sport field, Dominican women, along with their allies across the Third World, secured their place on national fields and their inclusion in the Olympic Movement.

CHAPTER 8

Dis-assembling the Logocentric Subject at the Paralympic Games

The Case of Colombian Powerlifter Fabio Torres

CHLOE RUTTER-JENSEN

In the world of sport studies much has been written about nation, nationalism, and other theories of belonging.[1] These theories have contributed to thinking about the ways in which a massively popular activity—watching sport—creates specific national narratives of inclusion and exclusion. The exclusions and inclusions crisscross intersectional identities, including gender, region, racial formation, social class, ability, and globalization. In this chapter I study an enfleshed disabled body that participates in international sporting events. I use the notion of enfleshed to insist that materiality matters as much as the narrated symbolic body; indeed they simultaneously create our experiences of bodies. It highlights the structural disabling of the body through spatial, material, and symbolic discourses. The body studied in this chapter, mutilated by a land mine, represents the physical experience (explosion, pain, scarring) as well as the political, racialized, and discursive violence. The concept of enfleshed allows a cultural, social, symbolic, material, economic, and spatial analysis of the practices that create, mobilize, demobilize, and constitute the disabled body: a body that is in constant excess when confronted by prescriptive and normative identities, but also a body that can only exist articulated with others (organic and nonorganic). Instead of an already essentialized and passive subject, the body and its identity are a process: an active assembling.

Using the frame of enfleshed bodies, I examine how the assembling (discursive and literal through prosthetics) of disabled athletes' bodies

DOI: https://doi.org/10.34053/scs2019.o.8

challenge prefixed "truths" such as national belonging, masculinity, and heroism. Specifically, I present Fabio Torres, ex-soldier of the Colombian military forces who was disabled by war, and his quest for a medal at the 2016 Rio Paralympics as a figuration in Colombia that defies the phallogocentric traditional Western subject position—static—and offers an affective and dynamic becoming. I hope to analyze the contradictory ways in which this national "other," racialized black, impoverished, disabled, and displaced body signal the dominant and subversive biopolitics at play. To explore Torres's excessive otherness that drives the appropriation of his body to be/represent Colombia, I will look at two images: one from mass media *Deportes RCN* and another from a photographic project done by Eduardo Leal called "Victims and Heroes" that portrays eight Paralympic Colombian athletes.

The history of international sporting events in which Colombia participates has long run on the gasoline of racial and regional stereotypes. Bodies are racialized and assigned to certain types of sports. The most obvious clichés show up in the main sports: black men play soccer, black women do track and field, white-mestizos swim, and mestizo men cycle. Any quick look at the Olympic rosters affirms that they illustrate this division. The racial stratification correlates to social class divisions. Certain regions are mined for their athletes, a process that extracts them from their hometowns, which are usually impoverished and precarious; then they compete in the Olympic Games as representatives of the nation. Nevertheless, while the individuals may be well fed and cared for, their regions remain undernourished and excluded. In his recent essay on race, sport, and Colombian regions, Héctor Fernández L'Hoeste points out that in the 1970s the Andean region and cycling were associated with the perceived hardworking mestizo while peasant and coastal regions and boxing were associated with the prejudice that "Afro-descendants of Caribbean extraction were ideal fodder for pugilistic aspirations."[2] He goes on to underline the disconnect between the success of Kid Pambelé in international boxing (light welterweight World Champion in 1972) and the "degree of abandonment" of Pambelé's home town, San Basilio de Palenque, a runaway-slave enclave founded in the seventeenth century. Pambelé's situation has not changed much forty years later compared to contemporary boxers. Colombian media continues to celebrate black athletes as examples of national glory while, institutionally and structurally, the penurious conditions of most Afro-Colombians are simultaneously maintained.[3]

In this chapter I look at Fabio Torres, whose otherization, certainly racialized and regionalized, goes on to reveal the structural and symbolic excess that a disabled body adds to the recipe. Torres is black, an ex-soldier, impoverished, and mutilated by a landmine in the Colombian conflict.[4] Studying this particular disabled soldier reveals many key dis-identifications. I reviewed the number of stories from August to October 2016 in Colombian mass media publications (*El Tiempo*, *El Espectador*, and *Semana*) to compare Olympic coverage with Paralympic coverage. These dates were selected to follow a build-up, a climax, and the conclusion to the Paralympic and Olympic period. I found that beyond the unbalanced coverage weighted toward Olympic stories, the narratives around them deployed clichés and stereotypes to tell formulaic tales that genderize, regionalize, and racialize bodies in negative ways.

I study two very distinct images, one from mass media and the other from an artistic photography project. As a Paralympic athlete in powerlifting, Torres's image exemplifies the paradoxes and contradictions of the national athlete and simultaneously excluded body. The detailed analysis of the portrayal of Torres through a frame of enfleshed subjectivity will be accompanied by critical feminist and critical disability studies, in addition to strategies of reading that range from close literary readings to traditional Marxism. The theoretical citations mostly come from Rosi Braidotti's work on "becoming." Braidotti's posthuman philosophy seeks to create a "positive vision of the subject as an affective, positive and dynamic structure, which clashes with the rationalist image traditionally projected by institutionalized philosophy."[5] I suggest that reading Torres as a subject in becoming, one that is dynamic and multiple, affirmatively contests the rationalist image.[6]

I look specifically at the 2016 Rio Paralympics to examine representations of an enfleshed experience of athletes. By recognizing the assembly of their bodies—the enfleshment—we can see not necessarily a breakdown of traditional narratives, but the ways in which the dynamic and excessive body actually push the normative structures of national identity to maintain its hegemonic narrative in more sophisticated ways. The heteronormative and capitalist representations of national belonging appropriate (make them property of the nation) even nonnormative bodies and thus diminish the possibility of these bodies manifesting political subversion. I propose that this "inclusion" reveals the narrative itself as failing hegemony, the recognition that the national subject, or any logocentric subject, crumbles upon inspection. The commodification of Torres's body exposes the fictional wholeness of nation. Torres is not white-mestizo, not middle-class, not normatively abled. The black, impoverished, and disabled body of Torres expresses the nonnormative despite attempted inclusion in a national narrative through the Paralympic Games. Indeed, this body shows how the logocentric subject/national narrative cannot ever really *be*.

The modern Olympic Games themselves exist through the concept of nation; to compete in them, you must first belong to a nation.[7] Yet racialized and disabled bodies make transparent that being born into a time/space does not guarantee access to national benefits, rights, and protections. In the case of people with disabilities, the access to practicing their citizenship is not given, and therefore competing for a nation requires a previous process of "nationalization," or even "naturalization." Lennard Davis develops the ways in which enforced normalcy and democracy are tied together and, furthermore, how that enforced normalcy permits some bodies to belong to the nation (to be citizens) and excludes others. He elaborates capitalism's ideological force for creating bodies that are interchangeable. These normalized bodies then fit the physical structures of, for instance, an assembly line or call center. Davis writes, "If all workers are equal and all workers are citizens, then all citizens must have standard bodies to be able to fit into the industrial-political notion of democracy, equality, and normality. Clearly people with disabilities pose problems to work situations in which labor is standardized and bodies conceptualized as interchangeable."[8] In this scenario the disabled athlete achieves where the disabled worker fails. The Paralympic Games offer citizenship to the disabled athlete. Nonetheless, the access to citizenship rights is only through sport and does not apply to all other disabled bodies. The same Torres can barely access education or training to seek employment in said call center or assembly line.

While the analysis of the first image introduced in this chapter shows how the disabled body is appropriated for/by the nation without changing the perception of subject location in society, the second image forms part of an effort to produce creative readings that can possibly represent more ethical subjects. I attempt to offer a reading that goes beyond the mere inclusion or extension of belonging, but rather recognizes infinite disruptions to the concept of enforced normalcy or wholeness as necessary prerequisites to citizenship. Indeed, following Donna Haraway's work, I propose subjects that are collective rather than individual, posthuman rather than human, and joyfully cyborg. "Cyborg" contests enforced nor-

malcy and allows for multiple and variable subjects.[9] Instead of categoriz-
ing bodies as disabled or abled, black or white, we can use the cyborg, the
machine plus organism, as a way to suggest more ethical narratives of the
body. I return to Torres's cybernetic organism at the end of this chapter
and concentrate on the ways that Torres has been supposedly included.

The dialectic reading of inclusion/exclusion, the relationship of the
"subject" (high-performance, able-bodied Olympic athlete) to the "other"
(Paralympic body with disabilities and a prosthesis) concentrates on a
marketable difference, one that in the case of international sport makes
possible the commodification of the disabled different body. After all,
Paralympic events also belong to commercial interests and sponsors.[10]
The commodification of the other generates revenue (as well as saleable
narratives of inclusion) in the form of commercials during the televised
events and indirectly through the advertisements that later include the
successful athletes.[11] Beyond marketable inclusion, I would like to show
how Torres's body challenges the nation as such and narrates an ethical
subjectivity that is radical and useful insofar as—in line with Gregory
Lobo's argument on the problematic of the nation in Colombia—its telos
is not the refounding of the nation in some more inclusive sense (which
always fails), but the necessary surpassing of it, since any idea of the
nation is always already burdened and indeed invalidated by an imma-
nent and thus inescapable authoritarianism. Braidotti states the dynamics
of commodification clearly when she discusses cyber-teratologies, the
perceived monstrous other in heteronormative hegemonies. She writes,
"In the political economy of postmodernity . . . the 'others' are simultaneously commodified into objects of material and discursive consumption. They are also, however, emerging in their own right as alternative,
resisting and empowering counter-subjectivities."[12] The nonnormative
body that I have chosen to study is in fact not "other" when seen in the
light of national Olympic/Paralympic celebration; it is appropriated and
commodified as a national hero. Yet it problematizes which experiences
are centered in the nation and which are marginalized. Thus, I propose
the Paralympic athlete as a figuration of the nation that can never *be*—as
an alternative subjectivity.

Part One: Torres, the Flag Carrying Individual

Men's football dominates the representation of Colombian sport.[13]
Football is *the* sport and all other sports are "other." This is useful for

understanding which sport bodies are important in the Colombian market. For example, on September 15, 2016, when two Paralympic athletes won silver and gold in "other sports" in Rio de Janeiro, the first three stories reported in the mass media were about men's football. Winning Paralympic silver and gold medals did not headline the news. As a matter of fact, it was not even a football game itself that supplanted the Paralympic medals, but rather administrative news about football that got top billing, with such items as "Fifa will no longer give out golden ball award" and "Medellín, despite losing to Lucumí, remains in the South American Cup."[14] In other words, a banal announcement about FIFA and a headline reminding the reader of Medellín's place in the regional tournament are placed in superior ranking to two Paralympic medals won by Nelson Crispin in 100 meters breaststroke and Mauricio Valencia in javelin throwing. Thus, my analysis of the first image, President Santos giving the "peace flag" to Fabio Torres, starts from a point of "otherness." The article and the image are from the section "other sports" in one of the most widely circulated news outlets, *Deportes RCN*.[15] The headline above the photograph states, "Santos entregó deportistas paralímpicos bandera Colombia-Rio 2016." The photo shows Santos at the podium giving a speech at a press conference, and a row of athletes next to him, the athlete sitting farthest away from him is Torres. In front of the athletes we see several rows of the backs of journalists (and perhaps other guests and dignitaries) taking pictures or writing notes. In other words, the photograph selected does not actually show the president handing a peace flag to Corporal Torres.[16] On reading the subheadline, the flag is defined as "allegorical."[17] Visually, Santos stands out (literally standing), and the five athletes *sitting* to his left are overshadowed by the backs of the public watching the ceremony. The other here, the disabled body, is still the other. Their wheelchairs or prosthesis can barely be seen, and only the tops of their bodies are visible. In societies in which mass media is a dominant tool for achieving hegemony, the regime of visibility correlates directly to hierarchies of power. In effect, Santos signifies the total power of this image, the only visually clear, standing, and unobstructed body, looking into the camera. Meanwhile, we only see backs and sides of the audience and the athletes (who are mainly looking at Santos).

The article that accompanies the photo reports: "El mandatario agradeció a Torres que porte esa bandera y aseguró que 'encarna el sentimiento de gratitud a los soldados y policías' que tienen todos los colombianos. 'Usted es ejemplo de lo que podemos los colombianos', apostilló [*sic*]."[18]

Remember, as the headline states and the photo shows, it is an allegorical peace flag. Beyond carrying this flag, I would venture to state that Torres's role is nonexistent in the peace process; after all, he was an armed soldier actively fighting the so-called enemy before being mutilated by a landmine. The word choice of assigning his representation of "all" Colombians through embodiment (*encarnar*) is contradictory at best, almost farcical when considering the three most salient identity categories of Torres. One, he is a person with disabilities, which in Colombia effectively means marginalized from normative work and education environments and almost all public spaces. Two, he is legibly racialized as black, therefore on the periphery in a racist nation whose black population is one of the most precarious groups. Three, he is from an impoverished region, economically disadvantaged, and, thus, further marginalized from participatory citizenship. Moreover, it is the intersection of black, male, and made-poor that compels his conscription into the armed conflict and exposes him to landmines. Most bodies that participate in the actual violence of Colombia's conflicts are impoverished, racialized, peripheral ones. The urban, white-mestizo, economically viable bodies can buy their way out of the military, or serve in less dangerous conditions (city offices, presidential guard, etc.).

Torres's intersectional subjectivity leads to the transfer of his leg flesh to the Colombian earth, an event for which Santos is "thankful" because now he can represent peace at the 2016 Rio Paralympics. This ironic gratitude for the mutilation, his leg literally being burned into the earth, implies a certain excess, as if he did not *really* need the leg. As we see in Santos's statement, Torres's enfleshing the earth deploys him as *the* Colombian, yet, as we know from studying the economic and symbolic conditions of black Colombians and Colombians with disabilities, this is at best fictional.[19] Paradoxically, he has been absent from most of the national political conversation through racial marginalization but, at the same time, he is present, literally *representing* (in sporting events) Colombia, because of his disability. Torres is a figuration of Eduardo Cadava's take on the ruin of representation. In his essay on the notion of assembling, Cadava writes that images are always about destruction and survival, that they are something that cannot tell a whole or true story. He proposes that instead they tell a story of assembling, becoming, an encounter. Images, such as photographs, only have the "capacity to bear the traces of what it cannot show, to go on, in the face of this loss and ruin, to suggest and gesture toward its potential for speaking."[20] In the suggestion or gesture toward speaking, we are in a dynamic process of becoming. Images like Torres's body suggest a potential for speaking, for presence, for action (powerlifting). Torres's photograph gestures toward this antinomy of presence/absence, war/peace in which the disabled athlete is present, but his disabilities are hidden. The contradiction intensifies when the president of Colombia suggests that this black and disabled athlete exemplifies what all Colombians could be: Santos says "*usted es ejemplo*" ("you are the example"). Yet I am sure that Santos does not mean that all Colombians should or could be disabled and black. Torres can only *be* this fictional example that Santos offers *through* disability. His image accepted at "face" value is the representation of ruin. His belonging required tragic and dramatic events, such as the landmine explosion that dismembered his body. Torres's heroism for surviving is what "members" him to the nation. The amputation of his leg is one type of loss, his marginalizations another, a loss of what he never had: social status.

In addition to Cadava's reading of loss, it is important to understand the ways in which Braidotti parses loss and its relation to subjectivity in her discussion of black subjectivity through the work of Edouard Glissant and Paul Gilroy. Braidotti analyzes the logocentric subject in Western philosophy and its interaction with blackness and black subjectivity. She points out how Glissant and Gilroy offer loss as becoming, a proposal that deeply questions thinking of black subjectivity as permanently tragic. Instead, these identities are perceived as already aware of becoming because of their marginalization, nostalgia, or loss. Thus, the construction of black subjectivity—and I extend it to disabled subjectivity—is no longer mired in tragedy. Judith Butler, in her reflection on precarious lives, also considers loss and mourning as part of subject construction. In response to the question of which lives one mourns, she proposes that "perhaps, one mourns when one accepts that by the loss one undergoes one will be changed, possibly forever. Perhaps mourning has to do with agreeing to undergo a transformation . . . the full result of which one cannot know in advance."[21] Loss, as well as marginalization and precarity, construct the subject in new ways. Despite the language of agency in the phrase "agreeing to undergo," I suggest that the becoming is through the corporeal change—Torres gets a new leg. The unknown future accompanied by a changed body allows for reassembling subjecthood. Fear of change is displaced by change as a dynamic process, complex and therefore stimulating and interesting. The new subject (never stable) practices new subjectivity (also only situational). Limb loss ratifies that "we have never been" complete. I remind the reader that Braidotti elaborates on Bruno Latour's statement "We have never been modern" to emphasize that modern meant some sort of completeness, framed through phallogocentric subjectivity. The loss of the limb as loss implies that an earlier Torres was "whole," "human," and "able bodied." Yet, as a black, impoverished person he was never complete. His body fictionalizes wholeness, even science-fictionalizes it, if we take into account his prosthetic leg. For President Santos, this body tells a story of *over*coming. Yet I argue that disability tells the story of constant *becoming* (taking off and putting on the prosthetic). Rather than tragedy determining the subject, disability points to how all bodies are assemblages, not just the legibly disabled one. Glissant and Gilroy also argue that, rather than blackness being emblematic of the failure to become modern/civilized/Western subjects, blackness shows the logocentric subject to be fictional and coreless. Torres may not be whole nor unified, as read through two minoritarian subjectivities, disabled and black. Nonetheless, it is not Torres who has failed to fulfill Western and colonialist subjectivity, but Western subjectivity that has eliminated and hidden the contradictions and paradoxes of all subjects. Thus, as a representative of Colombia in the international arena of sport, we can analogically read Colombia as neither whole nor unified. Torres's body stands in, or does not stand, sits in, for all bodies. Again, as Santos says, "you are the example" of all bodies. Unwittingly, Santos offers the fractured body, the body in assembling, the impossibility of wholeness or unification as the possibility of nationness.

Santos's reading of Torres pronounces his nationness through masculinity.[22] He "overcomes" landmine mutilation and reifies masculinity through powerlifting. By representing the nation successfully at international powerlifting competitions he has achieved a national masculinity that would actually be denied him if he were "simply" a black, impoverished regional man. Furthermore, the very name of the sport conjures up the image of dominant masculinity. If Torres can lift power for the nation, he precisely embodies what a Colombian should strive to be, yet, only through the explosion (of bones, tendons, ligaments, etc.) of his previously powerless black body. The heroic soldier athlete who lost his leg in the conflict is symbolically included by carrying a peace flag with him to the 2016 Rio Paralympics and represents the aspirational wholeness that Santos and the state appear to desire.

It seems rhetorically shrewd to offer Torres a flag, as if he were getting a clear signal of entry or acceptance into Colombianness. While contemporary uses of flags refer to or establish national identities, implicit in our use of flags as communication are the elements and protocols pertinent to battlefields and war. Long before the flag-waving glory of a gold medalist dominated our television screens, the flag conveyed elements of conflict and limits, indeed traffic signals of war and trade (on land and sea). The materiality of the flag itself refuses to "be" and only is legible in a state of assembling (i.e., blown by wind or air; no wind means an illegible flag). It only acquired meaning in conversation with other boats, armies, or nations. The peace flag given to Torres by Santos is allegorical, we must imagine it, we do not experience its silky billowing, nor does Torres carry the weight of its staff. Instead, the flag is a phantom limb.[23] This is a particularly coherent communication for Colombia, a country in which peace is both a material imaginary and a symbolic real. In the same way that access to peace is obstructed in Colombia, Torres's access and absence are imprinted on the flag.[24] And here I hark back to the necessity of the peace flag in the hands of a black and amputated soldier in the first place—his body materially exists, the Colombian one cannot. We can therefore see how the Colombian universal shatters in the actual context of citizenship in the country. He portrays the myth of Colombianness: a political fiction that is racially marked, Andean, literate, pro-Europe. In other words, it is not universal, and competing in the Paralympics will not change the situation for Afro-Colombians.

Torres, an impoverished and racialized Colombian, a member of a significant part of the country's population, becomes one with the land through the flesh literally burning into the earth. Torres's stump and new leg cannot be reconnected in a smooth and comfortable way; they will always have a point of contact, one in which the stump will create skin lesions from the constant friction, including blisters, calluses, and fungal infections. The uncomfortable rub, the gap—literally, the articulation between prosthesis and stump—serve as a way to imagine the also incoherent and discontinuous narrative of a subject. Torres's blasted leg, and now his new one (with an image of his football team América de Cali printed on the prosthesis), can be read as "the site for multiple display, as each [body] part became meaningful in itself, not as synecdoche for larger more coherent forms, but as unintegrated bits of information that did not reassemble themselves into classic narrative."[25] In other words, the leg disintegrates in the same way as the analytical category of "other." The leg becomes liquid, ashes, pieces of bone, skin, irreparably bits of information that cannot be rejoined nor put back together to form a leg or the legitimacy of a classic narrative. The landmine explodes not only the leg, but also the dialectic possibility between self and other. Braidotti calls this the others of Other, which in her argument is the actual material and enfleshed experience of the nonnormative subject: transparently cyborg. Torres's leg stopped being his leg after the blast, but his leg exists anew in the form of a prosthesis, and it is this prosthetic leg that brings him out of poverty and into national glory. The incoherent narrative signals the fractured national body, or the fictional ideal of a whole. I suggest that his body parts cannot be re-assembled into a coherent narrative; they can only be-come, just like the attaching/detaching of his new leg.

Briefly returning to the concept of loss, Torres's vaporized leg and the prosthetic one indicate a simultaneous understanding of the conflict in Colombia as loss and not loss. The epistemologies of the West perceive loss as nostalgia, melancholy, absence, and the need to fill emptiness with something/one. This thing/one is usually the capitalist consumption of fetishized goods to alleviate the loss (sporting events and the athletes themselves being some of the most popular something/someone of consumption). Dominant national discourses deploy violence in which people, their bodies, and the land they inhabit are forced to participate in the phallogocentric desire to be whole, coherent, and singular. I suggest that the conflict in Colombia stems as much from agrarian conflicts of ownership as from the exercise of enforced normalcy inherent in the colonial dialectic of the civilized/barbaric dyad. This is the tension between civilized and barbaric, the violence to become civilized as well the violence of "being" barbaric. If such is the case, the ending of the conflict could only happen not through a disarmament of weapons, but through the practice of posthuman subjectivity. Torres's loss might then be read as a multiple and rhizomatic becoming, precisely in the black and disabled body. As it is, the Colombian conflict has no winners that participate in the battlefield; indeed the winners are the capitalist market and economy that circulate during and after the conflict (including everything related to actual battle such as firearms, landmines, uniforms, gas, cars, trucks, canvas for camps, food, communications, and those costs related to postconflict reintegration projects, such as nongovernmental organization workers, housing, food, transportation, education, and so on). Another winner is the Paralympic Games: while it is now an international media and economic event for people of diverse types of disabilities, it was born out of war injuries (post–World War I amputations) and continues to be a primary space in which ex-combatants of all nations participate.[26] In a posthuman philosophy the dialectic of winner/loser would be uncreative and unproductive. Loss could be affirmative and creative. After all, it is Torres's loss that propels him to power "lift" for Colombia. It almost sounds fantastical that a "superpowerlifter" plays the role of savior of Colombia from itself by refusing the notion of a "whole" Colombia. Yet the rescue explicitly comes through the impossibility of assimilation to Colombia—except, of course, his leg, which is now assimilated into the earth.

Part Two: Torres, Embodying the Collective

One leg now part of Colombia, a new leg stepping in to fill the shoe of what the logocentric subject could not. Fabio Torres's new leg places him transparently as the enfleshed experience of the cyborg human. In the second part of the chapter, I intend to take advantage of Torres and his prosthesis as a figuration of machine-plus-man powerlifter, the cyborg. Torres's loss and disintegration serve to interpret him as a contradictory yet affirmative subjectivity. In the photographic project titled "Victims and Heroes" by Eduardo Leal we get a very brief textual history of eight Paralympic athletes whose entry into sport as a career resulted from either literal mutilation by firearms and landmines or displacement from the armed conflict in Colombia.[27] The artist chose specifically these two conflict-related activities as the subject of his pictures. Indeed, in the case of Maritza Arango, the first subject of Leal's portraits (and the only woman and only nonsoldier), the text states that had she not been displaced by the conflict she would never have become an athlete. She is a civilian, a woman, whose blindness results from a congenital condition, yet the quote about her is related to her displacement and ensuing introduction to athletics: "She confesses that before [being forcefully displaced] she did not even know what Track and Field or Olympics was. 'Leaving my town was like a blessing. When I lived there I thought that would be my life. I never imagine this or even getting into a plane. Never, ever.'"[28] Arango is ironically grateful to the conflict. Her athletic career is made possible through her blindness, and paradoxically through violence. In a better world, we could imagine a blind person who has always had opportunities to participate in public life, including education, work, and sport, but without experiencing forced displacement, impoverishment and/or other tragic and traumatic events. But in Colombia it is the violence and blindness that paves the road for a "better" life. Had she not been blind, not forcefully displaced, and had instead lived a "regular" life, she would have no international sport career, and thus would not be a *hero*. The earlier reference to Gilroy and Glissant on black subjectivities helps us understand that, similar to a racist society, in an ableist society a blind person already occupies minoritarian subjecthood and thus experiences enfleshed becoming. An ableist society locates disability in the individual not "in social attitudes, institutional structures, and physical or communicational barriers that prevent full participation as citizen subject."[29] As individuals who *overcome*, many Paralympic athletes appreciate and express gratitude for the conflict (the nation) instead of anger or resentment at the structure that disabled them.[30] In this narrative they actually thank Colombia for their disability, which has now given them a "new and better" life. This idea exemplifies the loss of normative physical abilities as a becoming, a different assemblage, rather than as nostalgia or melancholy for the perceived wholeness of the body before disability.

One of the possible readings of the photographic project, starting from the title "Victims and Heroes," is the commodification of the disabled body. Commodification not only in the sense of capitalistic profit but an attempt, through the figure of the hero, to make these bodies legible, coherent, and worthy of representation. Difference (in this case physical) establishes some sort of disruption to the viewer of the images. Yet the difference is subsumed through heroics. The body in question—the disabled war veteran, for example—comes into the fold of nationalism through the blast. In the case of Torres, as mentioned earlier, his body is burned into Colombia's earth, literally naturalized. Most of the people portrayed in this project are physically disabled by the conflict, with the exception of Arango, who is congenitally blind, but whose athletic career depends on forced displacement. Her inclusion suggests the ableist individual reading of disability in which she is a "victim" to her body, not to the structure or to the conflict. Nevertheless, what connects her to the project is her heroism (perceived as individual). She overcomes the challenges of war and displacement with the additional barrier of also being disabled by society's ocular centric structure. She, like the ex-soldiers, emerges from her disabilities to become an international athlete. Thus, she is a hero because she has succeeded as an individual despite the institutional and war-related obstacles she faces. The competitive international athlete who is *able* to be appropriated into the national symbolic system serves as a symbol of heroism. The bodies of the athletes in "Victims and Heroes" are metonymic of the conflict through their insertion into consumption, and into the international circuit of sporting events such as the Paralympic Games. In effect, they are heroes because they have overcome the bellicose within themselves, thus converting the disability into an asset. I briefly offer this analysis of Martiza because I suggest that Leal's inclusion of her in the project signals that much broader victimizations are occurring in Colombia, such as poverty, racism, misogyny, colonialism, and elitism. The athletes in his project are not merely victims of disability or armed conflict, but also of these structural oppressions. Arango's material body seems to be a combination of everything other, rather than the centered subjectivity of Western dominant masculine heroism.

Torres is also an example of everything other in the hegemonic Western subject construction—as I have said numerous times, black, impoverished, regionally marginal, and disabled. Yet he too is part of the photographic project as a victim and a hero. The legibility of a hero in Colombia must be further considered for a moment here in light of the conflict and the public-relations television and billboard campaign that "heroes really do exist." Like Leal, the Colombian military mediates the portrayal of their soldiers through a campaign that emphasizes their heroism. Gregory Lobo analyzes this campaign in his article about Colombia's mediation of its commitment to the military option during the conflict. He signals how the commercials quietly admit that the non-unified narrative of the conflict in Colombia reveals the instability of "nation." In his examination of the "heroes really do exist" series of commercials produced by the armed forces of Colombia, he states that "the need to insist on the existence of heroes stems from . . . the absence of the sort of (glorious) history that would actually have produced them."[31] The Colombian audience for these advertisements must be convinced that there are heroes. Hence, the Colombian military tacitly recognizes the nonexistence of a unified narrative of Colombian subjectivity (and therefore nation in Lobo's argument). It is not only Torres's body that needs to be made legible as hero in Colombia; Lobo argues that it is all of its soldiers. Ironically, Torres does not defeat the guerrilla as the military might desire—rather, he is de"feet"ed by them. As we saw above, all soldiers lose in this conflict without battlefield winners. Nevertheless, Torres does vanquish his enemy in the form of institutionalized poverty, institutionalized racism, and the social and physical structures that disable. Torres is both victim and hero. He is both the making of a Colombian hero *for* the nation, and a making of a Colombian hero *despite* the nation that impoverishes and disables him. In this way he is excessively Colombian.

The assembly of difference without commodification is not achieved through heroicization (or flag-carrying bearer of peace). Heroicization depends on the notion of the individual will to overcome structural hardship. While the title of Leal's project and the text that follows it signal dominant masculinity and individual will, the images from the photographer counter the text and title that accompanies it. Unlike the peripheral appearance of Torres in the photo with Santos, in Leal's photos Torres is in shared space with others, both human and machine. In search of multiple becomings, the photo I have chosen from Leal might fit this difference as affirmative.

There are four images of Torres; each shows him training, surrounded by a team of paid caregivers, also known as coaches. The image I analyze here shows one of his team, his collective, also a black man, carefully stretching or massaging Torres while he sits at a training machine. I find that the visual narratives signal care and desire in affirmative ways, contradicting the textual narrative of "victim and hero masculinity." The encounters that emerge between the athletes and their trainers are locations of affirmation, of each one becoming through the interconnection that defies the fiction of the self-generating individual. The work of an athlete intimately involves the coach or trainer. Athletes are not "self-made persons," independent of the care of others. An entire team of support surrounds athletes, including nutritionists, coaches, masseuses, doctors, physical therapists, sport journalists and photographers, sponsors, lawyers, industrial designers, dermatologists, machines, pharmaceutical substances, and, of course, in Torres's case, the minerals (mining/miners) that make up his prosthesis. In this photo of Torres, I encounter a highly intimate moment between him and a caregiver. Torres has his eyes closed in perhaps relaxation and/or deep concentration, and the hand of the other man delicately (with only three light fingers) touches his neck and face. It is a moment of "we are all in this together": a contact zone diminishing violence through affect. In this way, I can see the powerlift, track and field event, or boxing round of an athlete as pertaining to the entire team, not the heroism of the individual subject. It would seem that the military would also function through this collectivity, yet the team is suppressed in favor of the individual hero. The images of Torres show his team in an affirmation of the collective and multiple coming together to signify. Could this be because one's prejudices against the independence of people with disabilities allows us to recognize the team, whereas with normatively abled persons one continues to insist and believe in the individual winner? If this is the case, then the photos of Torres allow us to remember and recognize all the participants in the global chains of care that drive contemporary capitalist economies, but, more important, all the encounters and affective venues involved in "the lift." The lift emerges as the moment of most intense becoming, the assembling of a temporal/spatial and affective subjectivity conjoining diverse human and nonhuman actors.

Part Three. Torres, Cyborg

In the first two sections of this chapter I examined the normative intent to include Fabio Torres in a national project and the challenge to this logocentric subjectivity through the idea of an affective and dynamic becoming. In this concluding section, I feel that one must, even if briefly, address the prosthesis itself that Torres wears.[32] Torres's disability is a direct consequence of armed conflict in Colombia, in which the leftist militant groups have fought a long battle against the military, state, and private militias. With over 11,000 landmine-mutilated persons in Colombia, his disability is one that occupies space in the public sphere. This is due in part to the ability to count them, whereas many people with disabilities not caused by the conflict have little to no institutional presence. The institutional access of soldiers to a prosthesis permits this occupation of public space, even international public space.

Prostheses can be problematic if interpreted as fixing or curing. Yet, instead of completing the fragmented body, Torres and his prosthesis are the obvious figuration of a cyborg body. I say obvious, because, as Haraway argues, all of us are cyborg, but many of us do not recognize our cybernetic selves. The prosthesis allows us to imagine "concretely" the cyborg. Haraway states that the cyborg functions "as a fiction mapping our social and bodily reality and as an imaginative resource suggesting some very fruitful couplings."[33] Torres and his prosthetic leg stamped with "América de Cali"—the football team—are a hybrid machine and organism, steel/titanium connected to and moved by muscle and flesh, as well as an individual enfleshed as a whole team. Torres attaches a prosthetic leg to his flesh, but not just a bland reproduction of skin but one that is the emblem and logo of his football team. The prosthesis exceeds a fix or cure of his disability and becomes the inscription of his affect toward a collective, the team itself, as well as all its fans (including himself). It is his social and bodily reality. The prosthesis is a totem, his belonging to a specific clan and tribe, América de Cali, and the Pacific coastal region of Colombia. He is individual and collective at once, rather than one or the other. Importantly, he can take the prosthesis off and disassemble and reassemble himself and therefore embrace what Haraway calls "the possibilities inherent in the breakdown of clean distinctions between organism and machine and similar distinctions structuring the Western self."[34] I remind the reader that the prosthesis and stump and the friction in their articulation are never a clean distinction between organism and machine. Perhaps, then, instead of the competition and hierarchy traditionally dominant in sporting events, one could conceive of these events as the assembling, the joy of the collective, not only in the way the spectators and players interact, but in terms of the body becoming— thus, nondialectic, nondualistic, not abled or disabled, neither part of nor excluded, but rather posthuman and cyborg.

CHAPTER 9

In Search of the Olympic Games' Future Significances

Contributions from Buenos Aires,
Mexico City, and Rio de Janeiro

LAMARTINE PEREIRA DACOSTA

Although the Olympic Games and their sporting foundations can be understood in terms of their educational, cultural, and economic values, among many others, the geopolitical complexities of these mega-events also deserve great focus. This is so because, ever since the creation of the International Olympic Committee (IOC), the Olympic Games have often engaged in the promotion of either specific countries' or continental interests. In this sense, one of the original intentions of the Olympic Games gained ground over time—that is, there was an effort to project nations once they were already part of the Olympic Movement as well as to showcase relevant performances during the Olympic Games, as has most recently occurred with, for example, Cuba and Jamaica.

This chapter argues for the increasingly important geopolitical significance of the Olympic Games with respect to Latin America and the Caribbean. This analysis covers the first decades of the twentieth century to the 2016 Olympics in Rio de Janeiro. The role of sport in relation to the power of nations, national identities, and geopolitics can already be found in 1911 in texts by Pierre de Coubertin, who revived the Olympic Games in the late nineteenth century.[1] In a previous work, I showed that Coubertin chose Latin America as one of the main axes for the international expansion of the Olympic Movement, especially in the 1910s and 1920s, making specific references to the sporting initiatives of Argentina, Brazil, and Mexico.[2]

DOI: https://doi.org/10.34053/scs2019.o.9

The geopolitical projection of Latin America and the Caribbean, in terms of Olympic sport, is evident when considering the increasing significance of the expanding Pan-American Games in recent decades. Taking into account a historical review by Vale Castro in 2007, the impact of the Pan-American Games regarding the integration of the different countries throughout the hemisphere has been more effective in terms of public image than the intercontinental agreements and conferences on political and economic cooperation since the first Pan-American congress in Panama called by Simón Bolivar in 1826.

Castro's argument for the important geopolitical significance of the Pan-American Games throughout their existence, beginning in 1951 in Buenos Aires, is based on the massive and ever-increasing adherence by countries of the three Americas and the Caribbean to this continental sport competition. Popular regional events like the Central American and Caribbean Games—first held in Mexico, in 1926, and later in Cuba, in 1930—anticipated this geopolitical construction of continental identity that continues to this day.[3]

Given the well-studied impact of the Pan-American Games as a platform for visibility and international projection—enabled by the Olympic Games—this chapter will review the experiences of Buenos Aires, Mexico City, and Rio de Janeiro as candidate cities for or hosts of the Olympic Games through a geopolitical framework. I selected these cities not based on the usual criteria regarding countries' participation rate in the event or their medal count, but primarily due to their local and national projection at an international level.

Ultimately, the central question of this chapter is whether the impact of past Olympic experiences could contribute to the future renewal of the Olympic Movement in Latin American and Caribbean countries. Therefore, the selection of Buenos Aires, Mexico City, and Rio de Janeiro is also meant to demonstrate models and strategies to host the Olympic Games in view of potential interest from other urban centers of the region.

Buenos Aires's Persistent Desire to Host the Olympic Games

The categorization of Buenos Aires as a "persistent candidate" to host the Olympic Games is attributed to Cesar R. Torres and his convincing and influential analysis of Buenos Aires's five candidacies and their failure to receive final approval by IOC members in the selection process for the Olympic Games of 1936, 1940, 1956, 1968, and 2004. For Torres, a philosopher and historian of sport specializing in Olympic studies, such persistence by Argentina represents its search for greater international status.[4]

Torres observes that one of Argentina's first Olympic aspirations was to participate in the Olympic Games and host the event in Buenos Aires. In fact, in 1907, there had been frustrated efforts by sport leaders in obtaining financial support from the Argentine government to send national representatives to the 1908 London Olympic Games. However, those same leaders—especially Manuel Quintana and Antonio De Marchi, pioneer proponents of a National Olympic Committee for Argentina—subsequently directed their efforts to carry out what was then called the "Centennial Olympic Games." This event took place in 1910 to commemorate Argentina's centennial celebration of its revolution for independence. With this effort, the public proposal to make Buenos Aires into an Olympic City had been partially fulfilled.[5]

In appraising this incomplete objective of Argentine desires to host the Olympic Games in Buenos Aires, it is worth mentioning that Torres has argued that the results of the Olympic city selection process should be considered as a legacy even if the ultimate objective wasn't met. Therefore, it is necessary to value the host cities' preparatory processes, although there are often political or managerial problems concerning the IOC, as was the case during Argentina's Centennial Olympic Games.[6]

In Argentina's attempt to host some sort of Olympic Games in 1910, the IOC and Coubertin's personal reaction was to inhibit the pretensions of the Argentine leadership, whose representatives were ex officio due to the fact that the country lacked a National Olympic Committee. According to Torres, the position of the IOC, after all, was to avoid weakening the Olympic Games through unauthorized local events. This restriction lasted until 1923, when an Argentine Olympic Committee was officially created. Furthermore, considering the upcoming 1924 Olympics in Paris, the new Argentine Olympic Committee prioritized the national representation of its athletes, thus delaying Buenos Aires's renewed Olympic aspirations.

Due to these changes, the desire to host the Olympic Games reemerged only in 1931, with the renewed push to host the 1936 Olympics in Buenos Aires. These controversial Games, contrary to Argentine aspirations, were granted to Berlin, which had offered better conditions for the mega-event.

This marked the first in a series of Olympic host rejections for Buenos Aires that continued until 1997, with the selection of Athens to host the 2004 Olympics.

However, the distinguishing factor to be considered respecting the 2004 Olympics is the innovative project developed by Buenos Aires to carry out this mega-event. In a rare alignment of public opinion and political elites—including the federal and local governments—with the support of the media and sport institutions, a movement to turn the city into a model of global impact emerged. Thus, as Torres argues, the Buenos Aires bid, which competed with ten other cities in the 1997 selection process, "was seen as a catalyst to showcase the progress of Argentina in the 1990s."[7]

Even without the expected success, the lesson of Buenos Aires can be understood through its significance in the projection of identity forces within the city and the country—forces that were mobilized by ideas emerging from the prevailing optimism of the time. In other words, a growing economy, sufficiently understood by the average citizen within the favorable political context of the end of the 1990s, ended up projecting the probable "conquest" of the Olympic Games.

The lingering aspirations associated with the candidacy for the 2004 Olympics, however, resurfaced in 2013 when Buenos Aires was selected by the IOC as the host city for the 2018 Youth Olympic Games (YOG). Since then, the earlier plans for an Olympic Buenos Aires have been revised and improved. Daniel de la Cueva, an Olympic Studies scholar, has constructed a narrative combining the conception of Buenos Aires for the 2004 Olympics with the updated versions for the 2018 YOG.[8] As such, this narrative confirms Torres's thesis, to whom the series of experiences undergone by the Argentine capital as a candidate for Olympic host city typify the concept of the Olympic legacy, as previously mentioned.

In fact, De la Cueva considers the YOG to be a mega-event very similar to the Olympic Games, since it brings together 3,800 athletes (fourteen to eighteen years old) and 206 nations, with competitions that are readapted by the very same twenty-eight international sport federations linked to the traditional Summer Olympics. In the specific case of Buenos Aires, the government—national and local—and the Argentine Olympic Committee (COA), took the opportunity of hosting the YOG to modernize the city, in continuity with the 2004 project. There was a return to the "Olympic Corridor" project, a three-kilometer extension bordering a zone adjacent to downtown, where sporting venues and green areas are located, along the Río de la Plata. The Estadio Monumental, the proposed original location of the opening and closing ceremonies of the event, is quite close to this corridor.

Furthermore, most of the facilities were already available at the time of the IOC selection process in 2013, thereby reducing costs and creating the objective conditions enabling Buenos Aires to beat Medellin and Glasgow, its competitors for the 2018 YOG. The use of the "Metrobus" (bus rapid transit) was also added to the project, improving traffic between the "centers"—that is, the facility aggregates for the twenty-eight modalities of the competition, including the Olympic Village, which would host the 3,800 athletes of the 2018 YOG.

According to de la Cueva, the new narrative of the YOG, building upon Buenos Aires's prior experiences in Olympic bids, referred to the YOG as a "catalyst" for both urban reform and improvements in transportation and living conditions for the city's population. These objectives were considered valid by locals in 2015, as highlighted in an opinion survey reported by de la Cueva showing that 82.3 percent of the population of Buenos Aires supported the YOG in the provision given to the public that same year.

Taking into consideration another distinguished Latin American sport historian, Joseph Arbena—who since the 1980s and for more than three decades has elaborated on the close relation between sport, national identity, and politics—Argentina's aspirations to influence the IOC and international sport in general also impacted that country's initiatives in leading the creation of the Pan-American Games.[9] As mentioned earlier, the Pan-American Games took shape in a congress held in Buenos Aires in 1940, bringing together countries from all of the Americas and the Caribbean. The first edition of the Pan-American Games was hosted in that same city in 1951, with two thousand athletes from twenty-one nations, generating increasing interest from more countries, as evidenced by the event's continuous expansion so far.

Facing the positive impacts of the Pan-American Games, Arbena's historiographical review highlights Buenos Aires's long struggle in its Olympic aspirations and geopolitical interests. Such aspirations and geopolitical interests have now lasted close to a century. These Argentine aspirations and interests within the Olympic Movement can be compared and contrasted with Mexico City and Rio de Janeiro. These comparisons generate increasingly important issues and significances, which will be addressed in the following sections.

1968 Mexico City Olympics: Identity and Change despite Political Confrontations

Regarding Mexico City's 1963 candidacy to host the 1968 Olympics, it is worthwhile to initially refer back to Joseph Arbena, who attributes this effort to the improvement of Mexico's image in the international sphere.[10] A very clear geopolitical project was thus developed, derived from typical Mexican strong nationalism, and was distinct from Argentina's search for national identity, as argued previously. Another difference between Argentina and Mexico revolves around the high number of researchers who have taken an interest in the 1968 Olympics in Mexico City. This wider attention on the first Olympic Games in Latin America contrasts to the experiences of Buenos Aires and Rio de Janeiro.

The explanation for wide-ranging research on the 1968 Mexico City Olympics, beyond the typical interests of Latin America and the Caribbean, is primarily linked to the international context of the Olympic Games during the 1960s. The Cold War between the then-existing Soviet Union and the United States and their respective allies projected itself onto the Mexico City Olympics, resulting in constant maneuvering by the IOC and other international entities aimed at settling diplomatic disputes before and during the Games.

Another specific aspect of the 1968 Olympics was the effect of Mexico City's altitude (2200 m) on the athletic competitions, which gave way to scientific controversies resulting, on occasion, in false news that compromised the organization of the event. The controversies and speculations of the Cold War, as well as the eventual ill effects of the high altitude, increased academic interest in the Mexican Olympics, which resulted in two early works of mine: one on the altitude issue published in 1968,[11] and another on the management of the Games published in 1969.[12]

Having mentioned these factors, it is worth leaving the specific aspects regarding the management of the 1968 Mexico City Olympics outside of the scope of this chapter to focus on the theme of national identity and geopolitics. This task was previously undertaken inter alia in 2015 by Brazilian researchers Barbara Almeida, André Capraro, and Wanderley Marchi, within a post hoc analytical perspective, to identify the factors of greater historical prominence of the Mexico City Olympics.[13]

In principle, Almeida and her collaborators coincide with Arbena in identifying that the explanation for awarding the 1968 Olympics to Mexico City, which is typically categorized as a "Third World" country by many, resided in the IOC's interest in raising the Games' international status. These Brazilian researchers concluded, after acknowledging that Mexico was experiencing an extraordinary period of economic growth in the decade of the 1960s, that

> the situation of the moment was one of growth for the country, which wasn't recognized internationally; on the other hand, external impressions were of continuous subordination and stereotypes of a dirty, desperate, unscrupulous people, or of vulnerable innocents, created years before by the American movie industry. The hope was of hosting a successful event to erase once and for all the image of corruption, inefficiency, and mistrust that clouded over Mexico and its people.[14]

From this standpoint, it isn't surprising that the leaders of the 1968 Mexico City Olympic project would act within a framework of national politics, differently from the Argentine case, whose leadership acted primarily in connection to sport and its circles. It is therefore possible to better understand the emphasis placed by Almeida et al. on the fact that the initial leadership of the Mexico City Olympic project was taken by Adolfo López Mateos (president of Mexico from 1958 to 1964), accompanied by José de Jesús Clark Flores (then-president of the Mexican Olympic Committee and future second Mexican member of the IOC) and Marte Gómez (former president of the Mexican Olympic Committee and member of the IOC).[15]

As a result, the 1968 Mexico City Olympic project became identified with its connections to the national government, incorporating the political attributes of the party in power at the time, the Institutional Revolutionary Party (PRI), and mainly of President Gustavo Díaz Ordaz (1964–70). This context was also pointed out by Arbena, who even placed a greater emphasis on the issue, stating that the 1968 Olympics highlighted aspirations that had been identified in Mexico since 1920, from a sport perspective, and even since 1910—the period of the Mexican Revolution—from a political perspective.[16]

The interplay between party politics and ideologies within the 1968 Olympics, however, resulted in the connection of this mega-event with assertive but controversial actions, as emphasized in the international repercussion of the antiracism protest by two African American athletes, Tommie Smith and John Carlos, during a track and field medal ceremony. Other important protests were promoted by students from the

National Autonomous University of Mexico during preparations for the 1968 Mexico City Olympics; these students created the famous chant: *¡No queremos olimpiadas, queremos revolución!* (We do not want Olympics, we want revolution!).[17]

The greater impact of the 1968 Mexico City Olympics was centered on the student movements. This was the result of a confrontation between activists and police forces of the Díaz Ordaz government on the eve of the event's opening ceremony, leading to more than two hundred deaths according to contemporary estimates, neither confirmed nor denied by the Mexican authorities. Almeida et al. provide some contextualization for this incident:

> The above-mentioned student protest, which was not exclusive to the Mexican case and was similar to others around the world, including in Brazil—the French protest known as May 1968 being the most notorious—was the result of the rejection of paternalistic authority and had multiple political contours from different fronts, such as the struggle for more democracy, freedom and jobs, and the fight against the wars of the period (this was the time of the Vietnam War, of armed struggles in Latin America and Africa and of the Cultural Revolution in China). The expression of this dissatisfaction in Mexico was happening in public spaces considered sacred by the government, and consisted of marches, speeches and physical confrontation. One of these protests, which took place days before the beginning of the Olympic Games and was concentrated in the *Plaza de las Tres Culturas,* would later be remembered as the Tlatelolco Massacre, which happened on the night of October 2, 1968.[18]

As often happens with political confrontations resulting in tragic results, the so-called Tlatelolco Massacre has received multiple interpretations. However, its contextualization within the Olympic Games has resulted in the formation of a group of specialized analysts that emerged at the end of the 1990s and the beginning of the 2000s, in North American and British universities. Within this context we can include scholars such as Eric Zolov (Stony Brook University, New York),[19] Amy Bass (The College of New Rochelle, New York),[20] Kevin B. Witherspoon (Lander University, South Carolina),[21] Keith Brewster and Claire Brewster (Newcastle University, United Kingdom),[22] and Luis Castañeda (Syracuse University, New York).[23]

Pertinent to my argument, Zolov maintains that the 1968 Mexico City Olympics helped to spearhead the prevailing idea of Mexican national identity, sometimes substituted by "modernization," which actually represents the common theme of the aforementioned scholars. A particularly significant conclusion in Zolov's work is that

> today, however, the 1968 Mexican Olympics are generally remembered either for the tragic massacre of unarmed students on the eve of the Opening Ceremony or alternately, for the image of silent protest by U.S. black athletes Tommie Smith and John Carlos at their awards ceremony five days into the Games. Moreover, these memories tend not to overlap. For Mexicans, images of repression have overshadowed all other aspects, while for Americans the Olympics have been largely telescoped into a single representation of black-gloved defiance. Lost in this narrowing of historical memory is a sense of the exuberance as well as conflicts and challenges that marked Mexico's staging of the Games.[24]

Taken together, the convergence of the current generation of North American and British analysts dedicated to the 1968 Olympics is characterized by the tendency to emphasize the political confrontations related to the event, but preserves as valid the "exuberant" narratives—as Zolov calls them—connected to the identity and change of the Mexican nation. As such, this interpretation is also highlighted in the work of Catañeda, an author from the most recent group of scholars on the Olympic Games in Mexico City.[25]

Of course, Castañeda's approach follows the timeline that brought the Olympic Games to Mexico City, as well as the political conflicts that derived from the event. However, Castañeda, an architect by profession and training, emphasizes the improvements in the Mexican megalopolis—with a population of 8.5 million in 1968—during the preparations for the Games, referencing the new subway lines that manage to sustain the growth of the city, whose current population is over 20 million. In summary, Castañeda brings to light the infrastructure improvements, emphasizing the creation of transportation systems in urban areas. To him, this represents innovation in design and technology that was equally successfully adopted in the sport venues of the Mexican Olympics.

According to Castañeda, the infrastructural improvements were developed under the leadership of Pedro Ramírez Vázquez, the architect who took over the direction of the Mexico City Olympic project from López Mateos, who, after finishing his presidential term, had become, albeit for a brief period, the head of the organizing committee. Ramírez Vázquez had one of the best technical portfolios of his country, and his conceptions guided the construction of all of the pavilions representing Mexico in World Fairs, as well as the main national museums of the 1960s. As Castañeda indicates, it is important to emphasize that Ramírez Vázquez took over all of the managerial responsibilities of the Mexico City Olympic project, which would help explain the positive results of the linkage between innovative concepts and practical applications displayed in Mexico City in 1968.

Coincidentally, my early study of the 1968 Mexico City Olympics published in 1969 follows a similar path to Castañeda's observations, paying greater attention to the improvements to the city's transportation system and to technological developments, especially with regard to sport competitions and management procedures.[26] In conclusion, the convergence of Castañeda and DaCosta, although separated by four decades, acknowledges and reinforces the vivid, constructive forces that were present in the midst of the political conflicts related to the Games.

This idea of local development could gain more relevancy upon considering the infrastructure aspects of the Buenos Aires experiences, as explained in the previous section, which would involve reasserting the core idea that sporting mega-events, especially the Olympic Games, create both positive and negative impacts. This theoretical proposal has received support from several scholars, such as Richard Cashman (University of New South Wales, Australia), a well-regarded researcher in Olympic Studies.[27]

The approach related to progress and retrogression is also found in the work of Claire Brewster, a historian and prominent member of the revisionist group of the Mexico City Olympics, who presents her conclusions on the "changing impressions" that occurred in the events of 1968:

> The Mexican Organising Committee wanted to use the 1968 Games to showcase its cultural, political and economic progress; to stand before the world as a nation very much in development; to promote Mexico as a great location to visit; a viable place in which to invest; a model of Latin American achievement and stability; a champion of Third World, non-aligned countries; the representative of the Spanish-speaking world; and, above all, a peaceful country that was at ease with itself. That the members of the Mexican Organising Committee were able to confound all the dire predictions made from Baden-Baden onwards was a credit to their organizational abilities, the support they received from political and sport authorities, and the goodwill of their own countrymen. In an effort to make sure

that Mexico's international image not only remained untarnished but actually improved as a result of hosting the Games, the Organizing Committee deployed everything at its disposal to stage-manage all aspects. Mexico had made considerable advances in the twentieth century. Certain sectors of society could, with some truthfulness, claim to have achieved First World status. Provided one did not dig too deeply, Mexico could claim to be a country that enjoyed good race relations; especially when compared to its Northern neighbour. Mexico City undoubtedly put on a good show for the duration of the Olympic Games. International impressions of Mexico did change, albeit only while the Olympic flame was burning in the national stadium. But as John Rodda has testified, the brutal suppression of the Student Movement revealed that the portrayal of Mexico as a peaceful country at ease with itself was nothing more than a thin veneer.[28]

In light of the insights by Brewster, and other scholars such as Cashman, it is fitting to consider that the Olympic Games and sporting mega-events in general should not be observed in terms of radical black-and-white views but through more nuanced, varied tonalities. In this search for coherence it is possible to acknowledge that the 1968 Mexico City Olympics—similar to Buenos Aires's long experience as candidate city to host the Olympic Games—resulted in guiding ideas and progress, as well as retrogressions, which are always subject to becoming lessons for building the future.

The organization of the FIFA Men's World Cup of 1970, also held in Mexico City and with a similar scale to the 1968 Olympics, reinforces the reinterpretation of multiple significances. This claim may be granted because there are still not enough analytical works to the 1970 mega-event exposed by mainstream English-speaking authors, as previously addressed. The same could be said for the FIFA Men's World Cup of 1986, another relatively successful mega-event that also took place in Mexico as a solution for the political and economic crisis affecting Colombia at the time, the original host country that had been selected by FIFA in 1974.

2016 Rio de Janeiro Olympics: Technological Change despite Economic and Political Crisis

In 2009, the city of Rio de Janeiro was chosen to host the 2016 Olympics through the bidding process established by the IOC and presented itself as the representative of South America, a subcontinent that had never hosted the Olympic Games. The calls for geographical recognition were widely reported in the international news media, and the argument was rewarded with a favorable vote by a majority of IOC members, who conceded Brazil's second-largest city the right to host the 2016 Olympic Games.

This fact reaffirmed Pierre de Coubertin's vision of sport as a geopolitical conduit, while also giving more significance to the search for improved international status on the part of Buenos Aires and Mexico City in their own candidacies to host the Olympics throughout the twentieth century. Arguably, also, the selection of Rio de Janeiro to host the 2016 Olympics offers an opportunity to compare and contrast the different positive and negative implications of the Olympic Games with the other two mega-cities analyzed so far in this chapter.

In retrospect, the assertion of Brazilian nationhood through Brazilian participation in the Olympic Games was initially researched by historian Marcia Neto-Wacker.[29] Neto-Wacker focuses her analysis on the creation in 1914 of the National Olympic Committee (CON) in Rio de Janeiro with the approval of the IOC; as it also addressed the nomination, in 1913, of the first Brazilian IOC member, Raul do Rio Branco, also made official by Coubertin. A distinguishing feature of this case is that the pioneering CON had members actively dedicated to sport, and Rio Branco was a career diplomat residing in Switzerland—both convenient factors for the geopolitical dimensions of the IOC, which, contrary to its claims, has always been a political institution.

From these starting points, the above-mentioned study reexamines Brazil's first participation in the Olympic Games with an official delegation present at the 1920 Antwerp Olympics (there had been a prior isolated participation by the Brazilian athlete Adolphe Klingelhoefer in the 1900 Paris Olympics). Neto-Walker overall documents the efforts by the delegation's chief, Roberto Trompowski, and by Rio Branco to convince Coubertin in face-to-face meetings to host the Olympic Games in Brazil. The opportunity for such an endeavor, which had been accepted, was for the Olympic event to coincide with the celebrations of the Brazilian Centennial of Independence in 1922.

Thus, the Brazilian petition reemployed the same strategy adopted by Argentina for the 1910 commemoration of that country's centennial celebration of its revolution for independence. But, in contrast to the unsuccessful attempt made by Buenos Aires, the IOC decided to support what was then called the "Regional Latin-American Olympic Games," which included an official recognition of the event.

According to Neto-Wacker, the interest by Brazilian leaders in obtaining greater international prestige was affecting other areas that could represent the country, not just sport. More recently, researchers including Neto-Wacker and Christian Wacker have concluded that the effort to bring the Olympic Games to Rio de Janeiro was also an alternative for the lack of both high-level athletes and the financial means to travel to faraway competitions. In other words, Brazilian sport was proving to be deficient and its leaders were appealing to compensatory alternatives, with the "importation" of the Olympic spectacle being the most viable, while meeting, on the other hand, the requirement for improved international status.[30]

In addition to Neto-Wacker's studies, it is important to mention a newspaper column that highlights the most salient consideration in hosting the Olympic Games in Brazil. In the July 2, 1919, edition of the newspaper *O Estado de São Paulo*, the writer seeks popular support for the Olympic Games in Rio de Janeiro or São Paulo. Reflecting the geo-politics of the event, this editorial attacked France, which was also seeking to host the Games in 1920, saying that France was "employing all its efforts to host the first Olympics of the post-War period in its territory, an Olympics to which we have now had the right to host for many years." The writer also mentions that "the French have argued that we are not prepared to compete for the Olympic Games nor to conduct them on our territory, which does not yet have a national stadium."[31]

Judging by the *O Estado de São Paulo* campaign—a very prestigious media outlet in the country at the time—the reactions to Brazilian Olympic ambitions at the beginning of the twentieth century were similar to the rejections suffered by Buenos Aires, and later by Mexico City. And, as with Buenos Aires, Rio de Janeiro experienced four unsuccessful attempts (the candidacies for the Olympic Games of 1936, 1940, 1956, and 2004) in addition to the rejection of Brasilia's candidacy for the 2000 Olympic Games.

Following the selection of Mexico City for the 1968 Olympics, Rio de Janeiro achieved its long-awaited victory in 2009, when it won the bid for the 2016 Olympics. Thus far, the context of the 2016 Rio de Janeiro Olympics did not present international pressures in the style of the Cold War, although there was a sort of international rebellion against the event due to the risks associated with the contagious Zika virus, an epidemiological threat later proved to be exaggerated.[32] In other words, the Zika virus played a similar role to the Mexican high altitude. This political crisis, reinforced by economic insecurity, created instability throughout Brazil, but without the serious conflicts that occurred in 1968 in Mexico City.

While taking into account the similarities between Mexico City in 1968 and Rio de Janeiro in 2016, there should also be an emphasis on the improvements in public transportation (the Metro and bus rapid transit) and the restoration of public spaces in the urban center of Rio de Janeiro, which were recognized nationally and internationally. However, these improvements occurred within an environment of corruption and suspicion, beginning with the selection of the city during the bidding process that resulted in the abandonment of important non-Olympics projects for the development of the city (e.g., the depollution of Guanabara Bay): a situation that did not occur under the much-admired management of Ramírez Vázquez in Mexico City in 1968.

With this in mind, the previously discussed analysis of Latin American and Caribbean sport historiography, which equated certain infrastructural advances and sociocultural improvements and contrasted them with retrogressions as an "eclectic" development, still applies. I raise this point in the conclusion of the book *Sport and Latin American Society: Past and Present*, which I coedited with James A. Mangan. Eclecticism is an approach that draws upon multiple theories combined by different analytical interpretations and is the framework found appropriate in the conclusion of the book for reviewing the history of sport in South and Central America in addition to some Caribbean countries.[33] There, I contend that the cultural specificity of sport in Latin American and Caribbean countries is similar to European social and cultural experiments: "sometimes perverse, sometimes productive, sometimes beneficial."[34] With this in mind, let us move to some concluding remarks.

Conclusion

The Olympic Games of Mexico City and Rio de Janeiro prove again the need to adopt a framework that allows for eclectic significances and interpretations, with distinct nuances in terms of progress and retrogression. In the latter example, according to post hoc observations I published recently, there was popular support for the Games, giving continuity to the success in attendance and the support of the local media that had characterized the 2007 Pan-American Games and the 2014 FIFA Men's World Cup, both hosted in the same city.[35]

There had been, then, a convergence of three mega-events within a ten-year period held in the same location, Rio de Janeiro. This arrangement had been previously tested in Mexico City, with the juxtaposition of the 1968 Olympics and the Men's World Cups of 1970 and 1986 on a possibly lesser scale than the events in Rio de Janeiro, but with the support of significant public groups, as mentioned previously.

The technological innovations, on the other hand, that had been so well developed for and implemented in the 1968 Olympics, especially when aligned with design projects in urban spaces and sporting venues, were not repeated in the 2016 Olympics. However, digital technology per se did dominate the Rio de Janeiro Olympics and its relationship with the city and its population, and included the full participation of the digital globalized world. As such, the assumptions of the present chapter are situated within unprecedented digital development, insofar as it emphasizes the benefits of digital technology as the greater influence of the 2016 Olympics, even in the face of an economic and political crisis of national scope.

A similar insight has been gained by the organizers of the 2018 YOG in Buenos Aires, who, as judged by Daniel de la Cueva, defended the proposition that Olympic mega-events serve as "catalysts" for the host cities' urban and social development. In this sense, there is an acknowledgement that the 2018 YOG also aim to: (1) act as a platform for initiatives within the Olympic Movement; (2) represent an event of the highest international level for youth; (3) connect youth to Olympic sport through digital technology; and (4) generate a platform to develop YOG and to offer true business innovation.

De la Cueva's observations effectively take up the recommendations of the so-called Olympic Agenda 2020, which has been and will continue to be addressed by the IOC session. These recommendations include that the committee establishes its priorities regarding youth and digital technology (virtual hubs) in building a future for the Olympic Movement. In other words, the experiences of Mexico City, Rio de Janeiro, and Buenos Aires converge in an axis that spans the period between 1968 and 2018, rendered historically significant by its long duration.

However, the lessons learned in this half-century show that several advances resulted from the innovations adopted by these three major cities, whereas setbacks were overcome by understanding the Olympic Games as catalysts for managerial and social transformation—expectations that were shared by the local populations of these large urban centers. Specifically, this acknowledgement also includes the constructive aspect of the Pan-American Games (which have been constantly renewed for over almost seven decades) and of the YOG, a more recent event but with prior commitment to local development, as exemplified in the initiatives of Buenos Aires.

In these dynamic experiences by Buenos Aires, Mexico City, and Rio de Janeiro there is a final definition of the contributions to be passed on to other cities of Latin America and the Caribbean as they search for a stronger and better relationship with the Olympic Movement. And if the objective of future relations is of a geopolitical nature, then the solutions experienced by the three cities reviewed here could provide updated implications and significances for the proposition that social and technological development anticipate and render feasible the projection of national and local power in the international sporting arena.

A Brief Excursion into the Future

Indeed, beyond the better international image long pursued by Buenos Aires, Mexico City, and Rio de Janeiro, there is a new era of social interactions. This change, from today's perspectives, may renovate sport mega-events, as Leonardo Mataruna et al. have recently demonstrated, in projecting the future of the Olympic Games as embedded in digital society.[36]

This new social and cultural environment, as previously depicted by sociologists Siti Ezaleila Mustafa and Azizah Hamzah, is "an era that emphasized interactive communication compared to oral, writing, print, and telecommunication in the previous development of human communication. This shows that communication modes are changing and has now crossed such distances with the help of computerization and digital technology especially the emergence of Internet and its various new applications."[37] For these researchers, the digital sphere today has reached all corners of the world, regardless of the stage of development of each particular nation.

Unsurprisingly, the 2016 Rio de Janeiro Olympics revealed themselves a showcase of digital technology. In this respect, postevent reports from the IOC highlighted the 2016 Olympics as the most consumed Games ever, taking into consideration coverage viewed on television and on digital platforms, as well as engagement on social media. Broadcasters around the world made more television coverage and more digital-based connections available than ever before: over 350,000 hours for the 2016

Rio de Janeiro Olympics, compared to almost 200,000 hours for the 2012 London Olympics. Moreover, half the world's population watched images and sounds from the former, which also brought up over seven billion views of official content on social media platforms.[38]

In light of these numbers, the IOC considers the 2016 Olympic Games in Rio de Janeiro a landmark in terms of the visibility and awareness of the Olympic Games.[39] This worldwide impact had local audiences as its point of departure, a cause and effect that I previously posited in 2016 in a public preview of the Games in Rio.[40] Certainly, since 1922 the city of Rio de Janeiro has been showing supportive connections with sport mega-events, as experienced by the already-extinguished Latin American Olympic Games—aforementioned in this chapter—shared by most of the local population. More recently, the 2007 Pan-American Games, also hosted by Rio de Janeiro, were again a successful undertaking in terms of shareholders, despite their management pitfalls.

Historically speaking, my predictive approach suggested that traditional support of sport spectators in Rio de Janeiro could have been made even more meaningful through the "inspirational" reaction and the civic self-valorization that emerged from the 2012 London Olympics' local audiences. This soft patriotism in the case of the 2016 Rio Olympics apparently stood as a scenario for local citizenship's symbolic actions. Aside from local idiosyncrasies, another similarity could be pointed out when reviewing the "inspiration" that emerged in the Mexican sport mega-events of 1968, 1970, and 1986, as already discussed here.

Regardless of the reason for these disruptions in the Rio de Janeiro Olympics without the participation of decision-makers from either the Games or the government, there is a growing acceptance of a theoretical approach to the 2016 Olympics as mixed with a World Fair–like promotion, mostly created by the Hospitality Houses, associated with an amplified digital connectivity of the city's life. Six months after the 2016 Rio Olympics, I collected data on the relationships of these Hospitality Houses with the main environment of sport events.[41] In this regard, the map in Image 9.1 delineates the connectivity belt exhibited by the Rio de Janeiro Olympics as seen in its four locations of venues by means of selected extraevent opportunities.

Arguably, Rio de Janeiro became a nonplanned "smart city" during the 2016 Olympics on account of a technological "invasion" in addition to "off-Rio 2016" events mostly carried on by Hospitality Houses and other marketing efforts. Symptomatically, data I forwarded in the 2017 post hoc

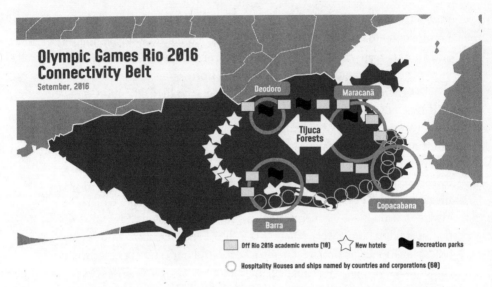

Image 9.1. Connectivity Belt, 2016 Rio de Janeiro Olympics. *Courtesy of the author.*

investigation revealed that four million people had accessed those participation opportunities, while eight million attended the sport competitions.

In conclusion, Rio de Janeiro's digital experience was a step forward in relation to Buenos Aires (urban renovation) and Mexico City (technological innovation), with connectivity as a guiding principle, as learned throughout the 2016 Olympics developments. These advancements, however, must be considered together with negative impacts, as previously addressed here, for these three megalopolises. Overall, the future Olympic Games are apparently turning into a multimedia platform shaped by outside innovative pressures with a digital step-change that now requires a major analytical reconfiguration from scholars dedicated to Olympic Studies.

Having said this, it is clear that the suggested directions of the Olympic Games are consistent with the new approaches of Olympic Agenda 2020 assumed by the IOC in 2014. As such, this new policy is a roadmap with a series of recommendations that should be adopted and managed in the coming years in order to make the Olympics even more appealing for our contemporary societies.[42] Therefore, putting the focus on Latin America and the Caribbean in order to meet the tri-cities experience of Buenos Aires, Mexico City, and Rio in addition to Olympic

Agenda 2020, there are point-specific recommendations to meet locally correct pathways toward future relationships with the Olympic Games' selective choices.

To put it briefly, recommendations 20 and 23 of Olympic Agenda 2020 promote "virtual hubs" as a major approach to implement or ameliorate management functions of all Olympic Movement's institutions, operations and stakeholders' functions, connecting athletes, volunteers, leaders, and sponsors, among others. In this sense, those new digital platforms are potentially able to bring national and international adherents of the Olympic idea closer together to seek online exchange of information, support, knowledge, and insights.

More important, the first recommendation of Olympic Agenda 2020 focuses on sustainability, proposing "maximum use of existing facilities and the use of temporary and demountable venues" by future host cities of the Olympic Games. [43] Also in the same pledge, the IOC is urged "to allow, for the Olympic Games, the organization of preliminary competitions outside the host city or, in exceptional cases, outside the host country, notably for reasons of sustainability."

In other words, after the 2016 Rio de Janeiro Olympics, the next generation of the event—hosted by any continent or region—is expected to be a lively digital marketing undertaking. Moreover, cities and countries with less political or economic power (especially from Latin America and the Caribbean) shall look forward to updated and low-cost, sustainable conditions as opposed to the high-cost requirements demanded in the past by megacities from the same continental region.

Ultimately, the challenges for the Olympic Movement's shareholders from Latin America and the Caribbean that lie ahead shall now center on Olympic geopolitical traditions from Buenos Aires, Mexico City, and Rio de Janeiro as well as the search of solutions to renew the Olympic Games and other mega-events by means of technological and cooperative management innovations. After all, future partnerships will need to inspire each other to change.

CONCLUSION

CHRISTOPHER GAFFNEY

The 2016 Rio de Janeiro Olympics brought into sharp relief the contradictions and permanent state of crisis of the Olympic Movement in Latin America. On the one hand, the 2016 Olympics were full of brilliant athletic and managerial achievements that used Rio de Janeiro as a highly functional stage for the latest iteration of the global spectacle. On the other hand, the 2016 Olympics were notoriously corrupt and destructive—an unparalleled opportunity for feckless politicians, Olympic officials, and brazen sport executives to raid public coffers and enrich cronies, leaving the city worse off than it was before. The lasting damage to the Olympic Movement in terms of image and prestige has been matched by a decline in the public funding of all sports in Brazil and a wretched legacy of abandoned venues, half-baked urbanization projects, and spiraling opportunity costs.

Yet, as the authors of the preceding chapters remind us, the inexorable connections between sport, politics, ideology, and the exercise of power have always been part of the Olympic Movement in Latin America. The case studies in this book reveal, yet again, that sport is much more than the tallying of records, achievements, statistics, and glories. The authors in this volume show us, once again, that sport is always political, personal, economic, and ideological. Indeed, these are the constituent elements that should always inform larger discussions about the games we play and watch.

As I write these remarks, in mid-2018, the Olympic Movement appears to be in an intractable and permanent state of crisis. Carlos Nuzman—longtime International Olympic Committee (IOC) member, former president of the Brazilian Olympic Committee, and head of the organizing committee of the 2016 Rio de Janeiro Olympics—is under house arrest and has had his assets frozen as part of an ongoing international investigation into corruption, bribery, and influence peddling. The Irishman Patrick Hickey, president of the European Olympic Committees, spent time in a Rio de Janeiro jail on charges of illegally selling tickets. The Russian Olympic team was (partially) banned from the 2018 Olympic Winter Games for state-sponsored doping. The Fédération Internationale de Football Association (FIFA) case being prosecuted in Brooklyn focuses on the corrupt practices of football officials from Latin America, many of whom have close connections to the Olympic Movements in their countries. It would appear that there are systemic problems in the governance of global sport as a whole and in Latin America in particular.

If we ignore the machinations of the *cartolas* (top hats) and focus on Latin American Olympic performance, we discover that there is also significant room for improvement. Taking the last three Olympic Games (Beijing 2008, London 2012, and Rio de Janeiro 2016), Latin American and Caribbean countries, including Jamaica, have won 7.9 percent, 6 percent, and 6.5 percent of all medals. If Jamaica is removed from the equation, the tally falls to 6.9 percent, 4.8 percent, and 5.1 percent of all medals awarded in those respective Games (see Image Conclusion 1). While there is more comparative research to be done in this regard (and it is important to remember that getting to the podium is not the only measure of success), there are indications that the cultural systems associated with Olympism either did not take deep root in the region, or that those roots have been degraded by feckless elitism and gross mismanagement.

The Olympic Games are elitist by design and popular acclamation. It is human nature to see who can run faster, jump higher, throw further, and lift more weight. The motto of the Olympic Movement—*citius, altius, fortius*—is a clarion call for ever-grander human performances, an ideology rooted in the paternalistic positivism of Pierre de Coubertin and his fin-de-siècle contemporaries. In the broad sweep of Latin American and Caribbean history, the Olympic Movement is a relative latecomer, but it did emerge onto the scene in a critical era of state formation and consolidation. As is well known, Latin American and Caribbean elites looked to Europe and the United States for social and political models where positivism and eugenics were in vogue. In relatively new nation-states with weak national traditions, sport (particularly football, and baseball in the Spanish Caribbean) was an important tool in consolidating populations that had few common traditions, symbols, and shared experiences. That the symbols and practices of Olympic sport were imagined and controlled by national elites is no surprise, but what we have learned in these pages is the extent to which those practices were embedded in national politics, identity constructs, governmental ideologies, and international

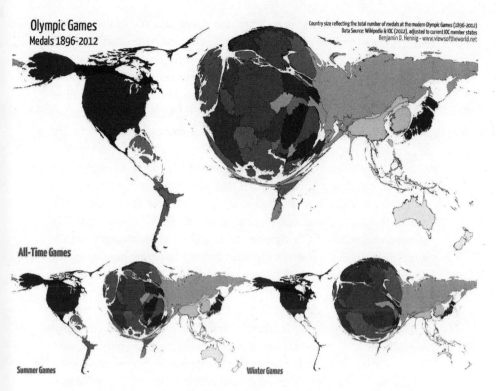

Olympic Games
Medals 1896-2012

Country size reflecting the total number of medals at the modern Olympic Games (1896-2012)
Data Source: Wikipedia & IOC (2012), adjusted to current IOC member states
Benjamin D. Hennig - www.viewsoftheworld.net

All-Time Games

Summer Games

Winter Games

Image Conclusion 1. Cartogram of Olympic Medals by country (1896–2012).
Courtesy of Benjamin D. Hennig and www.viewsoftheworld.net[1]

geopolitics. In the world's most murderous region, where the basic questions of civil rights, sanitation, education, housing, and transportation are far from being resolved, the performance of and adherence to the Olympic ideal can only further the systemic and acute crises that define Latin America and the Caribbean.

Within this context, however, we are inevitably drawn to the fascinating and inspiring trajectories of athletes as they reduce and expand human agency. On the one hand, athletes are quintessential representatives of the nation: donning the colors, saluting the flag, and engaging in proxy wars vis-à-vis competitions for the accumulation of precious metals. In this sense, they are no longer themselves but reductive objects onto which national desires, hopes, and aspirations can be pinned. On the other hand, athletes are bigger than themselves and have to negotiate sporting, political, and media spheres in uncomfortable and impactful ways. They may obtain heroic or iconic status—a condition that masks reality but ensures cultural longevity while opening avenues for appropriation. They establish connections across space and time, travel the world, and are active agents of internationalization, no matter how humble or rural their origins.

Yet it is not just athletes who make connections, but also the fans, the mayors of cities that host events, those that work to construct and operate sport facilities, and those embedded within sport bureaucracies. The persistent corruption, sexual-abuse scandals, unfulfilled promises, and deliberate underdevelopment of robust and transparent sporting institutions guarantee cycles of crisis and public recrimination. Making sense of the transits between personal narratives and the messy spaces of institutions is at the crux of critical analyses of sport. Add to this the mediated spectacles of Olympic events and their associated opportunities for international networking among politicians, sport managers, and businesspeople, and the world of sport looks more like a wormhole than an identifiable field of research.

However, you are not holding a wormhole, but a thoughtfully crafted collection of scholarship that takes us through the history and culture of Olympism in Latin America and the Caribbean. In what follows, I will offer my comments and reflections on the chapters here presented, identifying what I see as critical issues raised and questions (perhaps) unanswered. As we move through Uruguay, Cuba, Mexico, Puerto Rico, Brazil, Argentina, Dominican Republic, Colombia, and back to Argentina, Brazil, and Mexico, I hope to offer both readers and authors food for further thought and reflection. My intention is to be summative and provocative, engaging the ideas and narratives presented in this volume as a commentator, critic, and practitioner of sport.

Starting with Uruguay, Shunsuke Matsuo reveals some of the earliest examples of the ways in which sport was integrated into the national bureaucratic apparatus. The incorporation of the Comisión Nacional de Educación Física (National Committee of Physical Education) and the Young Men's Christian Association (YMCA) into the core of state bureaucracy was a mechanism through which the paternalistic Uruguayan state pushed visions of the nation through racial and class categories. Positively, the government demonstrated itself capable of developing public sport grounds and integrating them into urban development, fostering sport education programs and sport institutions, as well as diffusing "healthy" practices and a wider sporting culture. Problematically, the politicians of early twentieth-century Uruguay used sport as a template to fashion a national narrative that suited their positivist, masculine (read: antifeminist) ideologies.

The Uruguayan case shows us how, from the beginning of the Olympic Movement, the IOC positioned itself as an arbiter of what could and could not be done in its member countries in regards to national sport policy. The neocolonialist reach of the Swiss nonprofit was bolstered by the eugenic ideology of many IOC members. However, in the Uruguayan case, we see an engagement with the redistributive possibilities of sport quite early in the twentieth century. The successes of the Uruguayan football team at the 1924 and 1928 Olympics remain the only gold medals that country has won. Importantly, these were official world championships and reflected the rootedness of an innovative sport culture along the banks of the Río de la Plata.

Matsuo explores how the nascent sporting cultures in the region were fertilized with the untiring efforts of key individuals who managed to create institutional frameworks within which they could gather resources and wield legitimacy. As Montevideo has always dominated Uruguayan politics, the concentrated efforts of key people in the leading political parties combined with the proselytizing zeal of the YMCA and the IOC to transform the capital into a serious contender to host the Olympic Games. While they ultimately failed in this attempt, it was no accident that Uruguay subsequently hosted the first FIFA Men's World Cup in 1930. One wonders what a more completely national policy of sport development would have looked like, and whether or not the starkly uneven development of Uruguay's urban, economic, and political systems could have been challenged, rather than reinforced, through sport.

In the context of Cuban nationalism, Thomas Carter ably demonstrates that "Olympism is a flexible ideological tool that allows for its adoption under a range of political ideologies." In the early twentieth century, this meant that the Olympic Games were used in the intertwined projects of industrial capitalism and settler colonialism. Carter suggests that Olympism is the ideological equivalent of water, which it will find its natural level and conform to the contours of its vessel.

That the Cuban government used sport as part of a nation-building project in the twentieth century will surprise no one. That political elites in the 1910s and early 1920s were so eager to spend lavishly to demonstrate Cuban "progress, civilization, and technological sophistication" lays bare the linkages between sport-related ideologies, internal political dialogues, and foreign perceptions of the Cuban nation.

Cuba's modern history can be read through the prism of sport like few others. The meetings between the Spanish Fascist and IOC president Juan Antonio Samaranch and Fidel Castro indicate the degree of power that leading politicians afford to the president of the IOC. Fidel's outsized role as the president-sportsman strongly influenced the trajectory of the Cuban sporting complex, but with the dissolution of the Soviet Union and prolonged economic troubles, there are neither finances nor facilities to train world class athletes. This may be just as well, as in times of scarcity, it is indeed hard to argue for high-caloric diets for a few thousand elite bodies. This is but one way in which the continually unfolding crisis of Cuba's political economy is reflected in sport. The tendrils of the revolution run deep, however, and Cuba continues to exhibit strong national emotions with its teams and sportspeople. How those relationships and cultures shift over the coming decades will tell us much about life on the island.

Keith Brewster and Claire Brewster's analysis of the development of sport as a tool in managing inter-American cultural diplomacy highlights the correlation between a set of Olympic values (not far developed from the positivist eugenics of Coubertin) with professed sporting values in post-revolutionary Mexico. The confluence of these ideological systems helped to create a sense of greater geopolitical stability not only in Mexico but throughout Central America. The authors' exploration of the early Central American Games reveals how Olympic sport provided national elites and international observers access to a mutually intelligible world. This ever-more-legible, official, and sanctioned sporting universe showed the international sporting and political communities that some Mexicans and Central Americans knew the rules of the Games and could perform rituals of national coherence (and international adherence) in modern sporting arenas.

Given that, in 1926, when the first Central American Games were hosted in Mexico City, the country's population was primarily rural and that the vast majority of urban residents were poor, with little access to institutionalized sport and perhaps even less familiarity with the norms and mores of Olympism, it is fair to question the extent to which these excursions in nation building and internationalism impacted upon cultural and political dynamics for the majority of Mexicans. For most, the emotional and affective reach of Olympism was probably decades away, reaching its brief apogee in 1968. In the 1920s, fútbol had only recently consolidated as an urban cultural phenomenon and was beginning to gain important associations with the nation-state and its symbolic system. Given this, we probably assume that the early Central American Games were not mass cultural events and as such had little diffusion beyond the literate (and limited) upper and middle classes.

However, what we can assume with more certainty is that these kinds of events were excellent opportunities for national, regional, and international political and economic elites to meet each other. The action in the directors' box and the resulting partnerships, alliances, business deals, and network-making is never reflected in medal tallies. Sport as a tool in nascent diplomatic relations between relatively young states (especially in post-1917 Mexico) could only be effective if there were people with power and influence there to wield it. Much of the history of Olympism in Latin America and the Caribbean can be told as a story of elites meeting each other within the ideological, geographical, and historical boundaries of sport. From the distance of a *hacienda*, the northern, pasty visages of Avery Brundage and Samaranch were indistinguishable from the *patrón* or *coronel*. They offer similar words about development and the "indigenous capacity" to organize (on time, please, never mind the budget), while professing that the nation is strong because patriotic, disciplined bodies meet in competition with brothers (not yet sisters) from the region in order to express mutual admiration and to contribute to ever-increasing human prosperity and wellness. It is righteous, it is good, and because it is the nation, it is yours. But was it? Is it?

Olympism is always operating on multiple, intersecting, and mutually constitutive levels. Politics, national rituals, and sport are pushed by geopolitical currents that shape media discourse and public perception. Hosting sporting events is projected by rights holders and national elites as an honor and an opportunity, but we should never lose sight of the fact that the Olympic Games are always an exercise in and of power. Those in power use the Olympic Games to consolidate the exercise of that power, exacerbating social and economic divides through populist spectacles.

Reading Antonio Sotomayor's chapter in the wake of Hurricane Maria, I was struck by the enervating and enduring colonial condition of Puerto Rico. That the United States has not been a good hemispheric neighbor is not news. What is surprising is the degree to which sport has functioned as an instrument of empire as US forces brought their baseball bats along with their rifles. Puerto Ricans were early practitioners of "politicized sport," and activists were able to link the massive anticolonial protests of the 1950s with open defiance from athletes, delegations, and officials.

In 1948, Puerto Rico's first Olympic medal was connected to the island's sovereignty movement. This made the Olympic Games an ironic site for the contestation of imperial power, linking Puerto Rico's tragic relationship with the United States to the history of sport and independence movements. In this context, Puerto Rican sport has long been a site where the islanders can negotiate US imperialism. However, and as is frequently the case, there was not much dialogue between national-level politicians of the Partido Nacionalista and the athletes relative to the adaptation or rejection of the mark of settler colonialism: the US flag. Eventually, once Puerto Rico became a US dependency and had its own flag, people woke up to the power of sport to articulate political resistance—sadly, though, the moment had passed.

All too often the Olympic Movement is used by large powers to position themselves geopolitically (Beijing 2008, Sochi 2014), to signal global emergence (Mexico City 1968, Seoul 1988, Rio de Janeiro 2016), or to turn a quick buck (Los Angeles 1984, Atlanta 1996, London 2012, Paris 2024). From the example of Puerto Rico we see that the Olympic Games have the potential to be used as a weapon of the weak, creating highly visible and politically fraught spaces for battles over national sovereignty. While the Games did not and cannot resolve Puerto Rico's enduring predicament, they can on occasion serve as a mechanism through which sociopolitical crises can be publically approached. It would be fascinating to understand the importance of Monica Puig's 2016 gold medal in tennis in relation to the ongoing social, economic, and political crises in Puerto Rico. One gets the sense that the moment of victory never endures long enough to make a difference.

Fabio de Faria Peres and Victor Andrade de Melo launch us into the world of Adhemar Ferreira da Silva, one of the mid-century heroes of the Brazilian Olympic Movement. In a period of national optimism, economic growth, and urban expansion, da Silva was a "typical" Brazilian: black, urban, working-class, and ascendant. What was not typical was his ability at the triple jump that helped him win gold at Helsinki in 1952 and Melbourne in 1956. If the public hand-wringing over Brazil's loss to Uruguay in the Maracanã was painful and unresolved, it was because *futebol* had already established itself by 1950 as the principle vehicle for national identity. What Peres and Melo show us is how similar projections came to be placed upon a single individual—perhaps without risking quite so much national pride.

The idea that "Brazil" was sending out one man to defend the nation might not have happened in similar ways if that individual were a white sailor or shooter. While it is interesting to look at the ways in which newspapers reported the story, the language used in relation to subaltern subjects should be compared to other representations. While there is no reason to doubt that da Silva was "a model of the abdication and dedication that characterize national martyrs," there is also a sense of tokenism lingering in the background, particularly in regard to the way he was treated by his employers and the Brazilian sport authorities. When Peres and Melo write that the "valorization of his achievements could not mask the injustices of various orders that surrounded the Brazilian population, including those of a racial nature," they confirm the limited power of sport to change fundamental social structures.

There is also the ever-present problem of conflating what "the Brazilians" thought or imagined by limiting the analytic frame to the major newspapers in the wealthiest cities. Even within the context of the relatively developed southeast, the interior of Rio de Janeiro and São Paulo States remained in the agrarian molds of the nineteenth century and in the 1950s Brazil's literacy rate was only about 50 percent. Thus, we need to constantly remind ourselves of the limited context and limited scope of influence that the press might have had. While it may be true that millions of Brazilians listened to da Silva's Olympic exploits on the radio, it is too much to claim that obtaining a gold medal in the triple jump was an expression of the country's desires. Similarly, the official narratives surrounding the 2014 FIFA Men's World Cup and 2016 Olympics naturalized the "necessity" of building world-class stadia and airports that the vast majority of Brazilians will never use.

It is not too much to say, however, that Brazilian elites measure the efficacy of their development model with the metrics of athletic performance on the global stage. This was one of the reasons that the *maracanaço* continues to haunt the Brazilian psyche: it was taken as an enduring sign of Brazil's mongrel complex, or *complexo de vira-lata*. The success of da Silva was an indication that all of Brazil's black, urban working class could succeed under the given structural conditions. Those that jumped to "defend the nation" were bearers of national virtue and became the unwitting standard bearers for the propagation of Brazil's myth of "racial democracy." Similarly, when Neymar flops, Brazil flops with him.

Cesar R. Torres boils the "problem of Argentine sport" during the 1940s and 1950s down to a few interrelated elements. Since the early years of Juan Domingo Perón, sport has been used as a social technology, as a tool for cultural diplomacy, a state-centric political control mechanism that indoctrinates and guides the body politic, a means to increase consumption, and a means of manufacturing consensus and engaging with the international community. If that seems like a lot to put on sport, think of the massive state apparatus that Perón and subsequent populist leaders in Argentina have had at their disposal.

Torres shows how Perón mobilized the Argentine state to diffuse and organize sport through institutional frameworks and public spectacles that operated in the service of state power. With this power ever more concentrated in his hands, sport became increasingly associated with the state and its figurehead. Thus, when the government, or the economy, entered into crisis, sport either anticipated or followed it. There was nothing organic about Perón's use of sport, and, after his overthrow, the wealthy institutions that he created wanted to maintain the status quo and resisted "heavy handed interventions." The IOC, expressing an inimitable tone-deafness, considered any state intervention into sport institutions as "undue influence" and threatened to prohibit Argentine participation in the 1956 Olympics. It was fine when Perón was using the state to disseminate their ideological delicacies, but when the Argentine state tried to regulate the actions of their state-centric predecessor, they were rebuffed by the Swiss nonprofit.

A series of internecine conflicts erupted in the wake of Perón's overthrow, with details of intrigue and double-dealing that are reminiscent of the 2017–18 FIFA trials in the United States. The corruption associated with Argentine football has been at the center of unfolding revelations in FIFAgate. Political figures such as Néstor Kirchner and Cristina F. de Kirchner had close contacts with Argentina's sporting dons and Argentina's current president, Mauricio Macri, was president of Club Atlético Boca Juniors. If, as was the case in the period explored by Torres, the depoliticization of sport can only be achieved through politics—something that no politician is ever likely to take up as an abiding cause—then Argentina will continue as an Olympic minnow. This may be the "problem of sport" writ large, and we can fruitfully examine the Argentine case to understand the likely outcomes.

In the 1960s and 1970s, the Dominican Republic was experimenting with forms of social justice inspired by Cuba and the Soviet Union. Strongman Joaquín Balaguer promoted his "Third Way" development model predicated on a heavy paternalistic hand and heavy public investment in infrastructure. April Yoder focuses on the realization of the XII

Central American and Caribbean Games in 1974 as a key moment in which to examine the geopolitical situatedness of athletic performance under extraordinary political conditions.

This story will be familiar to Argentines who lived through the 1978 FIFA Men's World Cup, to Chileans under Augusto Pinochet, to Nicaraguans under the Somozas, to Cubans under the Castros, or to late Imperial Romans. But the hosting of "Games" in the Dominican Republic in 1974 was used explicitly as a mechanism to deliver popular projects as a means of avoiding political crisis and "facilitated this paternalism in the Third Way by creating a dialogue between the Balaguer government and the people about popular needs and desires for sport."

The case of the Dominican Republic is interesting in that it appears that sport authorities drew inspiration from the Cuban example of state-sponsored sport and encouraged Balaguer to adopt some of its most redistributive practices. One early success, and a legacy of the XII Central American and Caribbean Games, was increased female participation in sport. It would appear that there were some social gains from hosting, particularly in a reimagining of the female body and the role of women in the body politic of the nation: "Wholesome women in a public and national interest." The significant gains made by women in the public sporting arena would not be matched in economic or political spheres, but the leverage provided by hosting an international sporting event afforded a significant shift in public policy and cultural perceptions about women athletes. This again raises the question of the pursuit of large-scale sporting events, with their inevitably exaggerated costs and social exclusions, as a mechanism to pursue nominal egalitarianism.

The Colombian powerlifter Fabio Torres is another example of a poor black male who entered into national consciousness through athletic exploits. Chloe Rutter-Jensen suggests that Torres was (is) able to complicate a normative biopolitics by challenging gender, racial, and physical stereotypes through extraordinary physical feats. What she calls "enfleshment" is acted out through the rituals of Olympism, transmitted through the media, and internalized into national consciousness. Interestingly, there are differences between the ways in which this happens in Olympic versus Paralympic bodies. The former are understood as extraordinarily normative in that they conjure ideal form and functions of the human body, and the latter are taken as examples of extraordinary nonnormativity, with performative limitations integrated into athletic performance.

Of particular interest in this case, the relative dysfunction of the

Colombian body politic created an athlete who "would like to show how his body challenges the nation as such, and narrates an ethical subjectivity which is radical and useful" as a larger political move to decouple that body from its national imprimatur. It is perhaps only through performing on an international stage that Torres's body, "black, impoverished, and disabled," can articulate the nonnormative in a country wracked by decades of civil war that is only now emerging from a seemingly intractable political crisis to come to terms with its recent past and present future. Torres is but one subject-victim of the nonnormative condition of civil war, but far from the only one. It is interesting to speculate about the relative equivalence given to Olympic and Paralympic athletes in Colombia, but, in a country with few Olympic traditions, it is difficult to tell the degree to which these debates have broader political resonance. Again, one element of the crisis of Olympism in Latin America and the Caribbean might be that no one pays much attention.

As we see throughout this study, the human body is a site of contestation, projection, and conflict—a hugely important focus for sport scholars. Yet we need to tread carefully when distinguishing between objects and subjects, Olympic and Paralympics, humans, more-than-humans, and cyborgs. It is far too easy to revert to fundamental binaries and to project our thoughts and philosophies onto those who may not have any idea what we are talking about. It would be interesting to hear what Torres has to say about his subjectivities, contradictions, and paradoxes, or whether he is at all comfortable representing "all Colombian bodies"—or whether or not he feels empowered for having lost his leg to a landmine.

Lamartine Pereira DaCosta explores the pervasiveness of Coubertin's ideological mandate among a Latin American and Caribbean elite that was trying to reshape their cities, citizens, and politics to reflect Western European ideas of "civilization" and social discipline. Of course, this meant white men performing actions in the public sphere for other white men. Within this paradigm, the Pan-American Games were seen as a mechanism for social integration through public imagineering. Much in the same way that the contemporary events of the 2014 FIFA Men's World Cup and 2016 Rio de Janeiro Olympics would deploy images of indigenous Brazilians to promote national conciliation at the same time that the ongoing genocide was being directed from Brasília, we can rightfully question if meaningful numbers were watching these early Pan-American Games and, if so, who, under what conditions, and to what effect?

The suggestion that Buenos Aires, Mexico City, and Rio de Janeiro were models for smaller cities within their respective national hierarchies to follow with sporting projects needs to be examined within the context of the elite coalitions that were driving these projects. Again, with reference to the contemporary period, it is never accurate to suggest that "a city bids for the Games," but, rather, it should be understood that coalitions of vested interests coalesce around a project that deploys urban space to advance their goals. Cities are not actors and do not have agency, but are proposed as stages upon which Olympic dreams can be enacted and from which wealth extracted. This enactment, of course, requires major state subsidies and significant physical, discursive, technological, and ideological interventions.

DaCosta's analysis of the Olympic Games as a kind of spearhead for technological innovation in host cities is consistent with other findings in relation to the symbiosis of mega-events and capitalism more generally. Indeed, it may be that the Olympic Games and the FIFA Men's World Cups always presage, or at least call into being, urban capitalist futures through their intertwinement with technological innovations (from stadiums to surveillance, to doping and detection), increasing planning windows, and future-orientated delivery. In so much as it is impossible to separate the Olympic Movement from multiscalar geopolitics, it is equally foolhardy to separate the processes of bidding, preparing for, and hosting the Olympic Games from economic contexts at any level. What is clear is that the vested interests that propose, promote, and pull off the Olympic Games will direct urban development, technological innovation, and political capital in their direction. This is simply the core function of mega-events, and we will be wise to pay attention to the places and spaces in which that happens, as well as to engage the consequences of hosting in transparent and deliberative ways.

The chapters in this volume are indicative of the wider trends in Latin American sport scholarship and the generalized crisis of the Olympic Movement in Latin America and the Caribbean. The authors are predominantly male, investigating men both on the field and in male-dominated institutional/political contexts. This is not to imply that the editors and authors are biased, gender-blind, or discriminatory (they are not) or to diminish the quality and importance of their scholarship in any way. It is simply a reflection of the status quo of sport scholarship. This may be especially true in a region where large public sporting contests involve majority male audiences going to stadiums named after men to watch all-male teams owned by men. Couple this with the persistent discrimination against Latin American and Caribbean female athletes in terms of funding, machismo, and institutional support and it is no wonder that scholarship is male-dominated. While we could no doubt identify these patterns in other world regions, we should be particularly aware of the political ramifications of our investigative methodologies and subject matter in our own work and analysis.

The Latin American and Caribbean tradition of machismo appears to be shifting, but women's sport is still neglected in the press and continues to suffer from disproportional financing. Brazil is one of the more egregious cases; even after the hosting of the 2014 FIFA Men's World Cup, there is no functional women's football league. Throughout the region (and also in the United States), sporting institutions are dominated by men, as is the sport media, and sport scholarship.

Many of the chapters highlight the historical trajectory of what is now called "Sport for Development and Peace" (SDP). This is a critical element of the operational logics of the IOC and FIFA as they justify their massive profits (and nonprofit status) by highlighting the redistributive mechanisms implicit in their foundational charters. In some cases, progressive change has come as a result of hosting regional events like the Central American and Caribbean Games and Pan-American Games. Individuals have used the opportunity afforded by the big stage for their personal aspirations, while politicians and commentators have used those performances and the athletes' bodies in diverse ways to promote visions of the nation, or in discursive framings of citizenship predicated upon Western European ideals that continue to trickle down from the nineteenth century. While there is much to be admired in individual athletic performances and in the web of relations that sustain them, in a region beset by galloping inequality, pervasive social violence, and uneven development the pursuit of elite sport should be reconsidered as a necessary social good. This is not to say that SDP projects are unnecessary, but unless they are connected to broader social initiatives that seek to promote social justice and promote more egalitarian societies, the pursuit of Olympism in Latin America and the Caribbean is unlikely to advance "development and peace." To the contrary, the hosting of major events has increased income inequality, eroded constitutional norms, and fostered militarization.

That said, it appears that there is evidence that Olympic sport has inspired or generated positive social change in a number of cases.

Grassroots initiatives such as the Associação Miratus de Badminton (Miratus Badminton Association) in the Chacrina favela of Rio de Janeiro have produced top-level international athletes. While they are not yet able to compete with the world's best, this successful initiative is an example of how bottom-up Olympism can transform lives and create deeply embedded cultures of sport in underserved urban areas. There are many such initiatives through the region that hold conquering a spot at the Olympic Games as a primary goal, yet the tangible conquests are won in the day-to-day interactions between participants, coaches, and the communities which they serve. As researchers and citizens, we could do worse than to focus our attention on these kinds of initiatives in the hopes of exploring the successful implementation of sporting practices as a path toward greater social integration.[2]

In my opinion, the hosting of large-scale sporting events is not a necessary evil to attain these goals. Under the current business model, the Pan-American Games, Youth Olympic Games, and Olympic Games are mechanisms for pushing forward elite visions of urban development that over-promise and under-deliver by design. The rhetorical devices of sustainability, inclusion, and progress are twenty-first-century versions of Victorian-era positivism that transform citizen-subjects into consumer-objects. As we negotiate the inherent contradictions of Olympism in Latin America and the Caribbean—moving between the poles of populism and elitism, democracy and demagoguery—we should always question the lofty ideals of Olympism with the practical wisdom of hindsight and the urgent necessity of promoting social justice. For this task, we can be grateful to the authors and editors of this volume, who have given us such rich food for thought and fodder for further investigation.

CONTRIBUTORS

Dr. CLAIRE BREWSTER is senior lecturer in Latin American History at Newcastle University. She specializes in Mexican history, especially twentieth-century Mexican political and cultural history, including sport, Mexican intellectuals, the 1968 Mexican Student Movement, and the 1994 Zapatista rebellion. Her books include *Responding to Crisis in Contemporary Mexico* (University of Arizona Press, 2005) and (with Keith Brewster) *Representing the Nation: Sport and Spectacle in Post-revolutionary Mexico* (Routledge, 2010). She is currently working on the social and political impact of sport in post-revolutionary Mexico.

Dr. KEITH BREWSTER is senior lecturer in Latin American History at Newcastle University and has previously worked at the University of Cambridge. His main area of interest and expertise is twentieth-century Mexican history and culture. His books include *Militarism, Ethnicity, and Politics in the Sierra Norte de Puebla 1917–1930* (University of Arizona Press, 2003) and (with Claire Brewster) *Representing the Nation: Sport and Spectacle in Post-revolutionary Mexico* (Routledge, 2010). He also edited *Reflections on Mexico '68* (Wiley Blackwell, 2010). He is currently working on the social and political impact of sport in post-revolutionary Mexico.

Dr. THOMAS F. CARTER is principal lecturer in anthropology and sport at the University of Brighton. He leads the Centre of Sport, Tourism and Leisure Studies and also directs the master's degree program in Sport and International Development. He has been conducting research on sport in Cuba for the last two decades. He is a prolific scholar who has published, among other work, the following book: *The Quality of Home Runs: The Passion, Politics, and Language of Cuban Baseball* (Duke University Press, 2008), which in 2009 was recognized by the North American Society for the Sociology of Sport with its Outstanding Book of the Year Award.

Dr. LAMARTINE PEREIRA DACOSTA is currently affiliated with the State University of Rio de Janeiro in the area of Sport Sciences. He has collaborated with the World Anti-Doping Agency as a member of the Education Commission (2001–9) and the Trim and Fitness International Sport for All Association (TAFISA) as a member of its Executive Board during the 1990s. From 2001 to 2009 he was a member of the Research Council of the International Olympic Committee's Olympic Studies Centre. His vast scholarly work of almost four decades encompasses physical education, Olympism, sport management, sport philosophy, and sport history.

Dr. CHRISTOPHER GAFFNEY is clinical associate professor in the School of Professional Studies at New York University. He researches at the intersection of urban political economy and sport mega-events and has published extensively on the impacts of hosting the 2014 FIFA Men's World Cup and 2016 Olympics in Brazil. In addition to his monograph, *Temples of the Earthbound Gods: Stadiums in the Cultural Landscapes of Buenos Aires and Rio de Janeiro* (University of Texas Press, 2008), he has published more than a dozen book chapters as well as academic articles in prestigious journals. He has also published editorials in numerous global media outlets.

SHUNSUKE MATSUO is an assistant researcher in the Department of Latin American Studies at the University of Tokyo. His research interest focuses on sport and political history of the *Cono Sur* countries. He is currently working on his PhD dissertation, tentatively entitled "Sports and the State in batllista Uruguay: A Political History from the National-Global Perspective (1911–1933)," in which he analyses the development of Uruguay's sport policy in light of the rise and demise of the radical reformism led by José Batlle y Ordóñez as well as the interplay with global actors such as the International Olympic Committee and the Young Men's Christian Association.

Dr. VICTOR ANDRADE DE MELO is a professor at the Federal University of Rio de Janeiro, where he works in the postgraduate programs in comparative history and education. He is a coordinator of "Sport": Laboratory of History of Sport and Leisure. He has edited several books, including (with Mary Del Priore) *Pesquisa Histórica e História do Esporte* (UNESP, 2009) and (with Maurício Drumond) *Brazilian Sports History* (Routledge, 2016) and published numerous articles on the history of sport in Portuguese-speaking countries. He is the founder of *Recorde: Revista de História do Esporte*, the first Brazilian journal on sport history.

Dr. FABIO PERES is a sociologist and pedagogical advisor at Oswaldo Cruz Foundation (Fiocruz) in Rio de Janeiro. He is a coordinator of "Sport": Laboratory of History of Sport and Leisure. His main research interests and publications are in the areas of history and sport studies.

Dr. CHLOE RUTTER-JENSEN is an independent scholar. Her current areas of scholarly interest include critical disability studies, feminist pedagogy, posthumanism, and assisted reproduction. Rutter-Jensen is the author of *Temblores: Notas sobre sexo cultura y sociedad* (Ediciones B, 2012). She is a middle-school teacher of language and literacy in Spanish and English and restorative justice in the Oakland Unified School District.

Dr. ANTONIO SOTOMAYOR is associate professor and librarian of Latin American and Caribbean Studies at the University of Illinois at Urbana-Champaign. He is the author of the award-winning book *The Sovereign Colony: Olympic Sport, National Identity, and International Politics in Puerto Rico*. His work appears in *Caribbean Studies*, *The Latin Americanist*, *The Americas*, and *Journal of Sport History*, among others.

Dr. CESAR R. TORRES is professor in the Department of Kinesiology, Sport Studies and Physical Education at The College at Brockport, State University of New York. He specializes in the philosophy and history of sport. Torres is a former president of the International Association for the Philosophy of Sport (IAPS) and the founding president of the Asociación Latina de Filosofía del Deporte. He is also a fellow in the National Academy of Kinesiology and a recipient of the State University of New York's Chancellor's Award for Excellence in Scholarship and Creative Activities. Torres has been awarded the Warren P. Fraleigh Distinguished Scholar Award by IAPS.

Dr. APRIL YODER is assistant professor of history and global studies at the University of New Haven. Her research interests center on the intersections of sport, politics, and society during the Cold War. She is currently completing a manuscript on baseball in the Dominican Republic, tentatively titled "Pitching Democracy: Dominican Baseball and Politics since Trujillo." A new project focuses on the influence of socialist sport policies, such as those in Cuba, on women's access to sport throughout Latin America.

NOTES

Introduction

1. See, among others, Joseph L. Arbena, "Sport, Development, and Mexican Nationalism, 1920–1970," *Journal of Sport History* 18, no. 3 (1991): 350–64; Claire Brewster and Keith Brewster, *Representing the Nation: Sport and Spectacle in Post-revolutionary Mexico* (London: Routledge, 2010); Ariel Rodríguez Kuri, "Ganar la sede. La política internacional de los Juegos Olímpicos de 1968," *Historia Mexicana* 64, no. 1 (2014): 243–89; Kevin B. Witherspoon, "Protest at the Pyramid: The 1968 Mexico City Olympics and the Politicization of the Olympic Games," (PhD diss., Florida State University, 2003); and Witherspoon, *Before the Eyes of the World: Mexico and the 1968 Olympic Games* (DeKalb: Northern Illinois University Press, 2008).

2. "La designación de sede produjo gran júbilo en la C. de México," *El Siglo del Torreón* (Torreón, Coahuila), October 19, 1963, n.p.

3. We are aware that during the nineteenth century there were national revivals of the ancient Olympic Games. Thus, the correct denomination of the event initiated by the International Olympic Committee in 1896 would be the modern international Olympic Games. For simplicity's sake, in this introduction we will refer to the event as the Olympic Games. See, among others, John J. MacAloon, *This Great Symbol: Pierre de Coubertin and the Origins of the Modern Olympic Games* (Chicago: University of Chicago Press, 1981); and David Young, *The Modern Olympics: A Struggle for Survival* (Baltimore, MD: Johns Hopkins University Press, 1996).

4. Candidature File for Rio de Janeiro to Host the 2016 Olympic and Paralympic Games (n.d.), vol. 1, 19.

5. "Temer: Rio 2016 Shows Brazilian Organizational Capacity," *Around the Rings* (Atlanta, GA), August 18, 2016. http://aroundtherings.com/site/A__57127/Title__Temer-Rio-2016-Shows-Brazilian-Organizational-Capacity/292/Articles.

6. "Buenos Aires se postuló como sede de los Juegos de la Juventud 2018," *DERF. Agencia Federal de Noticias* (Santa Fe), August 29, 2011. http://www.agenciaderf.com/despachos.asp?cod_des=441124.

7. Mariano Ylarri, "Camino a los Juegos Olímpicos de la Juventud," *El Cronista* (Buenos Aires), June 9, 2017. https://www.cronista.com/especiales/Camino-a-los-Juegos-Olimpicos-de-la-Juventud-20170609-0017.html.

8. "The Olympic Rings Arrive at Buenos Aires to Celebrate One Year to go to the Youth Olympic Games," *Buenos Aires 2018*, October 5, 2017. http://www.buenosaires2018.com/en/news/los-anillos-olimpicos-llegan-al-corazon-de buenos-aires-para-celebrar-el-ano-hasta-los-juegos-de-la-juventud.

9. "The Olympic Rings Arrive at Buenos Aires."

10. See, for example, Kátia Rubio, "Postulações brasileiras aos Jogos Olímpicos: Considerações acerca da lenda do distanciamento entre política e movimento

olímpico," *Biblio 3W. Revista Bibiolgráfica de Geografía y Ciencias Sociales* 15, no. 895 (2010): 1–22; Cesar R. Torres, "Stymied Expectations Buenos Aires' Persistent Efforts to Host Olympic Games," *Olympika: The International Journal of Olympic Studies* 16 (2007): 43–76; Witherspoon, "Protest at the Pyramid"; and Witherspoon, *Before the Eyes of the World. See also* the chapter by Pereira DaCosta in this book.

11. See the chapter by Thomas Carter in this book.

12. Pablo J. Maldonado, "Atenas 2004: ¿hubiera sido distinto en Puerto Rico?," *Primera Hora* (Guaynabo), August 14, 2014. http://www.primerahora.com/deportes/otros/nota/atenas2004hubierasidodistintoenpuertorico-1028726/.

13. John J. MacAloon, "Double Visions: Olympic Games and American Culture," *Kenyon Review* 4, no. 1 (1982): 98.

14. See, for example, Sigmund Loland, "Coubertin's Ideology of Olympism from the Perspective of the History of Ideas," *Olympika: The International Journal of Olympic Studies* 4 (1995): 49–77; and MacAloon, *This Great Symbol.*

15. Cesar R. Torres, "Results or Participation?: Reconsidering Olympism's Approach to Competition," *Quest* 58, no. 2 (2006): 242.

16. Pierre de Coubertin, "Olympic Letter III: Olympism and Education," in *Olympism: Selected Writings*, ed. Norbert Müller (Lausanne: International Olympic Committee, 2000), 548.

17. Pierre de Coubertin, "Why I Revived the Olympic Games," in *Olympism*, 542–43.

18. International Olympic Committee, *Olympic Charter* (Lausanne: International Olympic Committee, 2017), 11.

19. *Olympic Charter*, 15.

20. See, among others, Richard V. McGehee, "The Origins of Olympism in Mexico: The Central American Games of 1926," *The International Journal of the History of Sport* 10, no. 3 (1993): 313–32; and Cesar R. Torres, "The Latin American 'Olympic Explosion' of the 1920s: Causes and Consequences," *The International Journal of the History of Sport* 23, no. 7 (2006): 1088–111.

21. Cesar R. Torres, "Mass Sport Through Education or Elite Olympic Sport? José Benjamín Zubiaur's Dilemma and Argentina's Olympic Sports Legacy," *Olympika: The International Journal of Olympic Studies* 7 (1998): 61–88; and Torres, "The Latin American 'Olympic Explosion' of the 1920s."

22. Gonzalo A. Mejía, *El deporte dominicano y su entorno hasta 1963* (Santo Domingo: Editora Búho, 2014), 18–22 and 31–38; and Cesar R. Torres, "Tribulations and Achievements: The Early History of Olympism in Argentina," *The International Journal of the History of Sport* 18, no. 3 (2001): 59–92.

23. Raanan Rein, "'El Primer Deportista': The Political Use and Abuse of Sport in Peronist Argentina," *The International Journal of the History of Sport*, 15, no. 2 (1998): 54–76; Cesar R. Torres, "The Limits of Pan-Americanism: The Case of the Failed 1942 Pan-American Games," *The International Journal of the History of Sport* 28, no. 17 (2011): 2547–74; Torres, "'Spreading the Olympic Idea' to Latin America: The IOC-YMCA Partnership and the 1922 Latin American Games," *Journal of Olympic History* 16, no. 1 (2008), 16–24; and Carlos Uriarte González, *De Londres a Londres: Juegos Olímpicos, una mirada desde Puerto Rico, 1948–2012* (San Juan: Editorial Deportiva Caín, 2012), 7–8.

24. For historical analyses of different editions of the Pan-American Games,

see the essays in *Historicizing the Pan-American Games*, ed. Bruce Kidd and Cesar R. Torres (New York: Routledge, 2017).

25. The list of authors, works, and countries would be simply too large to include here. We point to Allen Guttmann, *Sports: The First Five Millennia* (Amherst: University of Massachusetts Press, 2004), whose wide chronological and geographical coverage as well as citation of secondary sources offer an excellent introduction to the increasing use of sport to understand the experiences of countries around the world.

26. It was not until roughly the last quarter of the twentieth century that scholars began to give a closer and sustained look at sport in Latin America and the Caribbean, mainly due to the rise of cultural studies and a novel scholarly focus on the experiences of the working classes. Despite C. L. R James's exploration of the politics of cricket in Trinidad in *Beyond a Boundary* (London: Stanley Paul, 1963), much of the early work on Latin American and Caribbean sport is centered on football and, to a lesser extent, baseball, including, but not limited to, Mário Rodrigues Filho, *O negro no futebol brasileiro* (Rio de Janeiro: Irmãos Pongetti Editores, 1947); Julio Mafud, *Sociología del fútbol* (Buenos Aires: Américalee, 1967); Juan José Sebreli, *Fútbol y masas* (Buenos Aires: Galerna, 1981); Janet Lever, *Soccer Madness* (Chicago: University of Chicago Press, 1983); Eduardo Archetti, *Masculinities: Football, Polo and the Tango in Argentina* (New York: Berg, 1999); and Roberto González Echevarría, *The Pride of Havana: A History of Cuban Baseball* (Oxford: Oxford University Press, 1999). Anthologies include Roberto da Matta, ed., *Universo do futebol. Esporte e sociedade brasileira* (Rio de Janeiro: Pinakotheke, 1982); Joseph Arbena, ed., *Sport and Society: Diffusion, Dependency, and the Rise of Mass Culture* (New York: Greenwood, 1988); Joseph Arbena and David LaFrance, ed., *Sport in Latin America and the Caribbean* (Wilmington, DE: Scholarly Resources, 2002); and Pablo Alabarces, ed., *Peligro de gol. Estudios sobre deporte y sociedad en América Latina* (Buenos Aires: Consejo Latinoamericano de Ciencias, 2000). Progressively, scholars started to expand their conceptual reach and analysis of sport in Latin America. Two recent examples, among a growing number, are David Sheinin, ed., *Sport Culture in Latin American History* (Pittsburgh: University of Pittsburgh Press, 2015); and Héctor Fernández L'Hoeste, Robert McKee Irwin, and Juan Poblete, ed., *Sports and Nationalism in Latin/o America* (New York: Palgrave Macmillan, 2015). However, there has not been a volume addressing the dynamics of the Olympic Movement in Latin America and the Caribbean. Although there has been an increase in the number of monographs focusing on the Olympic Movement in a single country—see, for example, Witherspoon, *Before the Eyes of the World*; Cesar R. Torres, *Jogos Olímpicos Latino-Americanos: Rio de Janeiro 1922* (Manaus: Confederação Brasileira de Atletismo, 2012); Antonio Sotomayor, *The Sovereign Colony: Olympic Sport, National Identity, and International Politics in Puerto Rico* (Lincoln: University of Nebraska Press, 2016)—and papers exploring different Olympic issues in the region, there is still not a volume that provides a broad regional approach to the Olympic Movement in Latin America and the Caribbean. For an investigation of the trajectory, status, contributions, and omissions of sport history in South America and sport philosophy in Latin America, respectively, see Cesar R. Torres, "South America," in *Routledge Companion to Sports History*, ed. Steven W. Pope and John R. Nauright (New York:

. Routledge, 2010), 553–70; and Cesar R. Torres and Daniel G. Campos, "Philosophy of Sport in Latin America," *Journal of the Philosophy of Sport* 37, no. 2 (2010): 292–309. For an account of the development of sport sociology in Latin America, see Pablo Alabarces, "Deporte y sociedad en América Latina: Un campo reciente, una agenda en construcción," *Anales de Antropología* 49, no. 1 (2015): 11–28; and the chapters on Argentina, Chile, and Brazil in Kevin Young, ed., *Sociology of Sport: A Global Subdiscipline in Review* (Bingley, UK: Emerald, 2016).

27. *Olympic Charter*, 11.

28. For the expansion of the Olympic Movement, see for example, Barbara Keys, *Globalizing Sport: National Rivalry and International Community in the 1930s* (Cambridge, MA: Harvard University Press, 2006); and Allen Guttmann, *The Olympics: A History of the Modern Games*, 2nd ed. (Urbana: University of Illinois Press, 2002).

29. As an example of this situation, consider, for instance, the topics covered in *The Palgrave Handbook of Olympic Studies* (New York: Palgrave Macmillan, 2012), edited by Helen Lenskyj and Stephen Wagg. For a Latin American perspective on Olympic studies, see Kátia Rubio and Roberto Maluf de Mesquita, *Os estudos olímpicos e o olimpismo nos cenários brasileiro e internacional* (Porto Alegre: EDIPUCRS, 2011). For a limited account of Latin American scholars engaged in Olympic studies, see also Torres, "South America." The list is fortunately growing, especially in Brazil, most probably due to Rio de Janeiro hosting the 2016 Olympics.

30. Benedict Anderson, *Imagined Communities: Reflections on the Origin and Spread of Nationalism* (London: Verso, 1991); and Sara Castro-Klarén and John Charles Chasteen, ed., *Beyond Imagined Communities: Reading and Writing the Nation in Nineteenth-Century Latin America* (Washington, DC: Woodrow Wilson Center, 2003).

31. For analyses of the term "Latin America," including its genealogy and problems, see, for example, Marshall C. Eakin, "Does Latin America Have a Common History?," *Vanderbilt e-Journal of Luso Hispanic Studies* 1 (2004): 29–49; Michel Gobat, "The Invention of Latin America: A Transnational History of Anti-Imperialism, Democracy, and Race," *American Historical Review* 118, no. 5 (2013): 1345–75; and Walter D. Mignolo, *The Idea of Latin America* (Malden, MA: Blackwell, 2005).

32. See Pierre de Coubertin, "Amateurism at the Prague Congress," in *Olympism*, 651–53; and Coubertin, *Histoire Universelle* (Aix-en-Provence: Société de l'Histoire universelle, 1926- 1927), vol. 4, *La Formation et le Développement des Démocraties Modernes*, 160–67.

33. See Peter Bakewell, *A History of Latin America, c. 1450 to the Present*, 2nd ed. (Malden, MA: Blackwell, 2004), 547–49.

Chapter 1

1. The author would like to thank the International Olympic Committee Olympic Studies Centre for support provided through the PhD Students Research Grant Programme, which enabled him to conduct this research.

2. Cesar R. Torres, "The Latin American 'Olympic Explosion' of the 1920s: Causes and Consequences," *The International Journal of the History of Sports* 23, no. 7 (2006): 1088–111; and Torres, "'Spreading the Olympic Idea' to Latin America: The

IOC-YMCA Partnership and the 1922 Latin American Games," *Journal of Olympic History* 16, no. 1 (March 2008): 16–24.

3. This marks a contrast to neighboring countries such as Argentina and Chile, where national sport were organized by recreational circles of social elites, such as the Sociedad Sportiva Argentina and the Federación Sportiva Nacional.

4. This reform was carried out only partially after a hard-fought debate. In 1919, the new constitution established that the president controlled only the diplomacy, the police, and the army, while a nine-member collegiate executive branch called the National Council of Administration (Consejo Nacional de Administración) was in charge of all the other governmental functions.

5. There is a vast historiography on the emergence of Uruguay's democratic institution and Batlle's political, economic, religious, and social reforms, as well as their consequences. Here we mention only the most canonical studies: Milton I. Vanger, *José Batlle y Ordóñez of Uruguay: The Creator of His Times, 1902–1907* (Cambridge, MA: Harvard University Press, 1963); Vanger, *The Model Country: José Batlle y Ordóñez of Uruguay, 1907–1915* (Hanover. NH: University Press of New England, 1980); Vanger, *Uruguay's José Batlle y Ordóñez: The Determined Visionary, 1915–1917* (Boulder, CO: Lynne Rienner, 2010); Göran G. Lindahl, *Uruguay's New Path: A Study in Politics during the First Colegiado 1919–33* (Stockholm: Bröderna Lagerström, 1962); José Pedro Barrán and Benjamín Nahum, *Batlle, los estancieros y el imperio británico,* 8 vols. (Montevideo: Ediciones de la Banda Oriental, 1979–87); and Gerardo Caetano, *La república conservadora, 1916–1929,* 2 vols. (Montevideo: Fin de Siglo, 1991–92).

6. It deserves mentioning that Batlle's original idea, which he had carried since the 1880s, was not the creation of a permanent institution but the celebration of an annual sport competition called Juegos Atléticos Anuales or, occasionally, Juegos Olímpicos Uruguayos. It was in the legislative process that the establishment of the CNEF was added. For more details, see *José Batlle y Ordóñez: Documentos para el estudio de su vida y de su obra, Serie I 1856–1893, El joven Batlle 1856–1885,* vol.1 (Montevideo: Imprenta Vinaak, 1994), 29–31; Diario de Sesiones de la H. Cámara de Representantes (hereafter DSCR), vol. 187, 452, July 10, 1906; DSCR, vol. 189, 289–96, December 4, 1906; and Diario de Sesiones de la H. Cámara de Senadores, vol. 95, 17–18, July 2, 1909; DSCR, vol. 211, 67–69, July 4, 1911.

7. Most of the seven designated members in 1911 were leaders of sport institutions. An exception was Juan Smith, a politician of the National Party and Batlle's personal friend, who served as chairman. See Actas de la Comisión Nacional de Educación Física (hereafter Actas CNEF), vol. 1, 1, August 7, 1911, Secretaría Nacional de Deportes, Montevideo.

8. Besides Batlle and Ghigliani, *batllista* politicians such as Atilio Narancio, César Batlle Pacheco, César Miranda, and Juan Blengio Rocca served as CNEF members from 1915 to 1923. The CNEF members during these years also included famed professionals like Alberto Galeano (physician) and Juan María Aubriot (architect), in addition to José María Delgado, a poet, follower of the National Party, and chairman of Club Nacional de Football. All the nomination decrees of CNEF members during this period can be found at Caja 0071, Paquete 0049, Carpeta 967, Fondo Ministerio de Instrucción Pública, Archivo General de la Nación (hereafter MIP-AGN), Montevideo; Caja 0112, Paquete 0100, Carpeta 0251, MIP-AGN.

9. For Ghigliani, his participation in the CNEF was one of the first steps in

his burgeoning political career. In 1917, he joined the staff of *El Día*, a newspaper founded by Batlle, as a writer of sport pages. Two years later, he was promoted to the chief editor position of the evening version of *El Día*. In the same year, he was elected deputy for Montevideo, and throughout the 1920s he acted as a hard-core *batllista* spokesman in the Chamber of Deputies.

10. Julio J. Rodríguez, *La educación física en el Uruguay* (Montevideo: Imprenta Artística, 1930), 12.

11. Julio J. Rodríguez, *Plan de acción de la Comisión Nacional de Educación Física y conclusiones que se derivan del mismo* (Montevideo: Imprenta Latina, 1923), 76.

12. See, for example, Actas CNEF, vol. 1, 232–45, February 5, 1913.

13. Julio J. Rodríguez, "Preparación de Maestros de Educación Física en el Uruguay," *Uruguay-Sport*, December 1921, 3141–59; Comisión Nacional de Educación Física, *Informes, horario, programa y otros detalles del curso intensivo teórico-práctico* (Montevideo: Imprenta Latina, 1923). *Uruguay-Sport* was an official bulletin of the CNEF published monthly from 1918 to 1926.

14. See Allen Guttmann, *From Ritual to Record: The Nature of Modern Sports* (New York: Columbia University Press, 1978).

15. Actas CNEF, vol. 1, 399, July 3, 1914; Actas CNEF, vol. 2, 36, February 19, 1915.

16. The twelve sports that participated in the foundation of the FDU were track and field, equestrianism, tennis, shooting, cycling, volleyball, basketball, wrestling, rowing, gymnastics, boxing, and aviation. Actas CNEF, vol. 2, 39–40, March 5, 1915; *El Día*, August 27, 1915, 7.

17. Actas CNEF, vol. 4, fols. 412r–413v, August 1, 1918.

18. For example, in his study on the birth of the Uruguayan Olympic Committee, Arnaldo Gomensoro asserts that during most of the 1910s "much importance was not given [to the Olympic Movement] by Uruguayan authorities and athletes." Arnaldo Gomensoro, "El borrascoso nacimiento del Comité Olímpico Uruguayo," *ISEF Digital* 2 (2004): 3.

19. Actas CNEF, vol. 1, 118, May 8, 1912.

20. Actas CNEF, vol. 1, 118, May 8, 1912.

21. Actas CNEF, vol. 1, 132–34, May 22, 1912.

22. Juan Smith, *Stadium Nacional de Montevideo* (Montevideo: Talleres A. Barreiro y Ramos, 1913). This project was never realized.

23. Juan Smith to Pierre de Coubertin, January 30, 1914, Correspondance 1913–79, NOC Uruguay, Olympic Studies Centre Historical Archives (hereafter OSC Archives), Lausanne, Switzerland.

24. Juan Smith to Pierre de Coubertin, March 1914, Correspondance sur la preparation et choix des délégués 1911–1914, 1914 Paris Congress, OSC Archives; Actas CNEF, vol. 1, 341–42, February 27, 1914; Actas CNEF, vol. 1, 344, March 5, 1914; Actas CNEF, vol. 1, 348, April 17, 1914; "Carnet du Congrès de Paris," *Revue Olympique*, May 1914, 78. Destombes and de Miero participated in the 1914 Congress as consultative delegates, since Uruguay was not able to be represented with full status because of the absence of a National Olympic Committee.

25. It is noteworthy that in 1916 Coubertin was appointed by the French government as the organizer of the country's war propaganda toward Latin America, and in this connection he was acquainted with many Latin American diplomats.

See *The International Olympic Committee—One Hundred Years: The Idea, The Presidents, The Achievements*, vol. 1 (Lausanne: International Olympic Committee, 1994), 136.

26. In 1924, a Salvadorian diplomat recalled that in 1917 a committee composed of members from Uruguay, Chile, Brazil, Colombia, Argentina, Cuba, Paraguay, Peru, and El Salvador had been created "for the propagation of the Olympic idea in Latin America." Most probably, this is the committee Colombo referred to in his report. "Conference des Jeux l'Amerique Centrale," Conférences sur les Juex de l'Amérique latine et les Juex de l'Amérique centrale, les 3 et 4 juillet 1924 à Paris: correspondance, procés-verbaux et charte fondamentale, OSC Archives.

27. "Informe del Dr. Angel Colombo," *Uruguay-Sport*, February 1918, 18–21.

28. Juan Carlos Blanco to Rodolfo Mezzera, February 20, 1918, published in "Juegos olímpicos," *Uruguay-Sport*, February 1918, 16–17.

29. In fact, Uruguay's bid can be considered as one of the "proposals emanating from America" that interested Coubertin during the war years. Atlanta, Cleveland, Philadelphia, and Havana put in a bid for the 1920 Games. See Pierre de Coubertin, *Olympic Memoirs* (Lausanne: International Olympic Committee, 1997), 169 and 170.

30. Actas CNEF, vol. 4, fol. 327r, February 27, 1918.

31. *La Mañana* (Montevideo), March 5, 1918, 5; Caja 0147, Paquete 0137, Carpeta 0335, MIP-AGN.

32. Elwood Brown to Pierre de Coubertin, May 7, 1920, YMCA correspondance 1919–1920, OSC Archives.

33. For example, Paola Dogliotti Moro, *Educación del cuerpo y discursividades en torno a la formación en educación física en Uruguay (1874–1948)* (Montevideo: Ediciones Universitarias, UCUR, 2015), 125–44.

34. The YMCA is not necessarily and exclusively a North American movement. However, in this chapter "YMCA" basically refers to the North American YMCA movement led by the International Committee headquartered in New York. To avoid confusion, we allude to the YMCA institution established in Montevideo as "YMCA Montevideo."

Recently, scholarly interest has been growing concerning the relationship between sport and the North American YMCA mission in early twentieth-century Asia. For example, Stefan Huebner, "Muscular Christianity and the 'Western Civilizing Mission': Elwood S. Brown, the YMCA, and the Idea of the Far Eastern Championship Games," *Diplomatic History* 39, no. 3 (2015): 532–57; and Huebner, "Donors and the Global Sportive 'Civilizing Mission': Asian Athletics, American Philanthropy, and YMCA Media (1910s–1920s)," *Itinerario* 40, no. 1 (April 2016): 29–54. Although the YMCA's missionary work in Latin America was much less extensive than in Asia, this topic deserves more attention, particularly in relation to sport history.

35. The other two were John Swift and David McConaughy, who were assigned to Japan and India, respectively.

36. Monteverde also served as CNEF member in the 1920s. For his public life, see *A la memoria de Eduardo Monteverde: Homenaje recordatorio de sus sobrinos* (Montevideo: Talleres Gráficos de A. Monteverde y cía, 1945).

37. Myron A. Clark to the Foreign Department of the International Committee, November 10, 1900, Reports 1893–1919, YMCA International Work in Latin

America (hereafter IWLA) Box 8, Kautz Family YMCA Archives, University of Minnesota Libraries (hereafter YMCA Archives).

38. "El Club Protestante y las Sociedades de Jóvenes Cristianos (Y.M.C.A.)," *La Reforma* (Montevideo), June 1908, 39.

39. Charles Hurrey, "Annual Report for Year Ending September 20, 1909," Reports 1893–1919, IWLA Box 8, YMCA Archives.

40. When told about the invitation of a North American physical director, Batlle reportedly answered in a cynical tone: "Are you sure he will not be a failure like other foreigners we have brought out?" Philip Conard to John Mott, August 29, 1911, Correspondence and Reports 1910–1917, IWLA Box 3, YMCA Archives.

41. Actas CNEF, vol. 1, 210, 211, December 11, 1912; Actas CNEF, vol. 1, 232, February 5, 1913; Actas CNEF, vol. 1, 254, March 1913.

42. One of these disciples was Julio J. Rodríguez, who entered the CNEF staff in 1915 as an assistant of a plaza. Two years later, upon Hopkins's recommendation he decided to study at Springfield College. After completing his studies, Rodríguez served for many years as the CNEF's technical director, a position which Hopkins once held. See Actas CNEF, vol. 3, fol. 53v, November 9, 1915; Actas CNEF, vol. 3, fol. 233v August 1, 1917.

43. Philip Conard, "Statement of Need of a Central Building," [1916?], 1917–22, YMCA International Work in Uruguay Box 1, YMCA Archives.

44. Jess Hopkins to Charles Ewald, September 30, 1919, South American Federation Correspondence and Reports 1918–20, IWLA Box 3, YMCA Archives.

45. Jess Hopkins to Charles Ewald, September 30, 1919.

46. See Torres, "'Spreading the Olympic Idea' to Latin America," 16.

47. After leaving the Philippines, Brown stayed in France as a YMCA representative to assist the US Army participating in World War I. "Elwood S. Brown," Elwood Stanley Brown Biographical Data, Biographical Records Box 23, YMCA Archives.

48. [Neil McMillan?] to Jess Hopkins, February 5, 1920, South American Correspondence and Reports 1918–20, IWLA Box 3, YMCA Archives.

49. Elwood Brown, "Memorandum on Trip to South America March-April-May 1920," South America 1915–29, IWLA Box 8, YMCA Archives.

50. In the letters they assiduously exchanged from 1920 on, Hopkins and Brown always called each other by their first names.

51. Actas CNEF, vol. 5, fols. 749v, 750r, May 6, 1920. It is worth noting the different tones and terms in which Brown spoke of his mission to the YMCA International Committee and the CNEF. In letters to New York, Brown carefully avoided giving an impression that the YMCA would work "under" the IOC's instruction, while in front of the South Americans he tended to emphasize that it was Coubertin who was pushing forward the initiative and often spoke on behalf of the IOC, undoubtedly with the intention of resorting to the authority and renown Coubertin and the IOC already had on the continent. He always used "South American International Athletic Federation" instead of "South American Olympic Committee" in correspondence to his YMCA colleagues.

52. Actas CNEF, vol. 5, fols. 750r, 750v, May 6, 1920. Emphasis in original.

53. Actas CNEF, vol. 5, fols. 750r, 750v, May 6, 1920.

54. Brown also recognized the sporting virtue of Ghigliani immediately. In

a report he sent to Coubertin, he praised Ghigliani as "a very progressive public official and a man who [had] by reading and study brought himself up to date with the progress of modern physical education." Elwood Brown to Pierre de Coubertin, May 7, 1920, Young Men's Christian Association 1909–27, OSC Archives.

55. Actas CNEF, vol. 5, fol.751r, May 6, 1920.

56. DSCR, vol. 295, 336–54, October 10, 1921; DSCR, vol. 296, 518–22, November 9, 1921; DSCR, vol. 296, 599–618, November 14, 1921.

57. Jess Hopkins to Elwood Brown, June 5, 1920, South American Correspondence and Reports 1918–20, IWLA Box 3, YMCA Archives.

58. For more details on the preparation of the South American Games, see Torres, "'Spreading the Olympic Idea' to Latin America," 17–19.

59. Jess Hopkins to Elwood Brown, January 2, 1922, South American Federation Correspondence and Reports 1922–33, IWLA Box 3, YMCA Archives; Jess Hopkins to Pierre de Coubertin, January 24, 1922, Young Men's Christian Association 1922–78, OSC Archives.

60. Procés-verbal de la 19e session du Comité International Olympique, June 5, 1921, OSC Archives; Actas CNEF, vol. 5, fols. 949v, 950r, June 9, 1921.

61. Elwood Brown to the Foreign Department of the International Committee, June 1921, Policy Conferences on Foreign Work 1919–31, International Work Administration Records Box 74, YMCA Archives. Ghigliani, however, seems to have found himself in a somewhat awkward situation. Hopkins wrote to Brown: "Ghigliani is more interested than ever in the I.O.C. but he has received little from Coubertin other than the letter of appointment. He asks me all kinds of questions which I answer to the best of my ability. I must have everything there is in print and more too, if I am to hold his interest in the I.O.C." Jess Hopkins to Brown, January 3, 1922, South American Federation Correspondence and Reports 1922–23, IWLA Box 3, YMCA Archives.

62. [Elwood Brown?] to Jess Hopkins, November 17, 1921, South American Federation Correspondence and Reports 1921, IWLA Box 3, YMCA Archives; Olympic Games—Paris 1924, Physical Education Program Record Box 36, YMCA Archives.

63. Actas CNEF, vol. 8, fols. 1299v, 1300r, June 20, 1922.

64. Actas CNEF, vol. 8, fols. 1378r, 1378v, August 15, 1922.

65. Actas CNEF, vol. 8, fols. 1390v, 1391r, September 5, 1922; Actas CNEF, vol. 8, fols. 1400r–1401v, September 16, 1922; Actas CNEF, vol. 8, fols.1417r–1420r, September 26, 1922.

66. Actas CNEF, vol. 8, fols. 1427v–1428v, October 10, 1922; Actas CNEF, vol. 8, fols.1433v–1436r, October 13, 1922. Citation is from fols.1435v, 1436r.

67. For Baillet-Latour's Latin American tour, see Torres, "The Latin American 'Olympic Explosion,'" 1095–98.

68. Actas CNEF, vol. 8, fol.1455v, October 24, 1922.

69. Actas CNEF, vol. 8, fols.1454v–1457v, October 24, 1922.

70. "Rapport fait par le Comte de Baillet-Latour sur la Mission qu'il a remplie pour le CIO dans l' Amérique du Sud, l'Amérique Centrale et l'Amérique du Nord," 22e session à Rome 1923: procés-verbal, correspondence, discourse, invitations, memes propositions, programme et rapport 1922–23, OSC Archives. A translation of this report appeared in the official bulletin of the CNEF. "Informe presentado por

el conde Baillet-Latour miembro del C.I.O. (Bélgica) sobre la misión que le cometiera el C.I.O. en América," *Uruguay-Sport*, August 1923, 1–7.

71. "Rapport fait par le Comte de Baillet-Latour sur la Mission qu'il a remplie pour le CIO dans l' Amérique du Sud, l'Amérique Centrale et l'Amérique du Nord."

72. Actas CNEF, vol. 10, fols.1918v, 1919r, August 7, 1923; Procés-verbal de la 22e session du Comité International Olympique, July 8, 1924, OSC Archives.

73. Pierre de Coubertin, "Letter to the Members of the International Olympic Committee," in *Olympism: Selected Writings*, ed. Norbert Müller (Lausanne: International Olympic Committee, 2000), 739 and 740.

74. Elwood Brown to the Foreign Department of the International Committee, January 1, 1921, Policy Conferences on Foreign Work 1919–31, International Work Administrative Records, YMCA Archives; Brown, "Memorandum on Trip to South America March-April-May 1920," South America 1915–29, IWLA Box 8, YMCA Archives.

75. For the complexity of Uruguay's party politics during this period, see Lindahl, *Uruguay's New Path: A Study in Politics during the First Colegiado 1919–33* and Caetano, *La república conservadora, 1916–1929*.

76. Actas del Consejo Nacional de Administración (hereafter Actas CNA) 1923, vol. 3, fols. 320r-320v, August 30, 1923, Archivo General de la Nación, Montevideo.

77. *El Día (Edición de la tarde)* (Montevideo), October 28, 1922, 3; Actas CNEF, vol. 11, fol. 2099v, November 6, 1922.

78. For more on this incident, see Gomensoro, "El borrascoso nacimiento del Comité Olímpico Uruguayo," 1–17.

79. Actas CNA 1925, vol. 3, September 11, 1925, fols. 446v, 447r.

80. For more details, see Lindahl, *Uruguay's New Path*, 129–133.

81. *El Día*, October 18, 1927, 6; Francisco Ghigliani to Enrique Rodríguez Fabregat, October 19, 1927, Caja 0112, Paquete 0100, Carpeta 0251, MIP-AGN.

82. See, for example, Actas CNEF, vol. 26, fols. 5932v, March 19, 1931.

83. In 1915, the Liga Uruguaya de Football was renamed Asociación Uruguaya de Football.

84. Jess Hopkins, "Administrative Report for 1926," April 25, 1927, South American Federation Budgets and Reports 1926, IWLA Box 8, YMCA Archives; Hopkins to Charles Ewald, January 7, 1926; Hopkins, "The International Olympic Committee," July 22, 1926; Hopkins, "International Developmental Regional Games," July 24, 1926, South American Federation Correspondence/Reports 1926, IWLA Box 2, YMCA Archives.

85. For the "contraction" of YMCA foreign work in the 1920s, see J. Edmund Heavens, "John R. Mott, John D. Rockefeller, Jr., and the Progressive Rationalization of the YMCA 1921–1934," unpublished paper.

86. Jess Hopkins to Herbert Coates, March 31, 1928, South American Federation Correspondence and Reports January 9, 1928–April 30, 1928, IWLA Box 3, YMCA Archives; Hopkins, "Administrative Report for 1927," April 20, 1928, South American Federation Budgets and Reports 1927, IWLA Box 8, YMCA Archives.

Chapter 2

1. Eduardo Torres-Cuevas, *En Busca de la Cubanidad,* vols. 1 and 2 (La Habana: Editorial de Ciencias Sociales, 2006) and Torres-Cuevas, *En Busca de la Cubanidad,* vol. 3 (La Habana: Editorial de Ciencias Sociales, 2016).

2. Files from the International Olympic Committee Archives (hereafter IOCA) will identify the collection, when not the Cuban NOC files, and location in that archival resource when appropriate. In this instance, Box D-RMO1-CUBA/011, SD1: correspondence 1989–95. Some records will also have a reference number, and when this is recorded on the file, it will be noted here as well.

3. John Hoberman, "Toward a Theory of Olympic Internationalism," *Journal of Sport History* 22, no. 1 (1995): 1–37.

4. John MacAloon, "Humanism as Political Necessity? Reflections on the Pathos of Anthropological Science in Olympic Contexts," *Quest* 48, no. 1 (1996): 69.

5. Hoberman, "Toward a Theory of Olympic Internationalism."

6. Benedict Anderson, *Imagined Communities: Reflections on the Origin and Spread of Nationalism* (London: Verso, 1991); Ernest Gellner, *Nations and Nationalism* (Ithaca, NY: Cornell University Press, 2008); Eric Hobsbawm, *Nations and Nationalism since 1780* (Cambridge: Cambridge University Press, 1990); and Anthony Smith, *Nationalism and Modernism* (London: Routledge, 1998).

7. Juan M. del Aguila, *Cuba: Dilemmas of a Revolution* (Boulder: Westview, 1994); Susan E. Eckstein, *Back From the Future: Cuba Under Castro* (Princeton, NJ: Princeton University Press, 1994); Louis A. Pérez, *On Becoming Cuban: Identity, Nationality, Culture* (Chapel Hill: University of North Carolina Press, 1999); and Robert Whitney, *State and Revolution in Cuba: Mass Mobilization and Political Change, 1920–1940* (Chapel Hill: University of North Carolina Press, 2001).

8. Ruth Behar, *Bridges to Cuba/Puentes a Cuba* (Ann Arbor: University of Michigan Press, 1995); Jorge Mañach, *La Crisis de la Alta Cultura en Cuba e Indagación del Choteo* (Miami: Ediciones Universal, 1991); José Martí, *Our America: Writings on Latin America and the Struggle for Cuban Independence,* ed. Philip S. Foner, trans. Elinor Randall, Juan de Onís, and Roslyn Held Foner (New York: Monthly Review, 1977); Manuel Moreno Fraginals, *The Sugarmill: The Socioeconomic Complex of Sugar in Cuba, 1760–1860,* trans. Cedric Belfrage (New York: Monthly Review, 1976); Fernando Ortiz, *"Los Factores Humanos de la Cubanidad,"* in *Etnia y Sociedad* (La Habana: Editorial de Ciencias Sociales, 1993); Gustavo Pérez-Firmat, *Life on the Hyphen: The Cuban-American Way.* (Austin: University of Texas Press, 1994); and Félix Varela, *Antología* (Barcelona: Red Ediciones, S.L., 2017).

9. Jonathan Friedman, *Cultural Identity and Global Processes* (Thousand Oaks, CA: SAGE, 1994), 201.

10. John Comaroff and Jean Comaroff, *Ethnography and the Historical Imagination* (Boulder: Westview, 1992), 257.

11. Anderson, *Imagined Communities,* 47–65.

12. Partha Chatterjee, *Nationalist Thought and the Colonial World: A Derivative Discourse?* (Minneapolis: University of Minnesota Press, 1986).

13. Roberto González Echevarría, *The Pride of Havana: A History of Cuban Baseball* (New York: Oxford University Press, 1999); Pérez, *On Becoming Cuban,* 77–83, 277–86.

14. Félix Alfonso López, *Béisbol y Nación en Cuba* (La Habana: Editorial Científico-Técnica, 2015); López, *El juego galante: Béisbol y sociedad en La Habana (1864–1895)*. (La Habana: Ediciones Boloña, Editorial Letras Cubanas, 2016); Wenceslao Gálvez y Delmonte, *El Base-Ball en Cuba* (La Habana: Imprenta Mercantil de los Herederos de Santiago S. Speneer, 1889).

15. UNEAC (Unión de Escritores y Artistas de Cuba), ed., *Cuba: Cultura e identidad nacional* (La Habana: Ediciones Unión, 1995), 39–40.

16. José Cantón Navarro, *History of Cuba: The Challenge of the Yoke and the Star* (La Habana: Editorial SI-MAR, S.A., 2001).

17. Louis A. Pérez, *Cuba: Between Reform and Revolution* (New York: Oxford University Press, 1988), 176–88.

18. Irene Forbes, Ana María Luján, and Juan Velázquez, *Famosos y desconocidos: Cubanos en Juegos Olímpicos* (La Habana: Editorial Pueblo y Educación, 2003).

19. Enrique Capetillo, Miguel Hernández, Miguel A. Masjuan, and Victor J. Ortega, *Cuba: Sus aros de gloria* (Melbourne: Ocean, 1996), 7–14 ; and R. J. Pickering, "Cuba," in *Sport under Communism: The U.S.S.R., Czechoslovakia, The G.D.R., China, Cuba*, ed. James Riordan (London: C. Hurst, 1981), 148.

20. Fabio Ruiz Vinageras, *Un siglo de deporte olímpico: Cuba y América Latina, 1896–1996* (La Habana: Editorial Deportes, 1998), 25–26.

21. Literally, "to take the bottle": a colloquial phrase that means to take on adverse situations and deal with them.

22. Letters dated December 23, 1914, and February 15, 1915, Box C-J04.1920/001, SD4, IOCA.

23. Letter dated October 18, 1915, Box C-J04.1920/001, SD4, IOCA.

24. Letter dated October 4, 1915, Box C-J04.1920/001, SD4, IOCA.

25. Pérez, *Cuba*, 224–27.

26. Letter undated, January 1915[?], Box C-J04.1920/001, SD4, IOCA.

27. Vinageras, *Un siglo de deporte olímpico*, 29.

28. Vinageras, 33–34.

29. Vinageras, 39–41.

30. Vinageras, 43–44, 51–54.

31. Forbes, Luján, and Velázquez, *Famosos y desconocidos*, 9–12; and Ruiz Vinageras, *Un siglo de deporte olímpico*, 31.

32. US-American football was a growing popular sport in Havana in the 1920s and 1930s with US universities playing matches against the University of Havana squad. See Fernando Ortiz, "Foot-ball," in *Entre Cubanos: Psicología Tropical* (La Habana: Editorial de Ciencias Sociales, 1993), 31.

33. Forbes, Luján, and Velázquez, *Famosos y desconocidos*, 13–14.

34. Pérez, *On Becoming Cuban*.

35. I am borrowing George Orwell's phrase here regarding international sport as a form of war, which he made after observing some tension in international sport (George Orwell, *Shooting and Elephant and Other Essays* [London: Secker & Warburg, 1950]). East Germany did not compete in the 1952 Helsinki Games and competed as a unified German contingent in the 1956–64 Games. The 1968 Mexico City Games was the first appearance of East Germany in the Summer Olympiads.

36. Forbes, *Famosos y desconocidos*, 23–34.

37. Toby C. Rider, "From Resistance to Revolution: The Struggle for Control of the Cuban Olympic Committee, 1953–1964," *Olympika* 18 (2009): 59–65.

38. Box 60, Film 36, Avery Brundage Collection (hereafter ABC).

39. Rider, "From Resistance to Revolution."

40. Fidel Castro, *Fidel sobre el deporte* (La Habana: Instituto Nacional de Deportes, Educación Física y Recreación, 1975), 104.

41. Castro, *Fidel sobre el deporte*, 102–3.

42. Box 124 and Box 125, ABC.

43. See Rider, "From Resistance to Revolution," 69–81, for an analysis of these events from the perspective of actors outside Cuba.

44. Telegram sent to Lord Kilanan September 19, 1973, Box D-RM01. Cuba/004, SD2, Correspondence, IOCA.

45. Letter dated November 1, 1973, Box D-RM01.Cuba/004, SD2: Correspondence, IOCA.

46. Letter from Fidel Castro to José Antonio Samaranch, December 4, 1984, Box D-RM01.CUBA/005, SD2, Ref No. 1351/84, IOCA.

47. Box D-RM01.ETATU/026, SD2, IOCA.

48. Telex from George Miller to José Antonio Samaranch, September 6, 1986, Box D-RM01.ETATU/026, SD 3, IOCA.

49. Minutes of the Meeting of the Executive Board, October 10–11, 1986, Annex 7, IOCA.

50. Fidel Castro, *El Movimiento Olímpico Internacional, la grave crisis que se va a generar en torno a los juegos a Seúl en 1988, y la única solución posible* (La Habana: El Palacio de las Convenciones, 1985).

51. José Luis Salmeron and Ricardo Quiza, "Por un nuevo orden deportivo internacional," xerox copy of unnamed periodical publication, Granma?, Box C-J01.1988/187, SD 1, IOCA.

52. Meeting with Fidel Castro, Box C-J01.1988/187, SD 8, IOCA.

53. Correspondence 1985, Box D-RM01.Cuba/005, SD3, IOCA.

54. Meeting with Fidel Castro, Box C-J01.1988/187, SD 8, IOCA.

55. Meeting with Fidel Castro, Box C-J01.1988/187, SD 8, IOCA .

56. Minutes of the Meeting of the Executive Board, October 10–11, 1986, 15, IOCA.

57. Thomas F. Carter, "New Rules to the Old Game: Cuban Sport and State Legitimacy in the Post-Soviet Era," *Identities: Global Studies in Culture and Power* 15, no. 2 (2016): 194–215.

58. Antonio Carmona Baez, *State Resistance to Globalization in Cuba* (London: Pluto, 2004).

59. Carter, "New Rules to the Old Game," 206–8.

60. Comité Olímpico Cubano, *Report from Havana, Cuba, Applicant City to Host the 2008 Olympic Games, June 7, 2000* (La Habana: n.p., n.d.); Comité Olímpico Cubano, *Applicant City Report for the 2012 Olympic Games, May 30, 2003* (La Habana: n.p., n.d.).

Chapter 3

1. Kofi Annan, U.N. Press Release SG/SM/9579, November 5, 2004. https://www.un.org/sport2005/resources/statements/kofi_annan.pdf

2. Brenda Elsey, "Cultural Ambassadorship and the Pan-American Games of the 1950s," *International Journal of the History of Sport* 33, nos. 1–2 (2016): 106.

3. Victor Arriaga, "México y los inicios del movimiento panamericanismo, 1889–1890," in *Cultura e identidad nacional*, ed. Roberto Blancarte (México: Fondo de Cultura Económica, 1994), 107–26.

4. José Martí, "Nuestra América," *La Revista Ilustrada* (New York), January 1, 1891.

5. Pedro González Olvera, "La difusión cultural mexicana en Centroamérica," in *Diplomacia y cooperación cultural en México: una aproximación*, ed. Eduardo Cruz Vázquez, (Tuxtla Gutiérrez, Chiapas: Universidad Autónoma de Nuevo León, 2007), 125–44.

6. Cited in González Olvera, "La difusión cultural mexicana en Centroamérica," 135.

7. Antonio Sotomayor, *The Sovereign Colony: Olympic Sport, National Identity, and International Politics in Puerto Rico* (Lincoln: University of Nebraska Press, 2016), 5 and 10.

8. Alfredo B. Cuellar, "Los Juegos Olímpicos en México empezaron a trabarse en 1924," *El Universal* (Mexico City), October 20, 1963.

9. Richard McGehee, "The Origins of Olympism in Mexico: The Central American Games of 1926," *The International Journal of the History of Sport* 10, no. 3 (1993): 315–16.

10. For examples of such cooperation, see Archivo General de la Nación (hereafter AGN), Obregón-Calles, 805-A-26, May 1921, letter from the YMCA in Mexico to President Calles, October 19, 1925; "Un nuevo departamento en la YMCA," *El Monitor Republicano* (Mexico City), December 22, 1919, 4.

11. McGehee, "The Origins of Olympism in Mexico," 316.

12. Mark Dyreson, "Paris 1924: The Games of the Eight Olympiad," in *Encyclopedia of the Modern Olympic Movement*, ed. John E. Findling et al. (London: Greenwood, 2004), 85.

13. McGehee, "The Origins of Olympism," 313–14. Interestingly, the IOC proposal and the subsequent 1926 Games deftly sidestepped the fact that the "first" Central American Games had already taken place several years earlier. In 1921, during centenary celebrations of its independence from Spain, Guatemala hosted a sporting competition to which all Central American countries were invited. Mexico was not included. See Richard McGehee, "The Rise of Modern Sport in Guatemala and the First Central American Games," *The International Journal of the History of Sport* 9, no. 1 (1992): 138.

14. McGehee, "The Origins of Olympism in Mexico" 316–17.

15. Little Ball, "México abre su casa para recibir a los atletas de Cuba y Guatemala," *Excélsior* (Mexico City), October 9, 1926, 2nd section, 1, 9, and 10.

16. Little Ball, "Antes que los lauros deportivos buscan los atletas de Guatemala buena amistad," *Excélsior*, October 10, 1926, 1 and 8.

17. "El presidente recibió ayer a los atletas," *Excélsior*, October 17, 1926, 1 and 9.

18. Fray Gerundio, "El interés de los juegos que se inauguran mañana," *Excélsior*, October 11, 1926, section 2, 2.

19. Rafael Cardona, "Los Juegos Olímpicos," *Revista de Revistas* (Mexico City), October 10, 1926, 1.

20. "Aspectos de la 'Olimpiada Internacional,'" *Excélsior*, October 15, 1926, 5.

21. *El Universal*, October 18, 1926, cited in McGehee, "The Origins of Olympism," 323.

22. "El 'México' derroto el Club Cubano en emocionante juego," *Excélsior*, October 29, 1926, 3, 4.

23. For examples of charitable bullfights, see *El Mundo Ilustrado* (Mexico City), August 28, 1897, 30–32, and January 17, 1909, 124–25. The first reports on a bull-fight organized for the "victims of Tehuantepec" and the second on a bullfight in which the proceeds were given to victims of an earthquake in Italy.

24. AGN Obregón-Calles, 802-C-77 memo from presidential office, September 25, 1927, and letters from the Club Deportivo Chapultepec to Calles dated November 26, 1927.

25. Marco Antonio Maldonado and Rubén Amador Zamora, *Pasión por los guantes: Historia del box mexicano I 1895–1960* (México: Clío, 2000), 24.

26. Friedrich E. Schuler, *Mexico between Hitler and Roosevelt: Mexican Foreign Relations in the Age of Lázaro Cárdenas, 1934–1940* (Albuquerque: University of New Mexico Press, 1998), 11.

27. Secretaria de Relaciones Exteriores, (hereafter SRE), Memoria de la SRE, 1932–33, 82–83. Mexico's support for the Sandino rebellion had previously soured relations with Nicaragua.

28. SRE, Memoria de la SRE, 1933–34, 270–72.

29. SRE, Memoria de la SRE, 1931–32, 205.

30. Fray Nano, "Comentarios," *La Afición* (Mexico City), November 15, 1934, 3.

31. Fray Kempis, "Los Centroamericanos fueron definitivamente pospuestos," *La Afición*, October 30, 1934, 1 and 7.

32. Don Chon, "No Habrá equipo mexicano de futbol en los III Juegos Centroamericanos," *La Afición*, January 29, 1935, 8; and Fray Kempis, "Es casi seguro que no vaya equipo de tenis femenino en los Centroamericanos," *La Afición*, February 1, 1935, 1.

33. Fray Nano, "Comentarios," *La Afición*, February 1, 1935, 3–4; and Fray Nano, "Comentarios," *La Afición*, February 5, 1935, 3 and 6.

34. Fray Kempis, "Si queremos triunfar en El Salvador," *La Afición*, February 15, 1935, 3–4.

35. AGN, Lázaro Cárdenas, 532.2/7, Genaro Casas, CDM report, 1934–35, November 20, 1935.

36. Sebastiaan Faber, "'La hora ha llegado': Hispanism, Pan-Americanism, and the Hope of Spanish/American Glory (1938–1948)," in *Ideologies of Hispanism* ed. Mabel Moraña (Nashville: Vanderbilt University Press, 2005), 68.

37. SRE, Memoria de la SRE, 1937–8, 3–6, 34.

38. Dennis Merrill, *Negotiating Paradise: U.S. Tourism and Empire in Twentieth-Century Latin America* (Chapel Hill: University of North California Press, 2009), 65–102.

39. Cesar R. Torres, "The Limits of Pan-Americanism: The Case of the Failed 1942 Pan-American Games," *The International Journal of the History of Sport* 28, no.7 (2011): 2547–74.

40. Fray Nano, "Comentarios de Fray Nano," *La Afición*, October 26, 1934, 3 and 4.

41. AGN, Lázaro Cárdenas, 532.1/18, telegram from Mexico City's chief of police to Cárdenas, July 31, 1939.

42. "Las bases para conseguir un intercambio deportivo entre México y Guatemala," *El Nacional* (Mexico City), August 4, 1938, 8.

43. SRE, Memoria de la SRE, 1939–40, 378–79.

44. AGN, Miguel Alemán Valdés, 532.2/51, report from Clark Flores to Alemán, March 20, 1950.

45. Enrique Montesinos, *Los juegos regionales más antiguos: Juegos Deportivos Centroamericanos y del Caribe* (n.p.: Organización Deportiva Centroamericana y del Caribe, 2013), 42. http://www.odecabe.org/wp-content/uploads/2016/09/Libro-CAC-WEB.pdf.

46. AGN, Ruiz Cortines, 532.2/22, "Palabras al inaugurar los séptimos Juegos del Centroamericana y del Caribe," March 5, 1954.

47. "Los diplomáticos en 'el mundo deportivo', del Mago Septien," *Esto* (Mexico City), March 7, 1954, 17.

48. "Los Juegos Centroamericanos," *Excélsior*, March 6, 1954, n.p.

49. SRE, Memoria de la SRE, 1959, 12–14; SRE, Memoria de la SRE, 1964–65, 15.

50. Montesinos, *Los juegos regionales más antiguos*, 54. *See also* correspondence between Marte Gómez and Brundage during April 1957, IOC, Brundage Archive, reel 17, folder "Regional Games, 1951–59," 61–62.

51. Alberto Reyes, "Habla Mr. Avery Brundage," *Esto*, March 8, 1954, 9.

52. David J. Wysocki Quiros, "*Una Antorcha de Esperanza*: Mexico and the 1955 Pan-American Games," *The International Journal of the History of Sport* 33, nos. 1–2 (2016): 46.

53. IOC, Avery Brundage Archive (hereafter IOCABA), reel 17, folder "Regional Games, 1951–59," 81.

54. IOCABA, reel 17, folder "Regional Games, 1951–59," 147–49.

55. IOCABA, reel 18, folder "Olympic Games—II Pan-American sporting Games—1955," 74, 81.

56. "La Copa Olímpica para México por los últimos Juegos Panamericanos," *El Nacional*, June 16, 1955, 3. For details of the internal divisions, see Wysocki Quiros, "*Una Antorcha de Esperanza*: Mexico and the 1955 Pan-American Games."

57. Elena Poniatowska, "El movimiento estudiantil de 1968," *Vuelta* (Mexico City), June 1977, 15.

58. AGN, Miguel Alemán Valdés, 532/6. See report from Beteta, August 14, 1948.

59. AGN, Miguel Alemán Valdés, 532/6. See letter from Alemán to Beteta, March 16, 1949, and Beteta's acceptance of the appointment on March 18, 1949.

60. "El Ing. Marte R. Gómez lucha por obtener para México la Olimpiada de 1956," *La Afición*, April 27, 1949, 6.

61. Frank O'Brien, "Melbourne será el sede de la Olimpíada de 1956," *Excélsior*, April 29, 1949, 17 and 19.

62. AGN, Miguel Alemán Valdés, 532/6. Ing. Marte R. Gómez, undated report.

63. Wysocki Quiros, "*Una Antorcha de Esperanza*: Mexico and the 1955 Pan-American Games," 46.

64. AEN, "Alberca, gimnasio y canchas de basquetbol alrededor el estadio del Seguro Social," *Excélsior*, May 19, 1955, 27A; AEN, "Se inician les trabajos de México para la XVI Olimpíada," *Excélsior*, May 19, 1955, 28a.

65. Interestingly, the lowest score (4 votes) was obtained by Tokyo, which would host the 1964 Olympics. See AFP, "Probablemente los Juegos de Invierno serán en Squaw Valley," *Excélsior*, June 17, 1955, 8.

66. IOC, Lausanne: Historical Archive, folder COM 1961–69, box 139. Letter from Brundage to Clark Flores, August 2, 1962.

67. For an in-depth discussion of this topic see Claire Brewster and Keith Brewster, *Representing the Nation: Sport and Spectacle in Post-Revolutionary Mexico* (Abingdon, UK: Routledge, 2010), 45–51.

68. Brewster and Brewster, *Representing the Nation*, 54–79.

69. SRE, Memoria de la SRE, 1964–65, 17.

70. SRE, Director General de Relaciones Culturales. See correspondence in folder DAC-107–2, 1965–66.

71. SRE, Memoria de la SRE, 1965–66, 17–19.

72. SRE, Memoria de la SRE, 1964–65, 35–44; SRE, Memoria de la SRE, 1967–68, 29–35.

73. Sotomayor, *The Sovereign Colony*, 162–80.

74. AGN, Comité Organizador de los Juegos Olímpicos (hereafter COJO), Caja 142, 39–200, interview Ramírez Vázquez and Julio A. Millan of *La Prensa Gráfica* of El Salvador.

75. AGN, COJO, Caja 300, 40, co-presidencia, speech by Ramírez Vázquez to the Society of Architects, November 15, 1967.

76. AGN, COJO, caja 403, Charlas Radiofónicas, nos. 1–104. "American" in this sense refers to all countries of the American continent.

77. Cited in Ariel Rodríguez Kuri, "El otro 68: política y estilo en la organización de los juegos olímpicos de la ciudad de México," *Relaciones* 76 (1998): 116.

Chapter 4

1. Carlos Narváez Rosario, "Mónica Puig paraliza a la 'Isla del Encanto,'" ESPN Digital, August 12, 2016, http://espndeportes.espn.com/tenis/nota/_/id/2757840/monica-puig-paraliza-a-la-isla-del-encanto.

2. "The World Reacts to Puig's Historic Win," WTA News, August 13, 2016, http://www.wtatennis.com/news/article/5804568.

3. José Sánchez Fournier, "Mónica Puig llega a Puerto Rico," *Primera Hora* (Guaynabo), August 20, 2016, http://www.primerahora.com/deportes/otros/nota/monicapuigllegaapuertorico-1171072/.

4. Rafael Matos, "Puerto Rico's Rude Awakening," *New York Times*, July 14, 2016, http://www.nytimes.com/2016/07/14/opinion/puerto-ricos-rude-awakening.html.

5. Ayeza Díaz Rolón, "Lúgaro prefiere la independencia," *El Vocero* (San Juan), September 2, 2016, http://elvocero.com/lugaro-prefiere-la-independencia/; Víctor Rodríguez Velázquez, "Natal, Dalmau y Lúgaro se unen para reclamar la soberanía de Puerto Rico," *Diálogo* (San Juan), March 15, 2017, http://dialogoupr.com/natal-dalmau-y-lugaro-se-unen-para-reclamar-la-soberania-de-puerto-rico/.

6. María Bárbara Zepeda Cortés, *Cambios y adaptaciones del nacionalismo puertorriqueño: Del Grito de Lares al Estado Libre Asociado* (Michoacán: Universidad Michoacana de San Nicolás de Hidalgo, 2015), 69–75.

7. Cortés, *Cambios y adaptaciones del nacionalismo puertorriqueño*, 17.

8. Martín Cruz Santos, *Afirmando la nación: Políticas culturales en Puerto Rico (1949–1968)* (San Juan: Ediciones Callejón, 2014), 47–91.

9. For more on "colonial Olympism," see Antonio Sotomayor, "Colonial Olympism: Puerto Rico and Jamaica's Olympic Movement in Pan-American Sport, 1930 to the 1950s," in *Historicizing the Pan-American Games*, ed. Bruce Kidd and Cesar R. Torres (New York: Routledge, 2017), 84–104; and Antonio Sotomayor, *The Sovereign Colony: Olympic Sport, National Identity, and International Politics in Puerto Rico* (Lincoln: University of Nebraska Press, 2016), 4–7.

10. Sotomayor, *The Sovereign Colony*.

11. José Trías Monge, *Puerto Rico: The Trials of the Oldest Colony in the World* (New Haven, CT: Yale University Press, 1997), 41–44.

12. Pedro Cabán, *Constructing a Colonial People: Puerto Rico and the United States, 1898–1932* (Boulder, CO: Westview, 1999), 118.

13. Aida Negrón de Montilla, *Americanization in Puerto Rico and the Public-School System, 1900–1930* (Río Piedras: Editorial Universitaria, Universidad de Puerto Rico, 1975); Amílcar Antonio Barreto, *The Politics of Language in Puerto Rico* (Gainesville: University of Florida Press, 2001); César J. Ayala and Rafael Bernabe, *Puerto Rico in the American Century: A History since 1898*. (Chapel Hill: University of North Carolina Press, 2007), 74–79.

14. Roberta J. Park, "From *la bomba* to *béisbol*: Sport and the Americanisation of Puerto Rico, 1898–1950," *The International Journal of the History of Sport* 28, no. 17 (2011): 2575–93.

15. Two institutions were crucial in helping the sport Americanization project: the public education system and the Young Men's Christian Association (YMCA). The schools adopted US sports as tools of physical education. The YMCA, which worked closely with the school leadership, introduced sports like basketball, volleyball, and tennis, among others, and helped define sports as a manly activity. If the schools adopted these sports to help transform Puerto Ricans into Anglo-American citizens, the YMCA, as a missionary institution, utilized sports as a tool to convert Catholic locals to Protestantism. For the most part, these sports were massively adopted and practiced, as people saw in them a modern form of education and entertainment. Sotomayor, *The Sovereign Colony*, 40–60.

16. Scholars have shown how sport and nationalism interact in special ways. The intersection between US colonialism and sport occurred during times of heightened worldwide nationalism in the early twentieth century. In Latin America, as seen in Joseph Arbena's pioneering work, sport aided nationalist projects. Physical education curriculums, school athletics, and National Olympic Committees played a role in teaching and fostering nationalism. More recently, scholars of Latin America have deepened the analysis by covering topics like sport and national imaginaries, sport and state policies, sport and nondominant practices and subjects, and sport and alterity. Arnd Krüger, "Germany: The Propaganda Machine," in *The Nazi Olympics: Sport, Politics, and Appeasement in the 1930s*, ed. Arnd Krüger and William Murray (Urbana: University of Illinois Press, 2003), 17–43; Luke Harris, *Britain and the Olympic Games, 1908–1920: Perspectives on Participation and Identity* (New York: Palgrave Macmillan, 2015); Steven W. Pope, *Patriotic Games: Sporting Traditions in the American Imagination, 1876–1926* (New York: Oxford University Press, 1997); Lou Antolihao, *Playing with the Big Boys: Basketball, American Imperialism, and Subaltern Discourse in the Philippines* (Lincoln: University of Nebraska Press, 2015); Sotomayor, "Colonial Olympism"; Mike Cronin, *Sport and Nationalism in Ireland: Gaelic Games, Soccer, and Irish*

Identity since 1884 (Dublin: Four Courts, 1999); John Hargreaves, *Freedom for Catalonia? Catalan Nationalism, Spanish Identity, and the Barcelona Olympic Games* (Cambridge: Cambridge University Press, 2000); Barbara Keys, *Globalizing · Sport: National Rivalry and International Community in the 1930s* (Cambridge, MA: Harvard University Press, 2006); Joseph L. Arbena, "Sport and the Promotion of Nationalism in Latin America: A Preliminary Interpretation," *Studies in Latin America Popular Culture* 11 (1992): 143–56; and Héctor Fernández L'Hoeste, Robert McKee Irwin, and Juan Poblete, ed., *Sports and Nationalism in Latin/o America* (New York: Palgrave MacMillan, 2015), 13.

17. Pedro Albizu Campos, *Cuatro discursos, dos extractos, una entrevista* (San Juan: Editorial Patria Nuestra, 1969); Campos, *República de Puerto Rico* (Montevideo: El Siglo Ilustrado, 1972); Laura Albizu-Campos Meneses and Mario A. Rodríguez León, ed., *Albizu Campos escritos* (Hato Rey: Publicaciones Puertorriqueñas, 2007); Juan Manuel Carrión, *Voluntad de nación: Ensayos sobre el nacionalismo en Puerto Rico* (Puerto Rico: Ediciones Nueva Aurora, 1996); Alberto Prieto, *Albizu Campos y el independentismo puertorriqueño* (La Habana: Editora Política, 1986); Margaret Power, "Nationalism in a Colonized Nation: The Nationalist Party and Puerto Rico," *Memorias: Revista Digital de Historia y Arqueología desde el Caribe* 10, no. 20 (2013): 119–37; Juan Angel Silén, *Pedro Albizu Campos* (Río Piedras: Editorial Antillana, 1976); Benjamín Torres, *Pedro Albizu Campos: Obras escogidas, 1923–1936*, tomo 1 (San Juan: Editorial Jelofe, 1975); Benjamín Torres, *Pedro Albizu Campos: Obras escogidas, 1923–1935*, Tomo II (San Juan: Editorial Jelofe, 1981); Benjamín Torres, *Pedro Albizu Campos: Obras escogidas, 1923–1936*, tomo 3 (San Juan: Editorial Jelofe, 1981); and Cortés, *Cambios y adaptaciones del nacionalismo puertorriqueño*.

18. "Champion puertorriqueño," *La Democracia*, December 6, 1912.

19. For more on Puerto Rican soccer, see Antonio Sotomayor, "Caribbean Soccer: Hispanoamericanismo and the Identity Politics of Fútbol in Puerto Rico, 1898–1920s," *Latin Americanist* 61, no. 2 (2017): 193–224.

20. Power, "Nationalism in a Colonized Nation," 119–37.

21. José Coll y Cuchí, *El nacionalismo en Puerto Rico* (San Juan: Gil de Lamadrid Hnos, 1923), 6.

22. Emilio E. Huyke, *Los deportes en Puerto Rico* (Sharon, CT: Troutman, 1979), 175, 195.

23. Huyke, *Los deportes en Puerto Rico*, 195.

24. Sotomayor, *The Sovereign Colony*, 10–20.

25. Pedro Albizu Campos, *La conciencia nacional puertorriqueña*, selección, introducción y notas de Manuel Maldonado-Denis (Mexico: Siglo Veintiuno, 1972), 65.

26. José Ayoroa Santaliz, "¿Quién es Juarbe Juarbe? ¿Por qué lo discriminan?," Museo Olímpico de Puerto Rico, unpublished, 2–3.

27. Juan Juarbe Juarbe confessed this incident in a conversation with reporter Elliott Castro. Elliott Castro, interview by Antonio Sotomayor, March 8, 2017.

28. Letter from Juan Juarbe Juarbe to Luis F. Sambolín, dated June 28, 1979. Courtesy of the Museo Olímpico de Puerto Rico.

29. Juan Juarbe Juarbe, *Autobiografía*, November 30, 1979, 1, unpublished.

30. Margaret Power, "The Puerto Rican Nationalist Party, Transnational Latin American Solidarity, and the United States during the Cold War," in *Human Rights*

and Transnational Solidarity in Cold War Latin America, ed. Jessica Stites Mor (Madison: University of Wisconsin Press, 2013), 21–47.

31. "Declara al Gobernador que ha dado 'instrucciones terminantes' en el caso de Ponce," *El Mundo* (San Juan), March 23, 1937.

32. For an extended analysis of the diplomatic implications of this incident, see Sotomayor, *The Sovereign Colony*, 88–94.

33. Sotomayor, 93–94.

34. Adriana de Jesús Salamán, "Rebekah Colberg: una mujer con cría," *Diálogo*, February 25, 2014, http://dialogoupr.com/rebekah-colberg-una-mujer-con-cria/.

35. Juan Juarbe y Juarbe, *El derecho de Puerto Rico a su independencia* (Mexico, Comité Mexicano Pro Independencia de Puerto Rico, 1954), 64.

36. José Ayoroa Santaliz, "Juan Juarbe está en Puerto Rico," *Claridad* (San Juan), February 20, 1976.

37. Santaliz, "Quién es Juarbe Juarbe?," 6–7.

38. Juarbe y Juarbe, *El derecho de Puerto Rico a su independencia*, 13.

39. Letter from Juan Juarbe Juarbe to Luis F. Sambolín, dated June 28, 1979. Courtesy of the Museo Olímpico de Puerto Rico.

40. Juarbe y Juarbe, *Autobiografía*, 2.

41. Sotomayor, *The Sovereign Colony*, 137; Juarbe, *Autobiografía*, 2.

42. Carlos Uriarte González, *80 años de acción y pasión: Puerto Rico and los Juegos Centroamericanos y del Caribe, 1930 al 2010* (N.p.: Nomos Impresores, 2009), 58.

43. Pedro Albizu Campos, "Discurso pronunciado por Pedro Albizu Campos en Ponce, P.R. el día 21 de marzo de 1950," in *La palabra como delito: Los discursos por los que condenaron a Pedro Albizu Campos, 1948–1950*, ed. Ivonne Acosta (Harrisonburg, VA: Editorial Cultural, 1993), 138 and 140.

44. José Manuel Dávila Marichal, "El Comandante Tomás López de Victoria y la Masacre de Ponce - Parte I," Instituto Hostosiano de Educación Política Juventud Hostosiana–MINH, June 29, 2011, http://inhep.blogspot.com/2011/06/alba -alianza-bolivariana-para-los.html.

45. José Enamorado Cuesta, *Fuera de ley: Denuncia de la hipócrita tiranía "democrática" en Puerto Rico* (San Juan: Editorial Puerto Rico Libre, 1957), 44.

46. Cuesta, *Fuera de ley*, 44.

47. Miñi Seijo Bruno, *La insurrección nacionalista en Puerto Rico* (San Juan: Editorial Edil, 1997).

48. Nelson A. Denis, *War Against all Puerto Ricans: Revolution and Terror in America's Colony* (New York: Nation Books, 2015), 194–95.

49. José Trías Monge, *Puerto Rico: The Trials of the Oldest Colony in the World* (New Haven, CT: Yale University Press, 1997), 109–18.

50. Rubén Berríos Martínez, "A manera de prólogo," in *En nombre de la verdad*, ed. Pablo Marcial Ortiz Ramos (San Juan: Instituto Gilberto Concepción de Gracia, 2007), 16–17.

51. Gilberto Concepción Suárez, *Los días con mi padre* (San Juan: Ediciones La Patria, 2010), 75.

52. Wilma Reverón Collazo, "Introducción a la historia del MPI en el 160 Aniversario del Natalicio de Eugenio María de Hostos," Movimiento Independentista Nacional Hostosiano-Zona Mayaguez, January 11, 1999. http://capaprieto.tripod.com/id12.html.

53. For an analysis of the negotiations that allowed Puerto Ricans to participate at the 1948 London Olympics, see Sotomayor, *The Sovereign Colony*, 113–29.

54. Pedro Juan Camacho, interview by Antonio Sotomayor, March 1, 2017.

55. Memorandum dated February 10, 1945, from Rafael Correa, 1133760-000-100-SJ-4014-Section 5, February 10, 1945. Partido Independentista Puertorriqueño Collection. FBI Library. Archives Unbound.

56. Concepción Suárez, *Los días con mi padre*, 118.

57. Elliott Castro, interview by Antonio Sotomayor, March 8, 2017. An extensive investigation of the newspaper *El Mundo* between 1944 and 1966, as well as other newspapers in the Colección Puertorriqueña at the Universidad de Puerto Rico in Río Piedras, did not reveal any expression by the PIP to any of Puerto Rico's international sporting events. Collections of speeches and biographies of Gilberto Concepción de Gracia also do not contain any reference to COPUR or the national delegation; Pablo M. Ortiz Ramos, *Gilberto Concepción de Gracia: En nombre de la verdad* (San Juan: Instituto Gilberto Concepción de Gracia, 2007). Only the biographical book by his son (see note 55) mentions Concepción de Gracias's liking of baseball.

58. Memorandum dated January 22, 1954, from SA Charles B. Peck to SAC, San Juan (100–3), 5, 1133760-000-100-SJ4014-Section 21, August 4, 1953-January 25, 1954. Partido Independentista Puertorriqueño Collection, FBI Library, Archives Unbound.

59. Juan Mari Bras, *Abriendo caminos* (San Juan: Editora Causa Común, 2001), 101–2.

60. Mari Bras, *Abriendo caminos*, 103.

61. Luis López Nieves, "Compañero Juan," *Claridad*, July 31, 1976, http://juanmaribras.org/escritos/sobre-juan-mari-bras/139-companero-juan.html.

62. Carlos Raquel Rivera, "Los deportes y la política," *Claridad*, December 21, 1959.

63. Sotomayor, *The Sovereign Colony*, 142–48.

64. Pedro Juan Camacho, interview by Antonio Sotomayor, March 1, 2017.

65. Ayala and Bernabe, *Puerto Rico in the American Century*, 230.

66. Ayala and Bernabe, 244 and 283.

67. Ayala and Bernabe, 283. In solidarity with El Salvador and in opposition to US support for the military there.

68. Ronald Fernández, *Los Macheteros: El robo de la Wells Fargo y la lucha armada por la independencia de Puerto Rico* (Río Piedras: Editorial Edil, 1993), 207 and 345–47.

69. Elliott Castro, "El '78 deportivo," *Claridad*, January 5 to 12, 1978.

70. John MacAloon, "La pitada Olímpica," in *Text, Play, and Story: The Construction and Reconstruction of Self and Society*, ed. Edward M. Bruner (Washington, DC: American Ethnological Society, 1984), 315–55.

71. "Hermanos panamericanos," *Boletín Nacional* (San Juan), July 1979.

72. Pedro Juan Camacho, interview by Antonio Sotomayor, March 1, 2017.

73. *A Step Away*, codirected by Carlos Zurinaga and Roberto Ponce (San Juan: A Step Away, [1980] 2010), DVD.

74. Rubén Berríos Martínez, *La independencia de Puerto Rico. Razón y lucha* (Coyoacán: Editorial Línea, 1983), 32.

75. Martínez, *La independencia de Puerto Rico*, 33.

76. Martínez, 33.

77. Martínez, 34–35.

78. "Nacionalismo y soberanía deportiva: A propósito de Mónica," Partido Nacionalista de Puerto Rico's Facebook page, August 15, 2016, https://www.facebook.com/partidonacionalistadepuertorico/posts/1375401242473206.

79. "El gobernador de Puerto Rico apoya a equipo béisbol tiñiéndose de rubio," Agencia EFE, March 23, 2017, http://www.efe.com/efe/america/deportes/el-gobernador-de-puerto-rico-apoya-a-equipo-beisbol-tiniendose-rubio/20000010-3215969.

80. Hermes Ayala, "Edwin Rodríguez y su admiración por los próceres de su patria," NotiCel, March 19, 2017. http://www.noticel.com/noticia/138996/edwin-rodriguez-y-su-admiracion-por-los-proceres-de-su-patria.html.

81. Antolín Maldonado Ríos, "Miles de fanáticos celebran en grande con el equipo de Puerto Rico." *El Nuevo Día* (Guaynabo), March 23, 2017, http://www.elnuevodia.com/deportes/beisbol/nota/milesdefanaticoscelebranengrande conelequipodepuertorico-2303734/#cxrecs_s.

Chapter 5

1. For more information, see Fabio de Faria Peres, Victor Andrade de Melo, and Jorge Knijnik, "Olympics, Media and Politics: The First Olympic Ideas in Brazilian Society during the Late Nineteenth and Early Twentieth Centuries," *The International Journal of the History of Sport* 33, no. 12 (2016): 1380–94.

2. Comitê Olímpico do Brasil, *Comitê Olímpico do Brasil. 100 anos, 1914–2014* (Rio de Janeiro: Casa da Palavra, 2015).

3. *Manchete Esportiva* (Rio de Janeiro), May 31, 1958, 4. Months earlier, the author had already referred to this feeling of inferiority in the newspaper *Última Hora* (Rio de Janeiro), February 7, 1958, 14. For more information, see Fátima Martin Rodrigues Ferreira Antunes, *Com brasileiro, não há quem possa!* (São Paulo: Editora da Unesp, 2004).

4. It was, in fact, a long and troubled political period. In 1930, Vargas was elevated to the head of the provisional government through a rebellion (called the Revolution of 1930). This was the result of the fragmentation of a political arrangement between government and regional elites that had lasted since 1894. Afterward, he was elected to the presidency by the indirect vote in 1934, when the new constitution anticipating some democratic and modernizing advances was promulgated. However, by the end of the following year, in 1935, Vargas, with political skill—approaching fascist social forces (such as the Brazilian Integralist Action) and, simultaneously, repressing and fomenting the fear of the communist "threat" through an expressive propaganda apparatus—managed to press the Congress, first, to approve the state of siege and, then, the state of war that was successively extended until 1937, the year in which the *Estado Novo* dictatorship was imposed until 1945. The ambivalence of this period reveals itself in the great legitimacy and prestige that Vargas possessed, combining the nationalism and modernization of certain social and labor policies (such as education, social security, culture, and health) with the restriction on political freedom and expression. Through the alliance between the Social Democratic Party (Partido Social Democrático, PSD) and the Brazilian Labor Party, among other things, his political prowess was able to

become unbeatable, electing three presidents of the Republic—Vargas being one of them (1951–54)—while ensuring the democratic order. For more information, see Lilia Moritz Schwarcz and Heloisa Murgel Starling, *Brasil: Uma biografia* (São Paulo: Companhia das Letras, 2015).

5. For more information on the historical period, see Jorge Ferreira and Lucilia de Almeida N. Delgado, ed., *O Brasil republicano. O tempo da experiência democrática* (Rio de Janeiro: Civilização Brasileira, 2003).

6. *Última Hora*, June 21, 1952, Suplemento Esportivo, 2.

7. *Última Hora*, June 21, 1952, Suplemento Esportivo, 2.

8. *Última Hora*, July 7, 1952, 8.

9. As a consequence of this context, Brazil saw the emergence of a series of intellectuals who sought to interpret and even name the "place" occupied by the country in the capitalist system, among them Caio Prado Jr., Florestan Fernandes, and Celso Furtado. For more information, see Plínio de Arruda Sampaio Jr., "Entre a nação e a barbárie: uma leitura de Caio Prado Jr., Florestan Fernandes e Celso Furtado à crítica do capitalismo dependente" (PhD diss., Universidade Estadual de Campinas, 1997).

10. For more information on the historical period, see, Ferreira and Delgado, *O Brasil republicano.*

11. The very realization of the Soccer World Cup of 1950 was viewed by the government and other Brazilian authorities—at that time, in a position contrary to a state monopoly in the exploitation of resources considered strategic for the country—as a means of projecting the image of Brazil abroad. For more information, see Alvaro Vicente do Cabo, "Copa do Mundo de 1950: Brasil X Uruguai— uma análise comparada do discurso da imprensa," in *História comparada do esporte,* ed. Victor Andrade de Melo (Rio de Janeiro: Shape, 2007), 47–60.

12. Presidência da República, "Decreto-lei nº 3.199, April 14,1941," accessed May 23, 2017, http://www.planalto.gov.br/ccivil_03/decreto-lei/1937–1946/Del3199.htm.

13. In a ceremony held in Finland, Brazilian Foreign Minister Jorge Latour said: "Tonight, we, Brazilians, are particularly happy for the victory of Adhemar Ferreira, who is a modest and simple athlete, who received the spontaneous consecration of the public that witnessed his brilliant victory." *Correio da Manhã* (Rio de Janeiro), July 24, 1952, 2º Caderno, 1, 2).

14. Maurício Drumond, "Sport and Politics in the Brazilian *Estado Novo* (1937–1945)," *International Journal of the History of Sport* 31, no. 10 (2014): 1252.

15. For more information, see Maria Celina D'Araujo, *O Segundo Governo Vargas 1951–1954: Democracia, Partidos e Crise Política* (São Paulo: Ática, 1992).

16. *Correio da Manhã*, July 24, 1952, 2º Caderno, 2, 2.

17. In the city of São Paulo, an initiative was even organized to offer a house for the family of Adhemar (*Diário de Notícias*, July 24, 1952, 3ª Seção, 1.) The donation, however, did not occur because it was believed that it could be viewed as payment, which would conflict with the amateur status of the athlete.

18. *Mundo Esportivo* (São Paulo), May 12, 1953, 2; and *Imprensa Popular* (Rio de Janeiro), January 1, 1954, 7.

19. *Revista do Rádio* (Rio de Janeiro) April 14, 1956, 14.

20. *Última Hora*, August 11, 1952, 7.

21. *Correio da Manhã*, July 25, 1952, 2º Caderno, 1.

22. *Correio da Manhã*, July 25, 1952, 2º Caderno, 1.

23. *Diário de Notícias* (Rio de Janeiro), July 24, 1952, 3ª Seção, 3.

24. *Correio da Manhã*, July 25, 1952, 2º Caderno, 1.

25. For more information, see Guillermo Giucci and Enrique Rodríguez Larreta, ed., *Gilberto Freyre, uma biografia cultural: A formação de um intelectual brasileiro (1930–1936)* (Rio de Janeiro: Civilização Brasileira, 2007).

26. A naturalized French citizen, originally American, the artist was a civil rights activist and attracted attention for her political attitude, lifestyle, and social preferences. Josephine Baker participated in several organizations that fought against racial discrimination. During her visit to Brazil, she met with intellectuals, among them Edgard Santana (a physician who "hesitantly" participated in what was known as "racial counterideology" to discuss racism and to articulate ways of supporting local groups (*Última Hora*, July 21, 1952, 2º Caderno, 12). On racial counterideology, see Florestan Fernandes, *A integração do negro na sociedade de classes*, vol. 2 (São Paulo: Globo, 2008).

27. *Última Hora*, August 2, 1952, 2º Caderno, 4.

28. An interesting study on how racism is mitigated through the use of metaphors in the Brazilian press can be found in Carlos A. F. da Silva and Sabastião J. Votre, "Racist Discourse of the Brazilian Sports Media at the World Cups," *Esporte e Sociedade* 7, no. 20 (2012): 1–22.

29. *Correio da Manhã*, July 24, 1952, 2º Caderno, 1.

30. *Correio da Manhã*, July 24, 1952, 2º Caderno, 1.

31. *Diário de Notícias*, July 24, 1952, 3ª Seção, 1.

32. *Diário de Notícias*, July 31, 1952, 3ª Seção, 3.

33. *Correio da Manhã*, July 25, 1952, 2º Caderno, 1.

34. *Última Hora*, August 11, 1952, 7.

35. *Última Hora*, August 2, 1952, 2º Caderno, 3; and August 11, 1952, 7.

36. *Última Hora*, December 14, 1956, Tabloide, 1.

37. *Diário Carioca*, December 19, 1956, 6.

38. *Diário da Noite* (Rio de Janeiro), December 10, 1956, 2ª Seção, 6.

39. *Última Hora*, December 14, 1956, 1. Shortly after the medal was won, Juscelino and the vice president João Goulart telegraphed the athlete, congratulating him on the conquest (*Diário Carioca*, December 2, 1956, 3ª Seção, Suplemento Dominical, 2).

40. For more information about the period, see Ferreira and Delgado, *O Brasil republicano*.

41. *Mundo Esportivo*, December 14, 1956, 6.

42. *Mundo Esportivo*, December 14, 1956, 6.

43. *Última Hora*, November 22, 1956, 16.

44. Adhemar's world record was only finally approved at the International Athletics Federation meeting in Melbourne during the Olympic Games.

45. *O Globo* (Rio de Janeiro), March 19, 1955, segunda seção, 1.

46. For more information, see Leslie Bethell, "O Brasil e a ideia de 'América Latina' em perspectiva histórica," *Estudos Históricos* 22, no. 44 (2009): 289–321. Although US international politics sometimes associated Brazil with so-called Latin America, part of Brazilian political society defended a certain prerogative and status differentiated from other nations.

47. At the Pan-American Games in 1955, Brazil ranked seventh seventh in the medal table, behind countries such as the United States, Argentina, Mexico, Venezuela, Canada, and Chile, whereas at the 1956 Olympic Games, Brazil was twenty-fourth. Although, on this occasion, it ranked ahead of all other South American countries, Brazil was behind Mexico, Ireland, Norway, Iran, Denmark, Turkey, and Japan, among others.

48. *Mundo Esportivo*, December 30, 1956, 13.

49. *Última Hora*, November 9, 1956, 16.

50. *Jornal do Brasil* (Rio de Janeiro) October 25, 1956, 13.

51. *Última Hora*, November 20, 1956, 8. According to the paper, Jesse Owens was in Melbourne as one of the representatives of US President Eisenhower.

52. *Diário Carioca*, November 27, 1956, 1 and 9.

53. *O Globo*, November 27, 1956, 1; and *Última Hora*, November 27, 1956, 1.

54. For example, the *Mundo Esportivo*, in the "Questions and Answers" column —dedicated to interviewing sport personalities, most of them from soccer—asked, "What is the greatest expression of sport in Brazil?." Often, the athletes chose the name of Adhemar, sometimes followed by terms as "indisputably" (see the editions from March 23, 1956, 2; April 27, 1956, 2; May 11, 1956, 2; May 25, 1956, 15; and June 15, 1956, 3).

55. *O Cruzeiro* (Rio de Janeiro), May 12, 1956, 118.

56. *A Noite* (Rio de Janeiro), August 31, 1956, 2º Caderno, 2.

57. *Última Hora*, August 28, 1956, 8.

58. *Última Hora*, November 27, 1956, 6.

59. The news refers to the statement of the minister of war (General Henrique Teixeira Lott) in honor of the soldiers who died in the Brazilian communist uprising that occurred in November 1935.

60. For more information, see Victor Andrade de Melo and Fabio de Faria Peres, "Primeiros ventos olímpicos em terras tupiniquins," *Revista USP* 108 (2016): 39–48.

61. *Última Hora,* November 28, 1956, 16.

62. *Última Hora,* November 28, 1956, 16.

63. *O Globo*, April 26, 1955, 12.

64. *O Globo*, April 26, 1955, 12.

65. Adhemar graduated in 1948 as a sculptor from the Federal Technical School of São Paulo.

66. *A Noite*, August 31, 1956, 3.

67. *Última Hora*, December 14, 1956, 8.

68. *Correio da Manhã*, September 22, 1956, 13.

69. *Correio da Manhã*, September 22, 1956, 13.

70. *Correio da Manhã*, November 4, 1956, 2º Caderno, 4.

71. *Última Hora*, November 28, 1956, 24.

72. *Última Hora*, November 28, 1956, 8.

73. *Última Hora*, November 28, 1956, 16.

74. Examples of Ademar's columns can be found in the editions of *Última Hora* of June 5, 1956, 8; June 6, 1956, 8; August 21, 1956, 8; and August 29, 1956, 8.

75. *Última Hora,* November 27, 1956, 6.

76. *Última Hora,* November 18, 1956, 1.

77. *Última Hora,* November 25, 1956, 6.

78. *Última Hora,* December 14, 1956, 6.

79. *Última Hora,* December 14, 1956, 6.

Chapter 6

1. ORO [Osvaldo Ricardo Orcasitas], "Cuentos del aro," *El Gráfico* (Buenos Aires), May 2, 2010, 95–96. *See also* "La primera exhibición del Hindú Club de Buenos Aires en Paris," *El Mundo Deportivo* (Barcelona), March 13, 1927, 2; and "El partido entre argentinos y catalanes," *La Vanguardia* (Barcelona), March 25, 1927, 14.

2. Alberto Petrolini, "Informe del Presidente de la Delegación Argentina a los XVI° Juegos Olímpicos de Melbourne," in Comité Olímpico Argentino, *Informe General del Equipo Argentino en los Juegos Olímpicos de Melbourne 1956* (Buenos Aires: Comité Olímpico Argentino, n.d.), 5.

3. Petrolini, "Informe del Presidente de la Delegación Argentina a los XVI° Juegos Olímpicos de Melbourne," 5.

4. Augusto J. Leonhardt, "Informe sobre la Organización de la Concurrencia Argentina a los Juegos de la XVI Olimpiada en Melbourne," in Comité Olímpico Argentino, *Informe General del Equipo Argentino en los Juegos Olímpicos de Melbourne 1956,* 15; and Cesar R. Torres, "Peronism, International Sport and Diplomacy," in *Diplomatic Games: Sport, Statecraft, and International Relations since 1945,* ed. Heather L. Dichter and Andrew L. Johns (Lexington: University Press of Kentucky, 2014), 162–63.

5. Unless otherwise noted, the material in this section is based on Raanan Rein, "Uso y abuso del deporte en la década peronista," in *La cancha peronista: Fútbol y política (1946–1955),* ed. Raanan Rein (Buenos Aires: UNSAM Edita, 2015), 21–45; Rein, "Turning the Country into an 'Immense and Clamorous Stadium': Perón, the New Argentina, and the 1951 Pan-American Games," in *Historicizing the Pan-American Games,* ed. Bruce Kidd and Cesar R. Torres (London: Routledge, 2017), 29–42; and Torres, "Peronism, International Sport and Diplomacy."

6. For an analysis of the creation of these institutions, see Cesar R. Torres, "Tribulations and Achievements: The Early History of Olympism in Argentina," *The International Journal of the History of Sport* 18, no. 3 (2001): 59–92.

7. Ricardo C. Aldao to Sigfrid Edstrøm, June 10, 1947, "Aldao, Ricardo. Correspondance. 1927–1958" (hereafter "Aldao, Ricardo"), International Olympic Committee Archives (hereafter IOC Archives), Lausanne, Switzerland. See Torres, "Tribulations and Achievements: The Early History of Olympism in Argentina"; Torres, "Ideas encontradas: La educación física y el deporte en el debate parlamentario sobre la participación argentina en los Juegos Olímpicos de 1908," *Olympika: The International Journal of Olympic Studies,* 11 (2002): 117–42; Torres, "Stymied Expectations: Buenos Aires' Persistent Efforts to Host Olympic Games," *Olympika: The International Journal of Olympic Studies,* 16 (2007), 43–75; and Torres, "The Limits of Pan-Americanism: The Case of the Failed 1942 Pan-American Games," *The International Journal of the History of Sport* 28, no. 17 (2011): 2547–74.

8. Matthew B. Karush and Oscar Chamosa, "Introduction," in *The New Cultural History of Peronism: Power and Identity in Mid-Twentieth-Century*

Argentina, ed. Matthew B. Karush and Oscar Chamosa (Durham: Duke University Press, 2011), 1–2.

9. David Rock, *Argentina, 1516–1987: From Spanish Colonization to Alfonsín* (Berkeley: University of California Press, 1987), 262.

10. Matthew B. Karush, "Populism, Melodrama, and the Market: The Mass Cultural Origins of Peronism," in *The New Cultural History of Peronism*, 21.

11. Rein, "Turning the Country into an 'Immense and Clamorous Stadium,'" 30.

12. For a study of how Peronism politically socialized children and youth through the educational system, see Mariano Ben Plotkin, *Mañana es San Perón: A Cultural History of Perón's Argentina*, trans. Keith Zahniser (Wilmington, DE: SR Books, 2003), 83–134.

13. María Cristina Pons, "Cuerpos sublimes: el deporte en la retórica de la 'Nueva Argentina,'" in *Políticas del sentimiento: El peronismo y la construcción de la Argentina moderna*, ed. Claudia Soria, Paola Cortés Rocca and Edgardo Dieleke (Buenos Aires: Prometeo, 2010), 49–65; and Ariel Scher, Guillermo Blanco, and Jorge Búsico, *Deporte nacional: Dos siglos de historia* (Buenos Aires: Emecé, 2010), 282.

14. Raúl Gómez Alcorta et al. to Fernando I. Huergo, November 8, 1955, "Legado Prof. Luis A. Martín," Centro de Documentación Histórica IEF N° 1, Buenos Aires, Argentina.

15. See José Bernardo Marcilese, "Sociedad civil y peronismo: Los clubes deportivos en el período 1946–1955," *Recorde: Revista de História do Esporte* 2, no. 2 (2009): 1–34; and the esays in Raanan Rein, ed., *La cancha peronista*.

16. Ricardo C. Aldao to Sigfrid Edstrøm, June 10, 1947, "Aldao, Ricardo," IOC Archives.

17. See Marcela Gené, *Un mundo feliz: imágenes de los trabajadores en el primer peronismo, 1946–1955* (Buenos Aires: Universidad de San Andres, 2005); and Plotkin, *Mañana es San Perón*.

18. There was a previous Consejo Nacional de Educación Física, created in 1937. See Jorge Saraví Rivière, *Historia de la Educación Física argentina* (Buenos Aires: Libros del Zorzal, 2012), 243–48. In late 1948, Aldao wrongly told Edström that the creation of the Consejo on November 6 of the previous year meant "dissolving the ARGENTINE OLYMPIC COMMITTEE." Ricardo C. Aldao to Sigfrid Edstrøm, December 20, 1948, "Aldao, Ricardo," IOC Archives.

19. *Mensaje del Presidente de la Nación Argentina General Juan Perón al Inaugurar el 85° Periodo Ordinaria de Sesiones del Honorable Congreso Nacional: Conceptos Doctrinarios* (Buenos Aires: Presidencia de la Nación, 1951), 178.

20. Raanan Rein, "'El Primer Deportista': The Political Use and Abuse of Sport in Peronist Argentina," *The International Journal of the History of Sport* 15, no. 2 (1998): 70.

21. Rein, "'El Primer Deportista.'"

22. "Títulos mundiales y olímpicos obtenidos por nuestros país," *Olimpia: Revista de Capacitación Deportiva* (Buenos Aires), April 1954, 36.

23. Roberto J. Monteverde to Armand Massard, April 17, 1952, "Argentine. Correspondance. 1907–1965," IOC Archives.

24. Unless otherwise noted, the material on the Revolución Libertadora and its investigation of sport in this section is based on Emilio Gutiérrez, *1956, Donde*

Habita el Olvido: Básquetbol Argentino (Buenos Aires: Aurelia Rivera, 2007); Marcos Novaro, *Historia de la Argentina, 1955–2010* (Buenos Aires: Siglo Veintiuno Editores, 2010); Rock, *Argentina, 1516–1987*; and Luis Alberto Romero, *A History of Argentina in the Twentieth Century*, rev. ed., trans. James P. Brennan (University Park: Penn State University Press, 2013).

25. Rock, *Argentina, 1516–1987*, 334.

26. Juan Domingo Perón, *Los Libros del Exilio, 1955–1973*, vol. 1 (Buenos Aires: Corregidor, 1996), 195.

27. Juan K. Lang to Otto Mayer, August 18, 1956, "Argentine. Correspondance. 1907–1965," IOC Archives.

28. For an analysis of these policies, see Eduardo Elena, *Dignifying Argentina: Peronism, Citizenship, and Mass Consumption* (Pittsburgh: University of Pittsburgh Press, 2011).

29. "No Irá el equipo de básquet a los Juegos Olímpicos," *La Nación* (Buenos Aires), Agosto 26, 1956, 12.

30. Avery Brundage to Enrique Alberdi, October 18, 1955, "Argentine. Correspondance. 1907–1965," IOC Archives.

31. Enrique Alberdi to Fernando I. Huergo, August 23, 1956, "Argentine. Correspondance. 1907–1965," IOC Archives.

32. Enrique Alberdi to Avery Brundage, March 27, 1956, "Alberdi, Enrique. Correspondance. 1952–1958," IOC Archives.

33. International Olympic Committee, *The Olympic Games* (Lausanne: International Olympic Committee, 1956) 18.

34. Enrique Alberdi to Avery Brundage, March 27, 1956, "Alberdi, Enrique. Correspondance. 1952–1958," IOC Archives.

35. Enrique Alberdi to Avery Brundage, March 27, 1956.

36. Avery Brundage to Raúl Aguirre Molina, April 30, 1956, "Argentine. Correspondance. 1907–1965," IOC Archives.

37. Enrique Alberdi to Fernando I. Huergo, April 28, 1956, "Argentine. Correspondance. 1907–1965," IOC Archives.

38. Enrique Alberdi to Fernando I. Huergo, August 23, 1956 and Enrique Alberdi to Avery Brundage, May 10, 1956, "Argentine. Correspondance. 1907–1965," IOC Archives.

39. See, for example, Fernando I. Huergo to Otto Mayer, May 9, 1956, "Argentine. Correspondance. 1907–1965," IOC Archives.

40. Avery Brundage to Enrique Alberdi, August 8, 1956, "Argentine. Correspondance. 1907–1965," IOC Archives.

41. Avery Brundage to Lewis Luxton, August 31, 1956, "Argentine. Correspondance. 1907–1965," IOC Archives.

42. "Argentina Is Excluded from Olympics," *New York Times*, August 17, 1956, 25.

43. Juan K. Lang to Otto Mayer, August 18, 1956, "Argentine. Correspondance. 1907–1965," IOC Archives.

44. Milton Bracker, "Argentina Finds Herself in an Olympic Dilemma," *New York Times*, August 18, 1956, 13.

45. Procès-verbal de la rèunion de la commission Exècutive, Cortina d'Ampezzo, IOC Archives.

46. Enrique Alberdi to Fernando I. Huergo, August 23, 1956, "Argentine. Correspondance. 1907–1965," IOC Archives.

47. Raúl Aguirre Molina to International Olympic Committee, August 23, 1956; Otto Mayer to Avery Brundage, August 28, 1956; Otto Mayer to Raúl Aguirre Molina, August 29, 1956; and Avery Brundage to Fernando I. Huergo, August 30, 1956, "Argentine. Correspondance. 1907–1965," IOC Archives.

48. Confederación Argentina de Deportes-Comité Olímpico Argentino, September 3, 1956, IOC Archives.

49. Avery Brundage to Mario L. Negri, September 4, 1956, "Argentine. Correspondance. 1907–1965," IOC Archives.

50. Confederación Argentina de Deportes-Comité Olímpico Argentino, "Acta Constitutiva del Comité Olímpico Argentino," n.d, IOC Archives. *See also* Comité Olímpico Argentino, *Memoria, Septiembre 1956-Septiembre 1957* (Buenos Aires: Comité Olímpico Argentino, 1957), n.p.

51. Enrique Alberdi to Otto Mayer, September 16, 1956 and Otto Mayer to Enrique Alberdi, September 20, 1956, "Argentine. Correspondance. 1907–1965," IOC Archives.

52. Fernando I. Huergo to International Olympic Committee, September 20, 1956, "Argentine. Correspondance. 1907–1965," IOC Archives.

53. Avery Brundage to Enrique Alberdi, September 22, 1956, "Argentine. Correspondance. 1907–1965," IOC Archives.

54. Enrique Alberdi to Otto Mayer, September 24, 1956, "Argentine. Correspondance. 1907–1965," IOC Archives.

55. Enrique Alberdi to Otto Mayer, September 24, 1956.

56. Fernando I. Huergo to Avery Brundage, Octubre 1, 1956, "Argentine. Correspondance. 1907–1965," IOC Archives.

57. Otto Mayer to Argentine Olympic Committee, September 16, 1956 and Otto Mayer to Enrique Alberdi, September 20, 1956, "Argentine. Correspondance. 1907–1965," IOC Archives.

58. See Leonhardt, "Informe sobre la Organización de la Concurrencia Argentina a los Juegos de la XVI Olimpiada en Melbourne," 13–15.

59. Leonhardt, "Informe sobre la Organización de la Concurrencia Argentina a los Juegos de la XVI Olimpiada en Melbourne, 15. *See also* "Van a Melbourne," *El Gráfico*, October 5, 1956, 54.

60. Damián Cáceres, "Osvaldo Suárez: 'La Revolución Libertadora me arruinó la carrera,'" *La Nación*, January 3, 2017, http://www.lanacion.com.ar/1971237 -running-atletismo-maraton-juegos-olimpicos-osvaldo-suarez-la-revolucion -libertadora-me-arruino-la-carrera (accessed February 20, 2017).

61. Petrolini, "Informe del Presidente de la Delegación Argentina a los XVI° Juegos Olímpicos de Melbourne," 5.

62. "Proemio," in Comité Olímpico Argentino, *Informe General del Equipo Argentino en los Juegos Olímpicos de Melbourne 1956*, 1.

63. Confederación Argentina de Deportes, *Boletín Oficial* (Buenos Aires), May 1957, 12–16.

64. Avery Brundage to Comité Olímpico Argentino, May 14, 1957, "Argentine. Correspondance. 1907–1965," IOC Archives.

65. Comité Olímpico Argentino, *Memoria, Septiembre 1956-Spetiembre 1957*, n.p.

66. Enrique Alberdi to Avery Brundage, May 2, 1957, "Alberdi, Enrique. Correspondance. 1952–1958," IOC Archives.

67. Cáceres, "Osvaldo Suárez: 'La Revolución Libertadora me arruinó la carrera.'"

68. Enrique Alberdi to Otto Mayer, September 24, 1956, "Argentine. Correspondance. 1907–1965," IOC Archives.

69. Félix D. Frascara, "Deportes," in *Argentina, 1930–1960*, ed. Jorge A. Paita (Buenos Aires: Sur, 1961), 381.

70. José Oriani and Alberto P. Petrolini to the Members of the International Olympic Committee, August 20, 1963, "JO Ete 1968. Correspondance Generale. 1957–1964," IOC Archives.

71. Jorge N. Parsons to Otto Mayer, August 17, 1962, "Argentine. Correspondance. 1907–1965," IOC Archives.

72. Frascara, "Deportes," 381.

Chapter 7

1. Tomás E. Montás, "El deporte es fuente de fortaleza de la juventud; El pueblo cumplió el compromiso—Martínez Brea; Calculan alrededor 30 mil asisten a apertura Juegos," *El Caribe* (Santo Domingo), February 28, 1974, 17.

2. Pedro Caba, "XII Juegos Centroamericanos y del Caribe: Extraordinaria responsabilidad nacional," *¡Ahora!* (Santo Domingo), December 21, 1970, 73–76.

3. Pedro Caba, "XII Juegos Centroamericanos y del Caribe," 73–76.

4. Presidente del COD Juan Ulises García Saleta y Secretario del COD Gregorio Domínguez H., REF. COD-15-71, al Presidente Balaguer, February 15, 1971, Secretaría de Deportes, Educación Física y Recreación (SEDEFIR hereafter), Box 16528, Archivo General de la Nación (AGN hereafter).

5. Roberto Cassá, *Los doce años: Contrarrevolución y desarrollismo*, Tomo I (Santo Domingo: Editora Buho, 1991), 260.

6. On Trujillo's populist appeals, see Richard Lee Turits, *Foundations of Despotism: Peasants, the Trujillo Regime, and Modernity in Dominican History* (Stanford, CA: Stanford University Press, 2002). On his popular ceremonies, see Lauren H. Derby, *The Dictator's Seduction: Politics and the Popular Imagination in the Era of Trujillo* (Durham, NC: Duke University Press, 2009). Jonathan Hartlyn, *The Struggle for Democratic Politics in the Dominican Republic* (Chapel Hill: University of North Carolina Press, 1998), 11–22, described the authoritarianism of the Trujillo Era as "neosultanist" for its complete control while calling Balaguer's greater constitutionalism and less complete control "neopatrimonial authoritarianism."

7. Elizabeth S. Manley, *The Paradox of Paternalism: Women and the Politics of Authoritarianism in the Dominican Republic* (Gainesville: University Press of Florida, 2017), 158.

8. Víctor Gómez Bergés, Secretario de Estado de Relaciones Exteriores, in "La RD Favorece Consolidación De la Libertad," *El Caribe*, November 14, 1973, 15. Citing figures from the International Committee for the Alliance for Progress, Gómez Bergés noted that the Dominican Republic's GDP (Gross Domestic Product) increased by 7.5% in 1971 and 12.5% in 1972.

9. Piero Gleijeses, *La revolución desgarrada: La rebelion dominicana de 1965 y la invasion norteamericana* (Santo Domingo: Editora Búho, 2012), tells

of Dominican politics after the assassination of Trujillo through the election of Balaguer in 1966; for the meanings Dominicans projected onto democracy, see April Yoder, "Pitching Democracy: Baseball and Politics in the Dominican Republic, 1955–1978" (PhD diss., Georgetown University, 2014).

10. Scholarship on the 1966 elections has long suggested that US officials favored Balaguer, interpretations echoed by Gleijeses after his examination of documents declassified in the early 2000s. See, for example, Daniel Lawler and Carolyn Yee, ed., *Foreign Relations of the United States, 1964–1968*, vol. 32 (Washington, DC: Government Printing Office, 2005), Document 80, 176, https://history.state .gov/historicaldocuments/frus1964–68v32/ch1.

11. Manley, *The Paradox of Paternalism*, 5–8.

12. Manley, 156–89.

13. Manley, especially 29–60; Lauren H. Derby, "The Dictator's Seduction: Gender and State Spectacle during the Trujillo Regime," in *Latin American Popular Culture: An Introduction*, ed. William H. Beezley and Linda A. Curcio-Nagy (Wilmington, DE: SR Books, 2000), 213–39.

14. Manley, *The Paradox of Paternalism*, 158.

15. Barbara J. Keys, *Globalizing Sport: National Rivalry and International Community in the 1930s* (Cambridge, MA: Harvard University Press, 2006); and Brenda Elsey, "Cultural Ambassadorship and the Pan-American Games of the 1950s," *International Journal of the History of Sport* 33, no. 1–2 (2016): 105–26.

16. Greg Grandin, *The Last Colonial Massacre: Latin America in the Cold War*, rev. ed. (Chicago: University of Chicago Press, 2011), 4. My framework also borrows from Gilbert M. Joseph, "What We Know and Should Know: Bringing Latin America More Meaningfully into Cold War Studies," in *In from the Cold: Latin America's New Encounters with the Cold War*, ed. Gilbert M. Joseph and Daniela Spenser (Durham, NC: Duke University Press, 2008), 1–46.

17. These debates often centered on government incentives for national industries. Building on Frank Moya Pons's findings that the public debates around incentives in the 1970s created a "business mentality" in the country, I argue that sportswriters, and then Dominicans of all classes, applied their criticisms of this corporate welfare to their discussions around sport. On the incentives and the debates surrounding them, see Rafael Francisco De Moya Pons (Frank Moya Pons), "Industrial Incentives in the Dominican Republic 1880–1983" (PhD diss., Columbia University, 1987). On the debates over amateur and professional sport in the Dominican Republic, see April Yoder, "Pitching Democracy," especially chapter 5.

18. Caba, "XII Juegos Centroamericanos y del Caribe," 74–76.

19. Antonio Sotomayor, "*Un parque para cada pueblo*: Julio Enrique Monagas and the Politics of Sport and Recreation in Puerto Rico during the 1940s," *Caribbean Studies* 42, no. 2 (2014): 3–40.

20. Raanan Rein, "*El primer deportista*: The Political Use and Abuse of Sport in Peronist Argentina," *The International Journal of the History of Sport* 15, no. 2 (1998): 54–76.

21. Yoder, "Pitching Democracy," 16–51.

22. On regional solidarity and the XII Games, see April Yoder, "Dominican Baseball and Latin American Pluralism, 1969–1973," in *Oxford Research Encyclopedia of Latin American History*, ed. William H. Beezley (New York:

Oxford University Press, 2016), http://latinamericanhistory.oxfordre.com/view/
10.1093/acrefore/9780199366439.001.0001/acrefore-9780199366439-e-355?rskey
=GjGmRv&result=1.

23. Tirso A. Váldez hijo, "Cuadrante Deportivo," *¡Ahora!*, February 20,
1965, 54.

24. Yoder, "Dominican Baseball and Latin American Pluralism."

25. Caba, "XII Juegos Centroamericanos y del Caribe," 74.

26. José Armenteros, Presidente, Fundación Dominicana de Desarrollo, Inc.,
Carta al Dr. Joaquín Balaguer, Hon. Señor Presidente de la República, 3 de octubre
de 1967, SEDEFIR, Box 16583, AGN; Alvaro Arvelo hijo, "Embajador de EU Agasaja
A Piratas de Pittsburgh," *El Caribe*, October 24, 1967, 4; and "Ejecutivo Califica
Valioso Aporte de Piratas de Pittsburgh," *El Caribe*, October 24, 1967, 6.

27. Tirso A. Váldez, "Cuadrante Deportivo," *¡Ahora!*, April 10, 1965, 55; and
Thomas F. Carter, *The Quality of Homeruns: The Passion, Politics, and Language of
Cuban Baseball* (Durham, NC: Duke University Press, 2008), 17–35.

28. Váldez, "Cuadrante Deportivo," 55; and Váldez, "Cuadrante Deportivo,"
¡Ahora!, February 20, 1965, 54.

29. Director General de Deportes Horacio A. Veras, "Proyecto de Resolución,
Creación de los Juegos Deportivos Nacionales," [s/f], SEDEFIR, Box 16545, AGN.

30. Horacio A. Veras G., Núm 00348: Memorandum al Excelentísimo Señor
Presidente de la República, 11 de marzo de 1969, SEDEFIR, Box 16545, AGN.

31. Peggy B. de Bautista, Gobernadora Provincial de La Vega; César Barche
Viñas, Senador; y Dr. Fausto Sicard Moya, Diputado, Carta al General Osiris
Perdomo R., Jefe del Cuerpo de Ayudantes del Presidente, 3 de diciembre de 1969,
SEDEFIR, Box 16545, AGN.

32. Gaspar L [Vilchez] Suero, José María D'Soto Sánchez, Dr. Felipe
Ant. Moquete C., y demás, Azua, Carta al Dr. Joaquín Balaguer, Presidente
Constitucional de la República Dominicana, 20 de marzo de 1973, SEDEFIR,
Box 16528, AGN.

33. Gaspar L [Vilchez] Suero, José María D'Soto Sánchez, Dr. Felipe
Ant. Moquete C., y demás, Azua, Carta al Dr. Joaquín Balaguer, Presidente
Constitucional de la República Dominicana, 20 de marzo de 1973, SEDEFIR,
Box 16528, AGN.

34. Banco Central, *Ejecución del Presupuesto* (Santo Domingo: Banco Central,
1971, 1972, 1973, 1974); Presidente Joaquín Balaguer, Núm 6887 al Director
Nacional del Presupuesto, 20 de febrero de 1970, SEDEFIR, Box 16534, AGN.

35. Secretario Administrativo de la Presidencia, Dr. J. Ricardo Ricourt,
Oficio Núm 19641 al Director General de Radio Televisión Dominicano, Asunto:
Concesión del Centro Social Obrero a la Dirección General de Deportes, 4 de julio
de 1972, SEDEFIR, Box 16572, AGN.

36. Carta, 16 de septiembre de 1971, and other requests for installations, equipment, and financial support by groups and officials from across the country during
1971, SEDEFIR, Box 16572, AGN.

37. See Eric Zolov, *Refried Elvis: The Rise of Mexican Counterculture* (Berkeley:
University of California Press, 1999); and Valeria Manzano, "The Creation of a
Social Problem: Youth Culture, Drugs, and Politics in Cold War Argentina," *Hispanic
American Historical Review* 95, no. 1 (2015): 37–69.

38. Domingo Saint-Hilaire hijo, citing Guillermo Henríquez from his show

Claridades Deportivas, "Deportes mejor camino para erradicar las drogas," *La Información* (Santiago de los Caballeros), March 4, 1975, 5.

39. Héctor Bullo Steffani, Carta al Apreciado Dr. Balaguer, 14 de noviembre de 1973, SEDEFIR, Box 16578, AGN; Héctor Bullo Steffani, "Informe Deportivo que Envia el Sr. Héctor Steffani al Dr. Quezada, Secretario Administrativo de la Presidencia," 30 de septiembre de 1969, SEDEFIR, Box 16545, AGN.

40. Héctor Bullo Steffani, Carta al Apreciado Dr. Balaguer, 14 de noviembre de 1973, SEDEFIR, Box 16578, AGN; Héctor Bullo Steffani, "Informe Deportivo que Envia el Sr. Héctor Steffani al Dr. Quezada, Secretario Administrativo de la Presidencia," 30 de septiembre de 1969, SEDEFIR, Box 16545, AGN.

41. Saint-Hilaire hijo, "Deportes mejor camino para erradicar las drogas," 5.

42. Espacio Pagado, "Directorios Provincial y Municipales Partido Reformista en la Provincia de San Juan de la Maguana Apoyan la Postulación del Doctor Joaquín Balaguer en 1970," *El Caribe,* August 13, 1969, 6–8.

43. Ramón Rodríguez, "Los XII Juegos de 1974 cumplen 40 años," *Listín Diario* (Santo Domingo), February 24, 2014, http://www.listindiario.com/el-deporte/2014/02/24/311957.

44. Wayne Wilson, "The IOC and the Status of Women in the Olympic Movement: 1972–1996," *Research Quarterly for Exercise and Sport* 67, no. 2 (1996): 185; and Jim Riordan, "The Rise and Fall of Soviet Olympic Champions," *Olympika: The International Journal of Olympic Studies,* 2 (1993): 25–44.

45. International Olympic Committee, *Factsheet: Women in the Olympic Movement. UPDATE-January 2016* (Lausanne: International Olympic Committee, 2016), https://stillmed.olympic.org/Documents/Reference_documents_Factsheets/Women_in_Olympic_Movement.pdf.

46. Comité Olímpico Dominicano, "Olímpicos Veranos," *Colimdo.org,* accessed June 23, 2017, http://colimdo.org/actuaciones-atletas-dominicanos/torneos-olimpicos-oficiales/olimpicos-verano/.

47. International Olympic Committee, *Factsheet: Women in the Olympic Movement. UPDATE-January 2016,* Table B; Enrique Montesinos, *Los juegos regionales más antiguos: Juegos Deportivos Centroamericanos y del Caribe* (n.p.: Organización Deportiva Centroamericana y del Caribe, 2013), http://www.odecabe.org/wp-content/uploads/2016/09/Libro-CAC-WEB.pdf; Comité Olímpico Dominicano, "Centroamericanos y del Caribe," *Colimdo.org,* accessed June 23, 2017, http://www.colimdo.org/actuaciones-atletas-dominicanos/torneos-olimpicos-oficiales/centroamericanos-y-del-caribe/.

48. Comité Olímpico Dominicano, "Centroamericanos y del Caribe."

49. Comité Olímpico Dominicano, "XII Juegos Centroamericanos y del Caribe: Santo Domingo 1974," *Colimdo.org,* accessed June 23, 2017, http://www.colimdo.org/actuaciones-atletas-dominicanos/torneos-olimpicos-oficiales/centroamericanos-y-del-caribe/santo-domingo-1974/.

50. Comité Organizador, *Docejuegos. Compromiso cumplido. Santo Domingo 1974,* vol. I (n.p.: Organización Deportiva Centroamericana y del Caribe, 1974), 157, accessed June 23, 2017, http://www.odecabe.org/memorias/.

51. Elsey, "Cultural Ambassadorship and the Pan-American Games of the 1950s," 105–26.

52. Joshua H. Nadel, *Fútbol: Why Soccer Matters in Latin America* (Gainesville: University Press of Florida, 2014), 219–22.

53. Carmenchu Brusiloff, "Villa Deportivo Adquiere Cada Día Más Movimiento; Atleta Azteca Lamenta: 'Muchachas no nos Hacen Caso,'" *El Caribe*, February 26, 1974, suplemento deportivo, 34.

54. "Delegación Boricua Llega a RD; Es Más Nutrida Sale de Borinquen," *El Caribe*, February 26, 1974, suplemento deportivo, 35.

55. Comité Organizador, *Docejuegos. Compromiso cumplido. Santo Domingo 1974*, vol. II, 323–37.

56. Comité Olímpico Dominicano, "Panamericanos," *Colimdo.org*, accessed June 22, 2017, http://www.colimdo.org/actuaciones-atletas-dominicanos/torneos-olimpicos-oficiales/panamericanos/.

57. Comité Olímpico Dominicano, "XII Juegos Centroamericanos y del Caribe."

58. "Mayobanex Mueses exaltado al Pabellón de la Fama RD," *Listín Diario*, Octubre 15, 2007, http://www.listindiario.com/el-deporte/2007/10/15/32799/mayobanex-mueses-exaltado-al-pabellon-de-la-fama-rd.

59. García Saleta, REF.COD-506–73 al Presidente Balaguer, 5 de noviembre de 1973; Director Departamento Nacional de Investigaciones, No. 3508 al Secretario Administrativo del Presidente, 14 de noviembre de 1973; García Saleta, N/REF. COD. 662–74, 9 de enero de 1974, SEDEFIR, Box 16528.

60. Comité Organizador del II Torneo de la Amistad, Carta al Presidente Balaguer, 2 de agosto de 1972, SEDEFIR, Box 16572, AGN; Comité Organizador Docejuegos, Carta al Presidente Balaguer, 29 de diciembre de 1973, SEDEFIR, Box 16528, AGN, requested permission for the arrival of Cuban delegation for the I Volleyball Championship of Dominican Fraternity for men and women in the month before the XII Games.

61. Manley, *The Paradox of Paternalism*, 7.

62. "Closer to Chaos," *Time*, April 13, 1970, 36.

63. Manley, *The Paradox of Paternalism*, 156–64.

64. Manley, 165–74.

65. Dr. J. Ricardo Ricourt, Sec Administrativo de la Presidencia, Núm 33349 al Ing Federico Medrano Basilis, Director General del Comité Organizador Docejuegos Deportivos Centroamericanos y del Caribe, 13 de noviembre de 1973, SEDEFIR, Box 16528, AGN.

66. Ing. Federico Medrano Basilis, Director General del Comité Organizador Docejuegos Deportivos Centroamericanos y del Caribe, Carta al Excelentísimo Señor Dr. Joaquín Balaguer, Presidente de la República, 3 de noviembre de 1973, SEDEFIR, Box 16528, AGN.

67. Ing. Federico Medrano Basilis, Director General del Comité Organizador Docejuegos Deportivos Centroamericanos y del Caribe, Carta al Excelentísimo Señor Dr. Joaquín Balaguer, Presidente de la República, 3 de noviembre de 1973, SEDEFIR, Box 16528, AGN.

68. Comité Organizador I Juegos Deportivos Nacionales y Juan Ulises García Saleta, CO/No. 74, al Presidente Joaquín Balaguer, 4 de marzo de 1968, SEDEFIR, Box 16518, AGN.

69. Gobernación Provincial de Dajabón: Gobernadora Civil Librada Baez de Socias, Coronel Ejército Nacional Francisco A Medina Sánchez, y Rafael Osiris Martínez, Carta al Dr. Domingo Porfirio Rojas, Presidente del Comité Nacional de los Primeros Juegos Fronterizos, 4 de abril de 1975, SEDEFIR, Box 16516, AGN.

70. Presidente Germán Peralta Nivar, Secretario de Relaciones Públicas, Héctor

Pdo Germosen, y Secretaria General del Club Cultural y Deportivo Amantes de Quisqueya, Carta al Presidente Balaguer, 11 de marzo de 1972, forwarded by Director General de Deportes Veras to the President, Núm 8276, 22 de marzo de 1972, SEDEFIR Box 16572, AGN.

71. Presidente Germán Peralta Nivar, Secretario de Relaciones Públicas, Héctor Pdo Germosen, y Secretaria General del Club Cultural y Deportivo Amantes de Quisqueya, Carta al Presidente Balaguer, 11 de marzo de 1972, forwarded by Director General de Deportes Veras to the President, Núm 8276, 22 de marzo de 1972, SEDEFIR Box 16572, AGN.

72. Paula J. Pettavino and Geralyn Pye, *Sport in Cuba: The Diamond in the Rough* (Pittsburgh: University of Pittsburgh Press, 1994), 107–13 and 121–26.

73. Gertrud Pfister, "Gender, Gender Equality and Women's Sport: Theories and Practices," in *Women and Sport in Latin America*, ed. Rosa López de D'Amico, Tansin Benn, and Gertrud Pfister (New York: Routledge, 2016), 39; and Gladys Bequer Díaz, Ana María Morales Ferrer, and Anneliese Goslin, "Women and Sport in Cuba," in *Women and Sport in Latin America*, 118–28.

74. Pfister, "Gender, Gender Equality and Women's Sport," 32–54; and Pettavino and Pye, *Sport in Cuba*, 110.

75. Manley, *The Paradox of Paternalism*, 219–42.

76. Julie Marie Bunck, "The Politics of Sports in Revolutionary Cuba," *Cuban Studies*, 20 (1990): 122–29; and Margaret Randall, *Exporting Revolution: Cuba's Global Solidarity* (Durham. NC: Duke University Press, 2017), 192–204.

77. Sotomayor, "*Un parque para cada pueblo*," 14–17.

Chapter 8

1. See, for example, Katya Wesolowski, "From 'Moral Disease' to 'National Sport': Race, Nation, and Capoeira in Brazil," in *Sports Culture in Latin American History*, ed. David Sheinin (Pittsburgh: University of Pittsburgh Press, 2015), 161–82; Renata Maria Toledo and Maria Tarcisa Silva Bega, "Nationalism and Public Policies of Sports in Brazil" and Hortensia Moreno, "Women Boxers and Nationalism in Mexico" in *Sports and Nationalism in Latin/o America*, ed. Hector Fernández L'Hoeste, Robert Irwin, and Juan Poblete (New York: Palgrave MacMillan, 2015), 125–39 and 181–200, respectively.

2. Hector Fernández L'Hoeste, "Race, Sports, and Regionalism in the Construction of Colombian Nationalism," in *Sports and Nationalism in Latin/o America,* 88.

3. Colombia has 27 Olympic medals, 17 of them won by black Colombians, 10 won by nonblack Colombians (mestizo, white-mestizo, no indigenous representation. There are no medals by black people that are not stereotypical "black" sports in Colombia (track and field, boxing, wrestling, and weightlifting). The majority of the medals won by nonblack people are for shooting and cycling. Only one of the 11 black athletes responsible for 17 medals is from an "Andean" region. All others are from traditionally black areas, and therefore impoverished regions. 9 of the 17 medals are black women, so overrepresented in medals, but also the least represented in economic and symbolic wealth. One more point: since entering the Paralympics (1976), Colombia has won 26 medals, sending disproportionately fewer athletes, as compared to Olympic medals (27) with more years and more athletes, yet the

media and marketing celebration of national athletes still goes to the conventional Olympic one, not the Paralympic one. See www.coc.org.co.

4. This chapter will not elaborate much on the peace process. For the article it is important to understand that the peace process and the Olympic/Paralympic cycle 2016 were chronologically concurrent events. The peace process between the FARC and the government of Santos can be easily investigated by the reader in other works, including Andrea Fanta Castro, Alejandro Herrero-Olaizola, and Chloe Rutter-Jensen, ed., *Territories of Conflict: Traversing Colombia through Cultural Studies* (Rochester: University of Rochester Press, 2017).

5. Rosi Braidotti, *Transpositions: On Nomadic Ethics* (Cambridge: Polity, 2006), 7.

6. Braidotti writes in her 2013 work *The Posthuman* (Cambridge: Polity), "We need to devise new social, ethical and discursive schemes of subject formation to match the profound transformations we are undergoing. That means that we need to learn to think differently about ourselves. I take the posthuman predicament as an opportunity to empower the pursuit of alternative schemes of thought, knowledge and self-representation. The posthuman condition urges us to think critically and creatively about who and what we are actually in the process of becoming" (12).

7. The 2016 Rio de Janeiro Olympic/Paralympic events had a refugee team and an independent athlete participation category for those athletes whose possibility of belonging to a nation has been eliminated or denied.

8. Lennard Davis, "Bodies of Difference: Politics, Disability, and Representation", in *Disability Studies: Enabling the Humanities*, ed. Brenda Jo Brueggemann, Sharon L. Snyder, and Rosemarie Garland-Thomson (New York: Modern Language Association, 2002), 105.

9. Donna Haraway, "A Cyborg Manifesto: Science, Technology, and Socialist-Feminism in the Late Twentieth Century," in *The Cybercultures Reader*, ed. David Bell and Barbara M. Kennedy (New York: Routledge, 2000), 316.

10. Colombia sent 39 Paralympic athletes versus 147 conventional Olympic athletes. Total participation for Rio 2016 was 11,237 Olympic athletes and 4342 Paralympic athletes. Tickets sold for Olympics over 5 million, tickets sold for Paralympics nearly 2 million. The prices for Olympic tickets were roughly 3 times the price of Paralympic tickets. Nevertheless, the Rio Games were the second most highly attended Paralympic games after London 2012.

11. Braidotti, *Transpositions*, 90.

12. Rosi Braidotti, *Metamorphoses: Towards a Materialist Theory of Becoming* (Cambridge: Polity, 2002), 198.

13. All references to football are "soccer" in US-American English.

14. "Santos entregó a deportistas paralímpicos la bandera de Colombia para Río 2016," *Noticias RCN* (Bogotá), September 1, 2016, http://www.noticiasrcn.com/deportes-otros-deportes/santos-entrego-deportistas-paralimpicos-bandera-colombia-rio-2016.

15. *Deportes RCN* and *Caracol* are the two most circulated and viewed sport reports available nationally on noncable television and the web.

16. In a medium with a much smaller circulation, *Cablenoticias*, there is actually a photo of Santos giving Torres a white material flag; again, the disability is not visible. "Santos entrega a deportistas paralímpicos bandera para Río 2016,"

Cablenoticias, September 1, 2016, http://www.cablenoticias.tv/vernoticiabb.asp ?WPLACA=81512.

17. The [national] leader thanked Torres for carrying this flag and assured that he "embodied the gratefulness towards the soldiers and police" that all Colombians feel. "You are the example of what we Colombians can be." (The translation is mine and corrects the grammar of the newspaper version, or what I assume is poor writing).

18. "Santos entrega a deportistas paralímpicos bandera para Río 2016."

19. In a 2010 document from the Ministry of Culture, among other inequalities they write that Afro-descended Colombians have 11% higher rates of basic needs unsatisfied, double the migration and displacement, and 7% higher infant mortality rates than nonblack Colombians. Mincultura, "Comunidades Negras, Afrocolombianas, Raizales y Palenqueras," accessed May 1, 2017, http://www .mincultura.gov.co/areas/poblaciones/comunidades-negras-afrocolombianas -raizales-y-palenqueras/Paginas/default.aspx DANE, and Universidad del Valle report that in the Cauca region, which has one of the highest percentages of black population, more than double the percentage of black Colombians have days of no food, as compared to non–ethnic-group-identified Colombians (14% versus 7%). DANE y Universidad del Valle, "Análisis regional de los principales indicadores sociodemográficos de la comunidad afrocolombiana e indígena a partir de la información del censo general 2005," accessed May 1, 2017, https://www.dane.gov.co/ files/censo2005/etnia/sys/Afro_indicadores_sociodemograficos_censo2005.pdf.

20. Eduardo Cadava, "*Lapsus Imaginis*: The Image in Ruins," *October* 96 (2001): 36.

21. Judith Butler, *Precarious Lives: The Powers of Mourning and Violence* (New York: Verso, 2004), 21.

22. Ingrid Bolivar, "El Oficio de los Futbolistas Colombianos en los Años 60 y 70: Recreación de las Regiones, Juegos de Masculinidad y Vida Sentimental" (PhD diss., University of Wisconsin, Madison, 2016). The normative press narrative is that of masculinity and national glory, yet Ingrid Bolívar's interesting work on regional football in the 1960s and 1970s points out that the types of masculinity and affective ties narrated by ex-footballers challenge homogenous discourses of masculinity and football that the press usually constructs.

23. Without elaborating further, I include the phantom limb as a gesture toward the conversation on representation and reproduction of Walter Benjamin, whose work is part of the genealogy of posthuman philosophies.

24. The peace treaty that "ended" a 60-year conflict between the FARC and the military took four years to negotiate, only to be rejected by a popular vote and then later ratified by Congress.

25. Susan Jeffords, *The Remasculinization of America: Gender and the Vietnam War* (Bloomington: Indiana University Press, 1989), 8.

26. The Paralympic Games have a range of classifications for physical disabilities. These do not cover cognitive disabilities. Deaf people can participate in World Deaf Games, now called Deaflympics, or Olympics, but not Paralympics.

27. I could not secure permission to reproduce the images. To view the images, see Eduardo Leal, "Victims and Heroes," http://www.eduardoleal.co.uk/victims -heroes (accessed November 10, 2016).

28. See "Eduardo Leal," www.eduardoleal.co.uk (accessed November 10, 2016).

29. Michael Davidson, "Universal Design," in *The Disability Studies Reader*, ed. Lennard Davis (New York: Routledge, 2006), 119.

30. I discuss the extent to which Paralympic athletes reproduce a corporeal construct that pretends that their disability is individual not structural in Chloe Rutter-Jensen, "Can I Have a Ramp with that Medal? Colombian Paralympics and the Prosthetic Lim(b)inality of Nation," in *Sports and Nationalism in Latin/o America*, 163–79.

31. Gregory Lobo, "Spectacular 'Nationism' in Modern Colombia: Mediating Commitment to the Military Option," *Media, War & Conflict* 10, no. 3 (2017): 268.

32. José Orlando Ascencio, "El cabo Torres, esperanza de medalla en Paralímpicos," *El Tiempo* (Bogotá), April 28, 2016, http://www.eltiempo.com/archivo/documento/CMS-16575363 (accessed November 10, 2016).

33. Haraway, "A Cyborg Manifesto," 292.

34. Haraway, 311.

Chapter 9

1. Pierre de Coubertin, "Géographie Sportive, Revue Olympique," in *Pierre de Coubertin: Textes Choisis*, ed. Norbert Müller, vol. 2 (Zurich: Weidmann, 1986), 452.

2. Lamartine P. DaCosta, "Olympic Globalization: Sport Geopolitics or IOC Power Politics?," in *Olympic Studies. Current Intellectual Crossroads*, ed. Lamaritne DaCosta (Rio de Janeiro: University Gama Filho, 2002), 91–105.

3. Fernando Vale Castro, "O Panamericanismo em Jogo," *Revista da Historia da Biblioteca Nacional* 22 (2007): 18–25.

4. Cesar R. Torres, "Stymied Expectations: Buenos Aires' Persistent Efforts to Host Olympic Games," *Olympika: The International Journal of Olympic Studies* 16 (2007): 43–75.

5. Cesar R. Torres, "Tribulations and Achievements: The Early History of Olympism in Argentina," *The International Journal of the History of Sport* 18, no. 3 (2001): 59–92.

6. Cesar R. Torres, "On the Merit of the Legacy of Failed Olympic Bids" (2011), accessed November 1, 2017, http://digitalcommons.brockport.edu/cgi/viewcontent.cgi?article=1003&context=pes_confpres.

7. Cesar R. Torres, "Stymied Expectations: Buenos Aires' Persistent Efforts to Host Olympic Games," *Olympika: The International Journal of Olympic Studies* 16 (2007): 63.

8. Daniel de la Cueva, "Buenos Aires, Ciudad Olímpica: Candidaturas y Proyectos desde 1936 a 2016," unpublished manuscript, 2017.

9. Joseph L. Arbena, "Sport and the Study of Latin American History: An Overview," *Journal of Sport History* 13, no. 2 (1986): 87–96.

10. Joseph L. Arbena, "Sport, Development, and Mexican Nationalism, 1920–1970," *Journal of Sport History* 18, no. 3 (1991): 359–64.

11. Lamartine P. DaCosta, *Planejamento México* (Brasilia: Divisão de Educação Física, Ministerio da Educação e Cultura, 1968).

12. Lamartine P. DaCosta, ed., *XIX Olimpíada Mexico 68-Aspectos Técnicos Evolutivos* (Brasilia: Ministerio da Educação e Cultura, 1969).

13. Barbara Schausteck Almeida, Andre Mendes Capraro, and Wanderley

Marchi Junior, "Os Jogos Olímpicos na Cidade do Mexico 1968: Discursos Oficiais, da Midia e da Literatura Científica," *Revista Brasileira de Educação Física e Esporte* 29, no. 3 (2015): 383–93.

14. Almeida, Capraro, and Marchi Junior, "Os Jogos Olímpicos na Cidade do Mexico 1968," 386.

15. Almeida, Capraro, and Marchi Junior, 385–86.

16. Almeida, Capraro, and Marchi Junior, 359.

17. Joana Lopes, "Não queremos olimpiadas, queremos revolução," *Caminhos da Memória*, October 2, 2009, https://caminhosdamemoria.wordpress. com/2009/10/02/%c2%abnao-queremos-olimpiadas-queremos-revolucao%c2%bb/ (accessed April 20, 2017).

18. Almeida, Capraro, and Marchi Junior, "Os Jogos Olímpicos na Cidade do Mexico 1968," 387.

19. Eric Zolov, "Showcasing the 'Land of Tomorrow': Mexico and the 1968 Olympics," *Americas* 61, no. 2 (2004): 159–188.

20. Amy Bass, ed., *In the Game: Race, Identity, and Sports in the Twentieth Century* (New York: Palgrave Macmillan, 2005).

21. Kevin Witherspoon, *Before the Eyes of the World. Mexico and the 1968 Olympic Games* (DeKalb: Northern Illinois University Press, 2008).

22. Keith Brewster and Claire Brewster. "Pride and Prejudice: Foreign Perceptions of Mexico as an Olympic Host," *The International Journal of History of Sport* 26, no. 6 (2009): 764–89.

23. Luis Castañeda, "Choreographing the Metropolis: Networks of Circulation and Power in Olympic Mexico," *Journal of Design History* 25, no. 3 (2012): 285–303.

24. Zolov, "Showcasing the 'Land of Tomorrow,'" 159–60.

25. Luis Castañeda, "Beyond Tlatelolco: Design, Media, and Politics at Mexico 68," *Grey Room* 40 (2010): 100–126.

26. DaCosta, *XIX Olimpíada Mexico 68-Aspectos Técnicos Evolutivos*, 1–46.

27. Richard Cashman, *Impact of the Games on Olympic Host Cities* (Barcelona: Centre d'Estudis Olímpics and International Chair in Olympism, 2010). http://ceo .uab.cat/pdf/cashman_eng.pdf.

28. Claire Brewster, "Changing Impressions of Mexico for the 1968 Games," *Bulletin of Latin American Research* 29, no. 1 (2010): 23–45.

29. Marcia de Franceschi Neto-Wacker, "A participação do Brasil no Movimento Olímpico internacional no período de 1896 a 1925" (PhD diss., Universidade Gama Filho, 1999).

30. Marcia de Franceschi Neto-Wacker and Christian Wacker, *Brazil Goes Olympic: Historical Fragments from Brazil and the Olympic Movement until 1936* (Kassel: Agon-Sportverlag, 2010), 105–27.

31. "Os Jogos Olympicos de 1922 – Será a Brasil Prejudicado pela França?," *O Estado de São Paulo* (São Paulo), July 2, 1919, 1.

32. Sarah Boseley, "Zika Virus Risk at Rio Olympics 'Negligible,' Says Yale report," *The Guardian*, July 25, 2016, https://www.theguardian.com/world/2016/ jul/25/zika-virus-risk-at-rio-olympics-negligible-says-yale-report (accessed July 31, 2018).

33. Lamartine DaCosta, "Epilogue: Hegemony, Emancipation and Mythology," in *Sport in Latin American Society. Past and Present*, ed. James A. Mangan and Lamartine DaCosta (London: Frank Cass, 2002), 181–96.

34. DaCosta, "Epilogue," 186–187.

35. Lamartine DaCosta, "O Dia Seguinte dos Jogos Olimpicos e Paralimpicos – Experiencias e novas Previsoes," in *Anuário Sou do esporte*, ed. Fabiana Bentes (Rio de Janeiro: n.p., 2016), 166–71.

36. Leonardo Mataruna, Thiago Melo, Andressa Guimaraes, Renen Petersen-Wagner, and Daniel Range, "Olympic Agenda 2020, Social Media and Online Strategies for the Social Value of the Olympic Games," in *The Future of Sports Mega-events*, ed. Andrea Deslandes, Lamartine P. DaCosta, and Ana Miragaya (Rio de Janeiro: Engenho Arte e Cultura, 2015), 422–34.

37. Siti Ezaleila Mustafa and Azizah Hamzah, "Online Social Networking: A New Form of Social Interaction," *International Journal of Social Science and Humanity* 1, no. 2 (2011): 96.

38. "How do We Know that Rio 2016 Was a Success," *IOC News*, December 6, 2016. https://www.olympic.org/news/how-do-we-know-that-rio-2016-was-a -success (accessed July 31, 2018).

39. "How do We Know that Rio 2016 Was a Success."

40. DaCosta, "O Dia Seguinte dos Jogos Olimpicos e Paralimpicos," 167–69.

41. Lamartine DaCosta, "E o que Realmente Aconteceu: Jogos Olímpicos ou Feira Internacional Olímpica?," in *Diferentes Olhares sobre os Jogos Rio 2016: A Midia, os Profissionais e os Espectadores*, ed. Ailton Oliveira and Marcelo Haiachi (forthcoming).

42. Andrea Deslandes, Lamartine P. DaCosta, and Ana Miragaya, ed., *The Future of Sports Mega-events* (Rio de Janeiro: Engenho Arte e Cultura, 2015).

43. International Olympic Committee, *Olympic Agenda 2020. 20+20 Recommendations* (Lausanne: International Olympic Committee, 2015). https://stillmed.olympic.org/Documents/Olympic_Agenda_2020/Olympic_ Agenda_2020-20-20_Recommendations-ENG.pdf. (accessed July 31, 2018).

Conclusion

1. See Benjamin D. Hennig, *Rediscovering the World: Map Transformations of Human and Physical Space* (New York: Springer, 2013) for an explanation of the cartographic technique used to develop this cartogram.

2. The *Journal of Sport for Development* is a good source for academics and practitioners.

INDEX

Boletín Nacional (Puerto Rico), 91
Bolivar, Simón, 166
Bosch, Juan, 132
boxing: Argentine Olympic athletes, 127; Brazilian athletes, 115; Cuban athletes, 34, 42, 50; Puerto Rican athletes, 76; racial stereotypes, 148, 239n3; Uruguayan athletes, 210n16
Bracker, Milton, 125
Braidotti, Rosi, 149, 151, 154, 155, 157
Brasília, Brazil, 66, 177
Brasil, Wilson, 104
Brazil: anti-Temer protests, 3, 4; Brazilian bid, 175–78; complexo de vira-lata, 193; economic development, 96, 98, 103, 178; elitism, 193; female athletes, 198; FIFA World Cup (1950), 10, 96, 98, 227n11; FIFA World Cup title, 103; global recognition and prestige, 3, 176, 177, 178, 192, 193; infrastructure improvements, 178; internal stability, 177–78; international sport competitions, 105; literacy rate, 193; medal performances, 10, 95, 97–106, 192–93; national anthem, 100, 101; national identity issues, 98–99, 104–6, 109–10, 176, 228n46; Olympic athletic delegation, 95, 97–106, 176, 192–93; Olympic Games bids and rejections, 11, 175–78, 197; Olympic Movement, 10, 95, 192–93, 211n26; organized athletic games, 6, 10, 96, 193; political transitions, 96, 103, 177–78, 226n4; Puerto Rican independence movement, 82; race relations, 100, 101, 106, 192–93, 228n28; South American Games (1922), 14, 24, 25–27; sport-politics relationship, 98–104, 177, 179, 227n11; World War II participation, 63; YMCA missionary work, 21. See also da Silva, Adhemar Ferreira; Rio de Janeiro; Rio de Janeiro Olympic Games (2016)
Brazilian Centennial of Independence (1922), 176

Brazilian Integralist Action, 226n4
Brazilian Labor Party, 226n4
Brazilian Olympic Committee, 95–96, 99, 176
Brazilian Press Association, 103
Brazilian Sports Confederation (CBD), 99
Brewster, Claire, 172, 174, 175, 190
Brewster, Keith, 172, 190
Bronx Marathon (1911), 77
Brown, Elwood, 14, 23–25, 26, 28, 29, 212n47
Brum, Baltasar, 20
Brundage, Avery: Argentine Olympic controversy, 123–26, 128–30; Olympic values, 191; sporting diplomacy, 62, 66; sport-politics challenges, 41–42, 65; support for Mexican Olympic bid, 68, 70–71; support for regional games, 65
Buenos Aires: Centennial Olympic Games (1910), 167; global recognition and prestige, 4, 167–68, 176; "Olympic Corridor" project, 168–69; Olympic Games bids and rejections, 11, 115, 117, 130, 166–69; Pan-American Games (1951), 97, 115, 117, 121, 122, 166, 169; urban reform and development, 168–69, 179, 182, 197; YMCA missionary work, 21; Youth Olympic Games (2018), 4, 5, 168–69, 179, 180
Buenos Aires (Argentine province), 117
bullfights, charitable, 59, 219n23
Bustos Morón, Horacio, 116
Butler, Judith, 154

C

Cablenoticias, 240n16
Cabo Rojo, Puerto Rico, 81
Cadava, Eduardo, 153, 154
Caguas, Puerto Rico, 86
Calles, Plutarco Elías, 56, 58, 59, 60
Camacho, Pedro Juan, 91
Canada, 229n47
Candidature File (Brazil), 3

Capraro, André, 170. *See also* Almeida, Barbara
Caracol, 240*n*15
Cárdenas, Lázaro, 62
Cardona, Rafael, 59
Caribbean: identity politics and scholarship, 207*n*26; importance of sport, 6–7, 8, 196; independence movements, 35–36, 37, 82; Mexican diplomatic initiatives, 63; nation formation and development, 7–9; Olympic Games bids, 11; Olympic Movement, 5, 6–9, 165–66, 197; Sport for Development and Peace (SDP) projects, 198. *See also* Central America; Cuba; Dominican Republic
Carlos, John, 171, 173
Carter, Thomas, 135, 189
cartolas (top hats), 186
Carvajal Soto, Félix "El Andarín", 37
Casa del Estudiante Indígena, 58
Cashman, Richard, 174, 175
Cásper Libero Social Communication School, 109
Cassá, Roberto, 132
Castañeda, Luis, 172, 173–74
Castellanos Vargas, Juanita, 143
Castillo Ibarra, Carlos, 83
Castro, Elliott, 90
Castro, Fidel: on Cuban Olympism, 41–42; Cuban Revolution, 5, 35, 41; death, 50; Korean Olympic Games controversy, 46–48; meeting with Juarbe Juarbe, 82; meeting with Samaranch, 190; Mexican political sympathies, 55; Pan-American Games controversy, 44, 45, 47; passion for sport, 35, 47, 50; sport-politics relationship, 195
Castro, Raúl, 50
Castro, Vale, 166
Catete Palace, 103, 109
Centennial Olympic Games (1910), 6, 167
Central America: cultural diplomacy, 54, 59, 190–91; geopolitical conflicts, 54–55, 71, 190; hemispherical sporting events, 62–63, 71–72; Mexican diplomatic initiatives, 60, 63, 66, 69–70; politicized relationships, 54, 191; sport-politics relationship, 57–64; U.S. influence and dominance, 54, 60. *See also* specific country
Central American and Caribbean Basketball Confederation, 141
Central American and Caribbean Games: anti-colonial demonstrations, 83–84; beneficial role, 190; Colombia (1946), 39, 85, 91; Cuban athlete ban, 69; Cuban domination, 135; delegate influence, 65; Dominican Republic (1974), 11, 131, 138–43, 145, 195; El Salvador (1935), 39, 61, 80, *81*, 84, 91; female athletes, 138–43, 195; games motto, 131–32; geopolitical significance, 166, 195; Guatemala (1921), 218*n*13; Guatemala (1950), 64, 83, 91; Havana (1930), 39, 58, 60, 78–79, 166; hosting controversy, 64, 65; increased female participation, 140; indigenous athletes, 58; Mexico (1926), 56, 57–59, 166, 190; Mexico (1954), 56, 64, 66, 72; newspaper coverage, 58; Olympic Movement inspirations, 6; Olympism values, 33; Panama (1938), 39, 81; Panama (1970), 140; Puerto Rican athletic delegation, 78–79, 80, *81*, 83–84, 91; Puerto Rico (1966), 69; Sport for Development and Peace (SDP) projects, 198; sport-politics relationship, 190–91; weather-related postponement, 61
Central American and Caribbean Sports Organization (CACSO), 6, 65, 131
Central American Games: . *See* Central American and Caribbean Games
Central Intelligence Agency (CIA), 65
Centrobasket tournaments, 141–42
Chamosa, Oscar, 113
charitable bullfights, 59, 219*n*23
Chicago Tribune, 83

Chile: coup d'état, 43; elitism, 209n3; medal performances, 229n47; Mexican diplomatic initiatives, 63; Olympic Movement, 211n26; Puerto Rican independence movement, 82; sport-politics relationship, 195

Claridad (newspaper), 88, 90

Clark Flores, José de Jesús, 65, 66, 68, 69, 171

Clark, Myron, 21

Club Atlético Boca Juniors, 194

Club Protestante (Protestant Club), 21

CNEF: . *See* National Committee of Physical Education (CNEF)

Colberg, Rebekah, 81, *82*

Cold War politics: Cuban Olympism, 42–48, 50–51; Cuban sport model, 135, 141, 145–46, 195; female athletes, 144–46; London Olympic Games (1948), 40; Olympic Movement, 11, 42–48, 106, 144–46, 170; sport-politics relationship, 42–48, 54, 133–34, 140, 144–46; transnational cultural events, 54

Coll y Cuchí, José, 77–78

Colombia: armed conflicts, 157, 158, 160, 162; athletic delegations, 58; Central American and Caribbean Games (1946), 39, 85, 91; female athletes, 158–60, 239n3; marginalized individuals, 151, 153–54, 160, 195–96; medal performances, 152, 239n3; men's football, 148, 151–52; Mexican diplomatic initiatives, 63; military campaign of heroism, 160; Ninth International Americas Conference (1948), 83; Olympic athletes, 148, 239n3; Olympic Movement, 211n26; Paralympic athletes, 11, 148–63, 239n3, 240n10; Puerto Rican independence movement, 82; racial and regional stereotypes, 148–49, 153–56, 160, 195–96, 239n3

Colombo, Ángel, 19

colonialism and imperialism: Colombia, 155; Cuban nationalism, 34, 35; Puerto Rico, 73–75,

76, 78–84, 94, 191–92; Spain, 54; sport-politics relationship, 222n16

colonial Olympism, 75, 94. *See also* Puerto Rico

Colorado Party, 15, 28–29

Comisión Nacional de Educación Física (CNEF): . *See* National Committee of Physical Education (CNEF)

Comisión Nacional de Investigaciones, 119–22, 127

Comité Olímpico Argentino, 4, 111, 112, 113, 123–30, 167, 168. *See also* Confederación Argentina de Deportes-Comité Olímpico Argentino (CADCOA)

Comité Olímpico Cubano (COC), 32, 36, 38, 41, 42, 49, 66

Comité Olímpico de Puerto Rico (COPR), 84, 141

Comitê Olímpico do Brasil, 95–96, 99, 176

Comité Olímpico Sudamericano, 19, 24–25

Comité Olímpico Uruguayo (COU), 14, 18, 29

commodification, 149–50, 151, 159, 161

Commonwealth of Puerto Rico: . *See* Puerto Rico

complexo de vira-lata, 193

compromiso de todos, 131–32, 134, 136, 138–39, 145–46

Conard, Philip, 21–22

Concepción de Gracia, Gilberto, 85, 86–87, 91

Conditti, Cecilio, 116

Confederação Brasileira de Desportos (CBD), 99

Confederación Argentina de Basket-Ball, 116, 121, 122

Confederación Argentina de Deportes, 113

Confederación Argentina de Deportes-Comité Olímpico Argentino (CADCOA), 113, 115, 116–17, 119, 120–26

Consejo Nacional de Educación Física, 117

Conselho Nacional de Desportos (CND), 99

Córdoba, Jaime, 90

Correa, Rafael, 86

Correio da Manhã (newspaper), 101

Corrientes (Argentine province), 116

corruption and bribery scandals, 185–86, 188, 194

Costa, Afrânio, 95

Costa Rica: athletic delegations, 57, 58; Mexican diplomatic initiatives, 60

COU: . *See* Uruguayan Olympic Committee (COU)

Coubertin, Pierre de: Argentine sport controversy, 167; contact with CNEF, 14, 18–19; contact with Uruguay, 20; goals and objectives, 23, 28, 81, 176, 186; Latin conceptualization of sport, 8, 165, 196; official representative credentials, 25; Olympism concept, 5; South American International Olympic Committee proposal, 19; value system, 32, 41; war propaganda responsibilities, 210*n*25

Coupe Olympique (Olympic Cup), 27, *27*, 30, 66

Crispín, Nelson, 152

Cuba: athletic delegations, 58, 69; Central American Games (1930), 39, 58, 60, 166; Cold War–era scholarship, 33; economic stability, 38, 48, 49, 50; elitism, 31, 34–37, 39, 189; female athletes, 39, 141–42, 144; friendly rivalries, 59–60; globalization impact, 48–49; gold medal performances, 36–37, 39, 50; independence movements, 35–36, 37; internal stability, 50; national identity struggles, 31–36, 40–41, 189, 190; Olympic athletes, 36–37, 39–43, 49–50; Olympic Games bids, 5, 36, 37–39, 49; Olympic Movement, 211*n*26; Olympism impact, 10, 31–44, 47–48, 50–51, 189; Pan-American Games controversy, 44, 45, 47; political instability, 60, 190; post-Soviet era, 48–50, 190;

Puerto Rican independence movement, 82; relationship with IOC, 43, 190; revolutionary violence, 5, 35, 41, 60, 83; sport participation and policy, 34, 36, 49, 50–51, 135, 141, 145–46, 195; sport-politics relationship, 10, 31–35, 41–48, 66, 189, 195; sport training facilities, 142; tennis tournaments, 39, 59–60; U.S. occupation, 36

cubanidad, 31

Cuban Olympic Committee (COC), 32, 36, 38, 41, 42, 49, 66

Cuban Revolution, 5, 35, 41, 83

Cuesta, José Enamorado, 84, 93

cultural diplomacy, 53–72, 190–91

cultural nationalism, 74–75, 80–81

cultural Olympiad, 40

cyborgs, 150–51, 157, 162–63

cycling events, 36, 127, 148, 210*n*16

D

DaCosta, Lamartine Pereira, 174, 196–97

da Silva, Adhemar Ferreira: athletic skills, 192; biographical background, 96; ceremonial reception, 103; Helsinki Olympic Games(1952), 98, 100–102, 192; labor and financial challenges, 99–100; Melbourne Olympic Games (1956), 95, 102–6, 192; nationalistic sentiments, 99–100, 102, 106, 109–10; news media coverage, 97–98, 100–110, 193, 229*n*54; Olympic medal performances, 10, 97–106, 192, 228*n*39; physical characteristics, 96, 100; popularity and public image, 103–9, 227*n*13, 229*n*54; post-Olympic career, 109; racial nuances, 101, 192–93; sense of fellowship and sporting spirit, 106–9

da Silva, Leônidas, 96

Davis, Lennard, 150

Deaflympics, 241*n*26

de Bautista, Peggy B., 136

de Faria Peres, Fabio, 192–93
de Kirchner, Cristina F., 194
de la Cueva, Daniel, 168, 169, 179
de la Puente, Luis, 83
Delegación de Puerto Rico, 88
Delegación Nacional de Puerto Rico, 88–89
Delgado, José María, 209n8
de Lima, Negrão, 103
de Miero, Rafael, 19
Democratic People's Republic of Korea (PRK), 44–48
de Moraes, Vinícius, 108
Denmark, 229n47
Deportes RCN, 148, 152, 240n15
Destombes, José, 19
Diário Carioca (newspaper), 103, 105
Diário de Notícias (newspaper), 102
Díaz, Manuel Dioniso, 36
Díaz Ordaz, Gustavo, 69, 171, 172
digital technology, 179–83, *182*, 197
disabled bodies, 11, 147–63
dominant masculinity, 148, 155, 160, 161, 197–98
Dominican All-Stars, 135
Dominican Olympic Committee, 136
Dominican Republic: amateur versus professional sports, 131, 133–37; Central American and Caribbean Games (1974), 11, 131, 138–43, 145; Cuban sport model, 135, 141, 145–46, 195; female athletes, 133, 138–46, 195; First Northeast Regional Games, 143; national sport federations, 140–41; Olympic athletes, 139–40; organized athletic games, 6, 143; political and economic development, 11, 132–35; revolutionary violence, 132; sport-politics relationship, 11, 131, 133–46, 194–95; sport program and infrastructure development, 135–38, 142–46; U.S. dominance, 132–33; women governors, 133, 136, 139, 142–46; "Year of Sport", 137
do Rio Branco, Raul, 96
Dortmund, Germany, 121

Drumond, Maurício, 99
Dyreson, Mark, 57

E

Eastern European nations, 40
East German athletes, 216n35
Ecuador, 44, 63
Edström, Sigfrid, 116
Ejército Popular Boricua (Los Macheteros), 89–90
El Día (newspaper), 210n9
El Espectador (newspaper), 149
elitism: Argentina, 113–17, 119, 209n3; Brazil, 193; Caribbean Olympic organizers, 5; colonialism and imperialism, 34, 35; Cuba, 31, 34–37, 39, 189; Latin American Olympic Movement, 3, 5, 196; sport participation and policy, 34, 36, 49, 50–51, 113–17, 119, 209n3; sport-politics relationship, 186, 190–91, 197, 199
El Mundo (newspaper), 80
El Relámpago del Caribe (Caribbean Lightning): . *See* Barrientos, José
El Salvador: athletic delegations, 57; Central American and Caribbean Games (1935), 39, 61, 80, *81*, 84, 91; female athletes, 141; Mexican diplomatic initiatives, 69; Olympic Movement, 211n26
Elsey, Brenda, 53, 54, 140
El Tiempo (newspaper), 149
El Universal (newspaper), 57, 59, 65
enfleshed disabled athletes, 11, 147–63, 195–96
enforced normalcy, 150
equestrianism, 210n16
Equipo Nacional de Puerto Rico, 89
Estado Novo dictatorship, 99, 226n4
Estivill, Alejandro, 55
Ethiopia, 48
European colonialism and imperialism, 34, 35, 54
Eva Perón Foundation, 114, 116
Evert, Chris, 73
Excélsior (newspaper), 57, 58, 59, 64, 67

F

Faber, Sebastiaan, 61
Façanha de Sá, Ary, 108
Fangio, Juan Manuel, 115
Far Eastern Games, 23
Federación Argentina de Natación, 111, 119
Federación Deportiva del Uruguay (FDU), 17, 24, 210n16
Federación de Universitarios Pro Indepedencia (FUPI), 89
Federación Sportiva Nacional, 209n3
Federal Bureau of Investigation (FBI) surveillance program, 86, 87
Fédération Internationale de Football Association (FIFA), 186
Federation of University Students of Cuba, 82
female athletes: Brazil, 198; Colombian Paralympic athletes, 158–60, 239n3; Cuba, 39, 141–42, 144; discrimination and neglect, 198; Dominican Republic, 133, 138–46, 195; fútbol, 186; increased female participation, 139–40, 195; medal performances, 73, 93, 140, 141, 144, 145, 192; Olympic Games, 139–40; Puerto Rico, 73, 81, 93, 141, 144, 192; recruitment and training issues, 140–41, 144, 198. *See also* gender
fencing events: Argentine Olympic athletes, 127; Cuban Olympic athletes, 36–37, 39; Mexican Olympic athletes, 59; Puerto Rican athletes, 77–78
Fernandes, Florestan, 227n9
Fernández, José Ramón, 44
Fernández L'Hoeste, Héctor, 148
Ferreira dos Santos, José, 96
FIFA World Cup: Argentina (1978), 195; Brazil (1950), 10, 96, 98, 227n11; corruption and bribery scandals, 186, 194; indigenous athletes, 196; Mexico (1970), 175; Mexico (1986), 72, 175; news media coverage, 152; Rio de Janeiro (2014), 178, 193, 196, 198; Sport

for Development and Peace (SDP) projects, 198; Sweden (1958), 103; Uruguay (1930), 13, 189
Finland: . *See* Helsinki Olympic Games (1952)
First Northeast Regional Games, 143
Fonst, Ramón, 36, 39
football: . *See* fútbol
football, American, 216n32
Foraker Act (1900), 76
Formula One Grand Prix, 115
Fraginals, Manuel Moreno, 33
France: . *See* Paris, France
Frascara, Félix D., 129, 130
French Olympic Games bids, 177; . *See also* Paris, France
Freyre de Andrade, Fernando, 37
Freyre, Gilberto, 100, 106
Fuchs, Jim, 98
Fuerzas Armadas de Liberación Nacional (FALN), 89
Fundación Eva Perón, 114, 116
Fundamental Charter of the Central American and Caribbean Games, 65
Furtado, Celso, 227n9
fútbol: Argentine athletes, 115; Brazilian athletes, 99, 193; Colombian athletes, 151–52; corruption and bribery scandals, 186, 194; Cuban athletes, 60; female athletes, 186; Mexican athletes, 60–61; nationalist sentiments, 77; national masculinity, 241n22; popularity, 6; racial and regional stereotypes, 148; sport-politics relationship, 186, 190–91, 194; Uruguayan athletes, 13, 16, 27, 29, 189, 214n83. *See also* FIFA World Cup

G

Gag Law, 1948–56 (Puerto Rico), 77, 87
Galeano, Alberto, 209n8
García Padilla, Alejandro, 73
García Saleta, Juan Ulises, 136, 137, 142, 143
Gauldichau, Marc, 108
gender: Brazilian athletes, 198;

Colombian athletes, 158–60, 239n3;
Cuban athletes, 39, 141–42, 144;
Dominican athletes, 133, 138–46,
195; Dominican politicians, 133,
136, 139, 142–46; equal rights,
140, 144, 145; increased female
participation, 139–40, 195; medal
performances, 73, 93, 140, 141, 144,
145, 192; Olympic Games, 139–40;
Olympic Movement, 11, 144–46;
Puerto Rican athletes, 73, 81, 93,
141, 144, 192; recruitment and
training issues, 140–41, 144, 198.
See also female athletes
geopolitical conflicts, 54–55, 71, 190
Gerundio, Fray, 58
Ghigliani, Francisco, *17*; assessment of
sports federations, 24–25, 212n54;
as CNEF leader, 19, 26, 27; as CNEF
member, 16; founding of COU, 29;
founding of FDU, 17; as IOC mem-
ber, 25, 213n61; IOC-YMCA-CNEF
triangle, 28; political career, 209n9;
political conflicts, 29
Gigante, Arturo, 80
Gilroy, Paul, 154, 155, 159
Glasgow, Scotland, 169
Glissant, Edouard, 154, 155, 159
globalization, 48–50
Gómez, Héctor, 26
Gómez, Marte, 65, 66, 67–68, 171
Gonçalves, Osvaldo, 97–98, 102
González García, Manuel, 32, 44
González Olvera, Pedro, 55, 64
Good Neighbor policy, 54, 60, 61,
62, 80
Goulart, João, 228n39
Grandin, Greg, 133
Great Depression, 80
Grito de Lares, 76
Guatemala: athletic delegations, 57, 58;
Central American and Caribbean
Games (1950), 64, 83, 91; Central
American Games (1921), 218n13;
Central Intelligence Agency oper-
ations, 64–65; friendly sporting
events, 63; Mexican diplomatic
initiatives, 60, 63; political conflicts,

65; Puerto Rican independence
movement, 82
Guayaquil, Ecuador, 44
Guevara, Ernesto "Che", 83
Guggenheim, Harry, 78
Guinle, Arnaldo, 96
gunboat diplomacy, 60, 62
gymnastics events, 138, 140, 141, 210n16

H

Hamzah, Azizah, 180
Haraway, Donna, 150, 162, 163
Havana, Cuba: Central American
Games (1930), 39, 58, 60, 78–79;
Olympic Games bids, 37–39, 49;
Pan-American Games (1991), 47,
48; regional Olympic-style sporting
events, 39; US-American football
popularity, 216n32
Hay, Eduardo, 62
Helsinki Olympic Games (1952):
Argentine athletes, 112, 115, 121,
122, 127; bidding and hosting pro-
cess, 67; Brazilian athletes, 95, 98,
100–102, 106, 192, 227n13; East
German athletes, 216n35; Soviet
athletes, 40, 122, 139
hemispherical sporting events, 62–63,
71–72
Hernández, Rafael, 80
heroicization, 160–61
heroic soldier athlete: . *See* Colombia;
Torres, Fabio
Hickey, Patrick, 185–86
Hidalgo Cup, 60
Hindú Club, 111
Hispanophone nations, 39
Homar, Lorenzo, 88
Honduras, 58
Hopkins, Jess, 22–30
Hospitality Houses, 181, *182*
Hostos, Eugenio María de, 93
Hotel Regis (Mexico City), 58
House of the Indigenous Student, 58
Huergo, Fernando I., 120, *121*, 123–26,
128–29
humanism, 31, 32–33, 41–42, 49, 56, 66

King, Billie Jean, 73
Kirchner, Cristina F. de, 194
Kirchner, Néstor, 194
Klingelhoefer, Adolphe, 176
Kubitschek, Juscelino, 103, 228*n*39
Kvitová, Petra, 73

L

La Afición (newspaper), 63
La Borinqueña (Puerto Rican national
    anthem), 80, 81, 83, 91
La Nación (newspaper), 122–23
Lang, Juan K., 120, 125
La pitada olímpica, 91
lap of honor, 13
La Prensa (newspaper), 80
Latin America: cultural diplomacy, 54,
    190–91; geographic designation,
    8; geopolitical conflicts, 54–55,
    71; hemispherical sporting events,
    62–63, 71–72; identity politics
    and scholarship, 33–35, 207*n*26;
    importance of sport, 6–7, 8, 196;
    independence movements, 35–36,
    37, 82; international regional sport
    organizations, 6, 56, 65–66; Latin
    conceptualization of sport, 196;
    Mexican diplomatic initiatives,
    60, 63, 66, 69–70; national iden-
    tity issues, 33–35, 98–99, 104–6,
    109–10, 169, 172–73, 207*n*26,
    228*n*46; national sport federations,
    14, 16–18, 24, 25, 29–30, 41; nation
    formation and development, 7–9;
    negative stereotypes, 69; "Olympic"
    explosion, 13–14; Olympic Games
    bids, 11, 115, 117, 130, 166–70, 197;
    Olympic Movement, 3–9, 165–66,
    169, 176–80, 185–86, 191–92, 197,
    211*n*26; politicized relationships,
    54, 191; Sport for Development and
    Peace (SDP) projects, 198; YMCA
    missionary work, 21–22, 30, 57,
    211*n*34, 222*n*15. *See also* Central
    American and Caribbean Games;
    Pan-American Games; specific
    country

Latin American Olympic Games, 181
Latour, Bruno, 155
Latour, Jorge, 227*n*13
Lausanne, France, 25, 45, 125
Law #53 (Puerto Rico), 77, 87
Leal, Eduardo, 148, 158, 160, 161
Ley de la Mordaza (Gag Law, 1948–56,
    Puerto Rico), 77, 87
Liberating Revolution, 112, 123, 129,
    130
Liga Uruguaya de Football, 16, 214*n*83
limb loss, 154–58, 159, 162
Lobo, Gregory, 151, 160
logocentric subjectivity, 149, 150, 154,
    155, 158, 162
Lonardi, Eduardo, 119–20
London, England: Olympic Games
    (1948), 40, 85, 112, 115, 120;
    Olympic Games (2012), 50, 181,
    186, 192
long-distance endurance competitions,
    37
López Mateos, Adolfo, 3, 68, 171, 173
Los Angeles: cultural Olympiad, 40;
    Olympic Games (1932), 29, 40;
    Olympic Games (1984), 44, 192
loss, representation of, 153–54, 159
Lott, Henrique Teixeira, 229*n*59
Luciano, Manuel, 80
Lucumí, Colombia, 152
Ludwing, Emil, 107
Luxton, Lewis, 124

M

MacAloon, John, 5
Machado, Gerardo, 60
Los Macheteros, 89–90
machismo, 197–98
Macri, Mauricio, 194
Madagascar, 48
Maldonado, Marco Antonio, 60
Mañach, Jorge, 33
Mangan, James A., 178
Manley, Elizabeth, 132, 133, 145
Manuel Fajardo Superior Institute of
    Physical Education, 142
maracanaço, 10, 96, 98, 193

Maracanã Stadium, 96, 104, 192
Marchi, Wanderley, 170. *See also*
    Almeida, Barbara
marginalized individuals, 151, 153–54,
    160, 195–96
Mari Brás, Juan, 75, 87, 88, 94
Martí Cup, 60
Martí, José, 33, 54
Martínez, Beatriz, 140
Martínez Brea, Bienvenido, 131
Martínez, Conrado, 45
Martin, Ricky, 73
masculinity, 148, 155, 160, 161, 197–98,
    241*n*22
Massard, Armand, 119
Massarino, Marcelo, 130
Mataruna, Leonardo, 180
maternalism, 133, 142, 145
Matsuo, Shunsuke, 188, 189
Mayer, Otto, 120, 124–25, 126
McConaughy, David, 211*n*35
McGehee, Richard V., 56, 57–58, 130
Medellín, Colombia, 152, 169
Medrano Basilis, Francisco, 143
mega-events, 93, 165, 174–75, 178–81,
    183, 197, 199
Melbourne Olympic Games (1956):
    Argentine athletes, 115, 126–28;
    Argentine sport controversy, 111–
    12, 123–26; Brazilian athletes, 95,
    102–6, 192; medal rankings, 229*n*47
Menocal, Mario, 37
Men's Football World Cup: . *See* FIFA
    World Cup
Men's World Basketball Championship
    (1950), 115, 121
Men's World Shooting Championship
    (1949), 115
Merrill, Dennis, 62
mestizaje, 8–9
mestizo athletes, 148, 239*n*3
Mexican Olympic Committee, 57
Mexican Revolution, 56
Mexico: athletic delegations, 61;
    Central American and Caribbean
    Games (1954), 64, 66, 72; Central
    American Games (1926), 57–59,
    166, 190; Central American Games
(1954), 56; cultural diplomacy,
55–56, 62–63; economic growth
and development, 63, 67, 171, 173;
female athletes, 141; FIFA World
Cup (1970), 175; FIFA World Cup
(1986), 72, 175; foreign policy, 62,
71; friendly rivalries, 59–60; global
recognition and prestige, 3, 5, 57,
61–62, 67–69, 71–72, 170, 174–75,
176, 192; gold medal performances,
64; hemispherical sporting events,
62–63, 71–72; infrastructure
improvements, 173–74, 178, 179,
197; internal stability, 70, 190;
international relations, 71; national
identity issues, 172–73; oil expropriation, 62; Olympic Games, 3, 5,
10, 40, 55–56, 69–71, 170, 229*n*47;
Olympic Games bids, 11, 63, 66–69,
170, 197; Olympic Movement, 10,
190; Olympic organizing committee, 174–75; overseas reputation,
56; Pan-American Games (1955),
56, 65, 66, 121, 122, 229*n*47; Pan-
American Games (1975), 141; political conflicts, 54–55, 71, 171–73;
post-revolutionary Mexico, 10,
53–72, 190; Puerto Rican independence movement, 82; regional
diplomacy, 60–64, 66, 69–70;
revolutionary violence, 56, 57–58;
sporting diplomacy, 53–72, 190;
sport mega-events, 181; sport policy development, 57; sport-politics
relationship, 171–73, 179, 190;
student-government violence, 70;
student protests, 172, 173, 175; tennis tournaments, 59–60, 61; World
War II participation, 63; YMCA
missionary work, 57
Mexico City: Central American Games
(1926), 57–59; FIFA World Cup
(1970), 175; high altitude effects,
170; infrastructure improvements,
173–74, 179, 197; Olympic Games
(1968), 3, 5, 10, 40, 55–56, 69–71,
170, 216*n*35; Pan-American Games
(1955), 56, 65, 66, 229*n*47; Pan-

American Games (1975), 141; student-government violence, 70; student protests, 172, 173, 175; technological innovations, 179, 182; urban reform and development, 182

Mexico City Olympic Games (1968): anti-racism protests, 171–72, 173; architectural responsibilities, 173–74, 179; Cold War politics, 170; geopolitical significance, 170–72; global recognition and prestige, 174–75, 176, 192; high altitude effects, 170; sport-politics relationship, 171–73, 179; student protests, 172, 173, 175; technological innovations, 179, 182, 197

Miller, George, 44

Minas Gerais, 106

minoritarian subjectivity, 155, 159

Miranda, César, 209n8

Miranda, Lin-Manuel, 73

Miratus Badminton Association, 199

Mizuno, 49

modernist Olympism, 38–40

Moenck, Miguel, 41, 42

Monagas, Julio Enrique, 84

Montero, Rafael, 37

Monteverde, Eduardo, 21, 22, 211n36

Monteverde, Roberto J., 119

Montevideo: Juegos Olímpicos Uruguayos, 18, 209n6; YMCA missionary work, 21–22

Montevideo National Stadium, 18

Montreal Olympic Games (1976), 139

Moreno Fraginals, Manuel, 33

Morris, Michael, 32d Baron Killanin: . See Killanin, Lord

Mott, John R., 20

mourning, 154

Movimiento Pro Independencia (MPI), 75, 87–88, 89

Mueses, Mayobanex, 142

Muguruza, Garbiñe, 73

Mundo Esportivo (sport magazine), 104, 105

Munich Olympic Games (1972), 42, 43

Muñoz Marín, Luis, 85, 134

Mustafa, Siti Ezaleila, 180

N

Nano, Fray, 61

Narancio, Atilio, 209n8

Nascimento, Edson Arantes do, 96

National Autonomous University of Mexico, 172

National Committee of Physical Education (CNEF): CNEF-YMCA partnership, 21–22, 188; goals and objectives, 16–18, 28; historical perspective, 15–18; IOC-YMCA-CNEF triangle, 28–30, 212n51; Olympic Movement, 18–20, 24–30; physical education teacher training programs, 16; political conflicts, 28–29; public sport grounds construction projects, 16, 22, 27, 28; South American Games (1922), 25–27; sport federations, 16–18, 24, 25; sport policy development, 14–16, 18, 28–30, 188; stadium construction proposal, 18

National Council of Administration, 28–29

National Council of Physical Education, 117

National Guard, 85, 90

National Institute of Sports, Physical Education, and Recreation (INDER), 45, 138

National Investigating Commission, 119–22, 127

Nationalist Party, 15, 28–29

Nationalists (Puerto Rico), 74–75, 77–85, 87–88, 90–92, 94

national masculinity, 148, 155, 160, 161, 197–98, 241n22

National Olympic Committees: Argentina, 4, 111, 112, 113, 115, 116–17, 119, 120–30, 167, 168; Brazil, 95–96, 99, 176; Cuba, 38–39, 41, 42; Democratic People's Republic of Korea (PRK), 44–45; Dominican Republic, 136; increased female participation, 139–40; international protests and disputes, 44–48; IOC meetings,

68–69; Mexico, 44, 57, 58, 171;
Non-Aligned Movement nations,
45–46, 48; Puerto Rico, 84, 141;
Republic of Korea (ROK), 45;
sport-politics relationship, 222*n*16.
See also Confederación Argentina
de Deportes-Comité Olímpico
Argentino (CADCOA)
national "other": Colombia, 11;
commodification, 151, 159, 161;
nonnormative bodies, 11, 149–51,
155–57, 195–96; racial and regional
stereotypes, 148–49, 153–56, 158–
60, 195–96, 239*n*3
national sport federations: Argentina,
113, 115–17, 120–30; Colombia,
149–51; Cuba, 41; Dominican
Republic, 140–41; enfleshed disabled athletes, 149–51; Mexico, 57;
Olympic Movement, 168; Uruguay,
14, 16–18, 24, 25, 29–30. *See also*
Youth Olympic Games (2018)
National Sports Council (CND), 99
Nation-building phenomenon, 33–35
Navratilova, Martina, 73
Negri, Mario L., 125
neocolonialism, 48–49
neoliberalism, 32–33, 48–50
Neto-Wacker, Marcia, 176–77
news media coverage: da Silva,
Adhemar Ferreira, 100–110; foot-
ball, 152; Olympic Games (2016),
180–81; Paralympic athletes, 148,
149, 152–54; technological innova-
tions, 180; Torres, Fabio, 148
New York Bronx Marathon (1911), 77
New York Herald Tribune, 83
New York Times, 83, 124, 125
Neymar, 193
Nicaragua: athletic delegations, 58;
Mexican diplomatic initiatives, 60;
political conflicts, 48, 83; sport-
politics relationship, 195
Nicolini, Oscar L., 116
Niemeyer, Oscar, 108
Nigeria, 109
Ninth International Americas
Conference (1948), 83

Non-Aligned Movement nations,
45–46, 48
nonnormative bodies, 11, 149–51,
155–57, 195–96
North American YMCA mission,
211*n*34
North Korea: . *See* Democratic People's
Republic of Korea (PRK)
Norway, 229*n*47
Nuzman, Carlos, 185

O

Obregón, Álvaro, 56, 57
O Estado de São Paulo (newspaper),
177
O Globo (newspaper), 104, 105
Ojeda, Alejandro C., 120
Ojeda Ríos, Filiberto, 89–90
*Olimpia: Revista de Capacitación
Deportiva* (magazine), 119
Olmo, Nicasio, 77
Olympic Agenda 2020, 179, 182–83
Olympic Committee of Puerto Rico
(COPR), 84, 141
Olympic Council of Asia, 45
Olympic Cup (*Coupe Olympique*), 27,
27, 30, 66
Olympic Games: Amsterdam (1928),
13, 29, 39, 189; anti-racism protests,
171–72, 173; Antwerp (1920), 20,
39, 95, 97, 176; Argentine athletic
delegation, 111–12, 115, 117, 119,
120–26, 128–30; Athens (2004), 127,
168; Atlanta (1996), 49, 192; Beijing
(2008), 49, 186, 192; beneficial
role, 5–6; Berlin (1916), 19; Berlin
(1936), 40, 111, 167; Brazilian athletic delegation, 95, 97–106, 176,
192–93; Cold War politics, 170;
Colombian athletes, 148, 239*n*3;
competing political ideologies,
40; Cuban athletes, 36–37, 39–43,
49–50; Dominican athletes, 139–40;
eclectic significances and interpretations, 178–79; female athletes,
139–40; future outlook, 180–83;
geopolitical significance, 165–66,

188, 213n54; YMCA missionary work, 21–22, 188, 222n15

physically disabled athletes, 11, 147–63, 195–96, 241n26

Pinochet, Augusto, 43, 195

La pitada olímpica, 91

Pittsburgh Pirates exhibition, 135, 136

Plan for the Promotion of Sport (*Plan Promocional Deportivo*), 137

Platt Amendment (1902), 36

plazas de deportes, 16, 22, 27, 28

political nationalism, 74, 80–81, 84, 86–94

polo tournaments, 63

Ponce Massacre, 80, 92

Poniatowska, Elena, 67

Popular Democratic Party (PPD), 84, 85, 134

Populist Parties of the Americas Congress (1936), 82

post-Cold War scholarship, 33, 207n26

posthuman condition, 149, 150, 157–58, 163, 240n6

post-Peronist Argentina, 119–30, 194

post-revolutionary Mexico: internal stability, 56; Olympic Movement, 10, 190; overseas reputation, 56; sporting diplomacy, 53–72, 190; sport policy development, 57, 190; sport-politics relationship, 171–73, 179

powerlifting competitions, 155, 158

Prado, Caio, Jr., 227n9

Prado Júnior, Antônio, 96

professional baseball, 134, 135–36

prosthetics, 147, 155, 156–57, 158, 161, 162–63

Protestant youth gatherings, 21

public sport grounds construction projects, 16, 22, 27, 28

Puerto Rican flag: Central American and Caribbean Games, 83, 84; importance, 92, 93; as nationalist symbol, 77, 79, 80, *81*, 84, 192; Olympic athletic delegation, 88, *89*; Olympic Games, 73, 85, 90; Pan-American Games (1979), 75, 90; World Championship athletic events, 91

Puerto Rico: Americanization project, 76, 77, 92, 222n15; anticolonial unity, 87–88, 93–94, 191–92; armed insurrections, 84–85, 87, 89–90; athletic delegations, 58, 78–81, *81*, 83, 84, 85, 91; Central American and Caribbean Games (1966), 69; cultural and political nationalism, 74–75, 80–81, 84, 86–94; female athletes, 73, 81, 93, 141, 144, 192; gold medal performances, 73, 81, 93, 192; Great Depression, 80; independence movements, 74–75, 76, 78–90; Mexican diplomatic initiatives, 69; national anthem, 73, 80, 81, 83, 90, 91, 93; national identity struggles, 73–94, 191–92; official coat of arms, 85–86, *86*; Olympic athletic delegation, 73, 78, 79, 85, 88–89, 90, 91–93; Olympic Games bid, 5; Olympic Movement, 10, 74–75, 81, 83, 84, 88–89, 90, 92–94, 141; Olympic sovereignty, 74, 88, 90, 91–93; organized athletic games, 6; Pan-American Games (1979), 75, 90–92; A Park for Every Town program, 146; Spanish colonialism, 74, 76, 77–78; sport policy development, 76; sport-politics relationship, 74–84, 86–94, 191–92; statehood versus independence debate, 88; U.S. influence and dominance, 54, 73–75, 76, 78–81, 82, 83–85, 92, 191–92

Puig, Mónica, 73, 93, 192

Puig, Yasiel, 73

Pye, Geralyn, 144

Pyongyang, 45

Q

Quadros, Jânio, 100

Quirot, Ana Fidelia, 50

Quito, Ecuador, 44

Puerto Rico, 74–84, 86–94, 191–92;
social change initiatives, 198–99;
Uruguay, 28–29, 189
Springfield College, Massachusetts, 21,
22, 212n42
Stadium Nacional de Montevideo, 18
Stevenson, Teófilo, 42, 50
St. Louis (Missouri) Olympic Games
(1904), 36, 37
structurally disabled bodies, 11, 147–
63, 195–96
student protests, 172, 173, 175
Suárez, Osvaldo, 127, 128
Suárez, Valentín, 116
Summer International University
Sports Week (1953), 121, 122
Sweden, 103
Swift, John, 211n35
swim teams: Argentine athletes, 127;
Colombian Paralympic athletes,
152, 239n3; Dominican athletes,
140, 141; female athletes, 140, 141;
racial stereotypes, 148, 239n3
Sydney Olympic Games (2000), 49
synchronized swimming, 140

T

table tennis, 140
taekwondo, 140
Teisaire, Alberto, 116
Teixeira Lott, Henrique, 229n59
Telles da Conceição, José, 108
Temer, Michel, 3, *4*
tennis tournaments: Cuban athletes,
39, 59–60; Dominican athletes,
140; female athletes, 73, 140, 141;
Mexican athletes, 59–60, 61; Puerto
Rican athletes, 73, 192; Uruguayan
athletes, 210n16; YMCA missionary
work, 222n15
Third Way model of government,
132–39, 142, 144–46, 194–95
Tlatelolco Massacre (1968), 172, 173
Torres, Cesar R., 13, 62, 166–67, 168,
193–94
Torres, Edelberto, 83
Torres, Fabio: caregiving team, 161–62;

commodification, 149–50, 151; as
cyborg, 162–63; as heroic symbol,
160–61; as national "other", 11, 149,
151, 196; nonnormative bodies,
11, 149–50, 155–57, 195–96; peace
flag presentation, 152–53, 155–56,
240n16; prosthetic legs, 155,
156–57, 158, 161, 162–63; racial and
regional stereotypes, 149, 153, 155–
56, 160, 195–96; war-related disabilities, 148, 149, 153, 155, 156–57, 158,
159. *See also* Paralympic Games
Towers, Pedro, 22
track and field events: anti-racism protests, 171, 173; Argentine athletes,
127, 128; Brazilian athletes, 97,
100–101, 102, 105, 192; Colombian
Paralympic athletes, 152, 239n3;
Dominican athletes, 140, 141; female
athletes, 140, 141; Puerto Rican
athletes, 79; racial stereotypes, 148,
239n3; Uruguayan athletes, 210n16
transnational sporting goods corporations, 49
triple jump event, 97–98, 102, 105, 192
Trompowski, Roberto, 176
Trujillo, Rafael, 132, 133, 134–35
Truman, Harry, 84
Tupi TV, 103
Turkey, 229n47

U

Última Hora (newspaper), 97, 98, 101,
105–6, 107, 108–9
underdog complex, 10, 96
Unión Deportiva de Cuba Libre, 42
United Nations International Women's
Year, 145
United States Olympic Committee, 44
University of Brazil, 109
University of Puerto Rico (UPR), 79
Uruguay: athletic delegations, 14; FIFA
World Cup (1930), 13, 189; FIFA
World Cup title, 10, 96; government
reforms, 209n4; historical perspec-
tive, 15; national sport federations,
14, 16–18, 24, 25, 29–30; Olympic

athletic delegation, 13–14, *27*, 189; Olympic Games informal bid, 19–20, 211*n*29; Olympic medal performances, 13–14, 189; Olympic Movement, 9, 13, 14, 18–29, 188–89, 211*n*26; sport history, 13–14, 188–89; sport policy development, 14–18, 24, 26–27, 188–89, 209*n*6; sport-politics relationship, 28–29, 189; YMCA missionary work, 21–22
Uruguayan Football Association, 29
Uruguayan Football League, 16
Uruguayan Olympic Committee (COU), 14, 18, 29
U.S. Congress, 84–85

V

Valencia, Mauricio, 152
Valenzuela, Rodolfo G., 117, *118*, 120
Van Zo Post, Albertson, 36–37
Varela, Félix, 33
Vargas, Getúlio, 96, 98, 99, 103, 226*n*4
Vassallo, Jesse, 91
Vázquez Raña, Mario, 44
Venezuela: athletic delegations, 58; medal performances, 229*n*47; Mexican diplomatic initiatives, 60; Puerto Rican independence movement, 82
Veras, Horacio, 136, 137, 144
Veríssimo, Érico, 108
volleyball: Dominican athletes, 140; female athletes, 140, 142; Puerto Rican athletes, 76; Uruguayan athletes, 210*n*16; YMCA missionary work, 222*n*15
vuelta olímpica (lap of honor), 13

W

Wacker, Christian, 177
Wainer, Samuel, 108
walking competitions, 37
weightlifting events: Colombian Paralympic athletes, 155, 158; Dominican athletes, 140
Werthein, Gerardo, 4

Western subjectivity, 148, 154, 155, 160, 163, 198
Witherspoon, Kevin B., 172
Wolf, Sebastião, 95
women politicians, 133, 136, 139, 142–46
World Baseball Classic, 93
World Championship athletic events, 90, 91, 115, 121
World Deaf Games, 241*n*26
World Tennis Association, 73
World War II, 63
wrestling, 127, 210*n*16, 239*n*3
Wysocki Quiros, David J., 65, 68

Y

Yaohan, 49
Yemen, 45
YMCA: . *See* Young Men's Christian Association (YMCA)
YMCA Manila, 23
YMCA Montevideo, 21–22, 30
Yoder, April, 194–95
Young Men's Christian Association (YMCA): CNEF-YMCA partnership, 21–22, 188; goals and objectives, 20–22, 28; historical perspective, 20–22; influence on sport and physical education policy, 20–22; IOC-YMCA-CNEF triangle, 28–30, 212*n*51; IOC-YMCA partnership, 13–15, 23–26, 28, 29–30; Latin American nations, 13–14; missionary work, 21–22, 30, 57, 211*n*34, 222*n*15
Youth Olympic Games (2018), 4, 5, 168–69, 179, 180, 199

Z

Zamora, José, 18
Zamora, Rubén Amador, 60
Zátopek, Emil, 98, 101
Zika virus threat, 177
Zocca, Ireneo V., 125
Zolov, Eric, 172–73
Zubiaur, José Benjamín, 6